LOVE'S LABORS

LOVE'S LABORS

A Story of Marriage and Divorce

DANIEL ROCHE

RIVERHEAD BOOKS

a member of

Penguin Putnam Inc.

New York

1999

Certain names and identifying characteristics
of individuals portrayed in this
book have been changed to
protect their privacy.

Riverhead Books
a member of
Penguin Putnam Inc.
375 Hudson Street
New York, NY 10014

Library of Congress Cataloging-in-Publication Data

Roche, Daniel, date.
Love's labors : the story of a first marriage / by Daniel Roche.
p.   cm.
ISBN 1-57322-067-1
1. Roche, Daniel—Marriage.   2. Married people—United
States—Biography.   I. Title.
HQ734.R628   1999
306.872'092—dc21   98-45432 CIP
[B]

Printed in the United States of America

1   3   5   7   9   10   8   6   4   2

This book is printed on acid-free paper. ∞

Book design by Carla Bolte

Acknowledgments

My agent, Jane Dystel, has cared for and encouraged this project from the beginning. I've been blessed with great editors at Riverhead—Nicky Weinstock and Wendy Carlton. The book is better because of the help of all three of these people.

Phil Terman and Karl Stukenberg not only lived through many of these experiences with me but were always willing to talk about them, read about them, and tell me what they meant. I continue to listen.

Many other wise and energetic people read drafts of this book, and I thank them all, especially Carl Klaus, Tom Simmons, Dee Morris, Patricia Foster, Les Margolin, and Susan Lohafer.

My family members never failed to chip in with stories when I needed them, and I owe my brother Steve a few beers for his long talks.

I am especially grateful to Julie Elman, who tactfully kept my memory honest, even going so far as to send me pages and pages from her journals. With rare generosity and humor, she understood that every marriage creates two storytellers, and kept insisting, "This is your story. Tell it." Her version would be different, but I trust that this one also feels true to her.

For Maura Brady to have been so patient as I spent countless hours rehashing my first marriage is an act of love beyond my comprehension. I hope it was worth it for her.

FOR MY PARENTS,
FORTY-TWO YEARS AND COUNTING.

Contents

Prologue   1

COMING TOGETHER   11

STARTS   51

DRIVING   75

IMMERSION   95

A MARRIAGE APART   121

PHANTOMS   137

SWERVING   157

WALKING   187

SYMPATHY   211

LAST MEALS   227

EARLY TERMINATION   239

WASHING AWAY   255

Epilogue   265

LOVE'S LABORS

PROLOGUE

WE'D HAD TO RUN, BUT WE MADE THE TWELVE-FORTY. THE Purple Line was a double-decker train with Greyhound-bus-like seats against which I could lean the back of my head. We sat upstairs, near a vent that blew warm air around our ankles, and watched the blue-jacketed conductor stroll down the aisle and take tickets from the half-dozen other passengers. It was November, brisk enough for bulky jackets but sharply sunny. Some of the other passengers looked as if they were going shopping, some as if steeling themselves to visit relatives for the Sunday afternoon. *I'm going,* I wanted to announce, *to have lunch with my wife and my ex-wife.* It would be their first meeting. *Who knows,* the sympathetic ones might have responded, *what to expect from an afternoon like that? Watch out for backbiting. Snide remarks. Maybe even water thrown in each other's faces! Isn't this,* they might have concluded prudently, *the kind of thing that sane and tactful people avoid? It's not too late to skip your stop. Go shopping instead.*

The train pulled out of South Station. The sun was bottle-green through the windows. Maura arched her eyebrows at me. "You two aren't going to spend the afternoon reviewing your marriage, are you?" She and I had been married six months, had been together for three years. One of my pet names for her was Enigma, which she liked and which I had cause to use a lot. I couldn't read her now, couldn't tell for sure how deep her seriousness ran under her humor.

"We'll spare you."

"Not that I'm not *interested*. I was interested last Christmas, when your mom made me look at your wedding pictures."

My mom. She'd been "trying to be helpful," only hoping, as she later put it, to give the new bride some extra ideas about dresses and table settings. We'd been heavy from lunch, and she had tossed off the question in a singsong voice while she leaned against the kitchen sink with her cup of decaf: "Maura, have you seen Dan and Julie's wedding pictures?" I groaned. She raised her arms innocently. "What? They're just pictures. I don't have Julie herself stored in the basement." I rolled my eyes. "Maura knows all about Julie," she said. "She's not a secret." I wasn't interested in secrets, I'd tried to explain. I was interested in tact.

"Well, I *did* want to see them," Maura said now.

"Yeah, you were good about that, flipping through 'the happiest day of my life.'"

"Happiest up till then, you mean."

Boston was empty, like a closed amusement park. The train cleared downtown and slowed to a stop in Newtonville. Julie was in West Newton, one more stop away. It was almost one o'clock, and we hadn't had anything to eat since a bowl of cereal at six. Maura is skinny, with a fast metabolism, and usually eats constantly, like a small child. But we'd been at a conference all morning, and then had run for the train.

I imagined her fainting.

"Today might be a little different," I warned her. "Julie will probably really move, you know, and talk."

"I hope so."

I imagined myself fainting.

Across the aisle from us was a man of about fifty with thick dark hair combed back so solidly it seemed not to be made up of individual strands. His face, tanned even this late in the year, was wrinkled, and heavy around the eyes. Maybe he'd been married two or three times himself, had to juggle the distinct sections of his own romantic life. When he sat down he pursed his lips and looked hard at us, then snapped open a *Globe. Why go at all?* I could imagine him asking me. Could I sort out my hodgepodge of motives, the curiosities and suspicions propelling me forward as forcefully as the train? I wasn't afraid to admit that I *was* curious. Heavily so.

Partly about Julie. Now and then we'd talked on the phone and exchanged letters, but it had been more than three years since I'd seen her. Bits of gossip had filtered their way through various channels. Her parents, for instance, sent Christmas cards to my parents. I knew the broad outlines of Julie's work (a new job as photo editor at a suburban newspaper) and love (most recent relationship ended, nothing in the works) and satisfaction with her life (mixed). And if I'd wanted to ask, I could have had as much detail as I could ingest. Julie showed no reluctance, no sign that she'd share any less with me now than she had when we were married. But I had never really known how she had reacted to the divorce—whether she felt anger or resentment or merely sadness. Or straight satisfaction. In our recent years apart she'd always struck me as kind and sensitive—even to the point, the previous winter, of tactfully easing away after I'd told her Maura and I were getting married. She wrote less often, let me decide whether to call her or not (I hadn't), gave me and Maura room. I let her drift off. But I always felt her out there, like a balloon tied by a hundred-foot string to my belt loop.

I had been the angry one. Lately, anyway. Or at least a few months before. I didn't feel it so much today, here in Boston (what good would it do to show up angry at my ex-wife?). But I had felt it. Weeks here and there of shudders and boiling gall. Spurts of anger that I didn't want to feel. They intruded. I didn't even understand them. They seemed lodged mostly in resentment, in the idea that a marriage—a good marriage, a marriage I still respected and felt proud of in many ways—could have turned me bitter. That idea scared me.

I'd long been the reluctant one. Through most of the divorce I had little appetite for details about Julie. Partly I was mad, but mostly I was tired. Or maybe I couldn't separate the two states, each feeding the other. I wanted only to turn my energies toward myself, and after that toward Maura. A retreat. A catching of the breath. But by the time Maura and I showed up in Boston, it had been three years. With no explicit "falling out," a reconciliation between me and Julie didn't seem in order. So instead I thought of the afternoon ahead of us as an opening up, a new attention to connections that hadn't disappeared simply because we'd gotten divorced. Not romantic connections but others, altered by time, by the disappearance of any romantic love, by Maura's presence. I was on this train to visit Julie because some connections still existed, and I was curious about them. Curious about their use, their reality, their health.

That was the part of my curiosity I could safely admit to aloud. It made me, I thought, seem generous and unself-conscious. There was other curiosity, of course. How would Julie and Maura get along? I was convinced that in a different world—that is, one without me—they would be friends. Why not? They had in common the broad qualities that had made me want each of them for a wife: intelligence, sense of humor, strength, even New England childhoods (Julie's in Boston, Maura's in Vermont). I was the male, Midwestern odd one out—proud of this small stab at matchmaking, and of my own willingness to be the yenta. And maybe, I hoped vaguely, the prospect of the afternoon was making Maura see me in as good and generous and liberal a light as I was seeing myself.

Even now, though, my pure-of-heart motives waggle in my mind like giant rationalizations. I ignored them then by concentrating on my own grand willingness to share with Maura some part of my life she could never get through stories or pictures. I hadn't actually asked whether she wanted me to share. I'd simply come back from a walk two nights before and reported that I'd called Julie from a payphone, that she had suggested lunch, and I asked Maura if she wanted to go. She'd yelled to her sister in the next room, "Hey Jennifer, I get to meet the ex-wife!" I took that as a good sign. But on the train she didn't look particularly impressed with my generosity and courage. We were passing the Museum of Fine Arts and the Harvard Medical School and the brown-brick neighborhoods of Brookline, and she was reading a magazine.

I looked at her profile. Maura is tall and lithe and delicate ("the most naturally beautiful woman I've ever seen," my aunt had once said). She's charming, funny, sociable. Sophisticated in ways that never occur to me until I see her play them out. She's better read than I am, and she's at ease with philosophical ideas. She knows classical music, but also the lyrics to songs from 1920s musicals, as well as the themes from schlocky 1960s and 70s TV shows. Ask her what they play when the Skipper and Gilligan are tiptoeing quietly backward around a palm tree, seconds away from scaring the wits out of each other, and she'll hum it. I suddenly realized that I wanted to brag, to show her off to Julie, a quiet exhibit of what it meant to be well matched.

I wouldn't have to say a word. Maura and I would simply get off the train in West Newton, and Julie would observe and come to understand, as I had, that life had evened itself out. The universe had aligned itself as it was meant to, and I was married to the right woman. Then we'd let it end right there. Closure.

Or maybe it would be the start of some other phase of our relationship. In vague ways I sensed that the tenor of this meeting would further define our divorce, which in turn would help to define, retrospectively, our marriage itself. And maybe, too, my marriage to Maura. I was trying to figure it all out.

The houses changed from charming to more rugged and working class, from luminous brown brick to faded green and yellow shingles. When the train slowed into West Newton, Maura and I were the only ones who stood. The thick-haired man across the aisle glanced up from his paper, and I gave him a somber nod. He didn't nod back. The train came to a full stop and the door opened. The conductor stepped momentarily onto the concrete platform with us, then pulled himself back up as the train began accelerating to the west. We turned and walked away slowly. No one was there.

"She's usually very punctual," I said.

Then Julie appeared over the hill on the other side of the tracks, windblown hair, then gray cloth coat, gray pants, white sneakers. She was waving. I saw her teeth, heard a faint "Hi-i-i!"

"That's her."

I saw myself, too, as if I were still sitting on the train looking down, every move rife with meaning and repercussions. Signals of preference. I walked slowly, almost came to a standstill, until Maura put her hand on my lower back and pushed me forward. Then Julie's cold cheek was against mine, her arms around my waist. I squeezed. When we let go she held a hand out to Maura, the gray cloth sleeve of her coat riding up above her wrist. She introduced herself. Then she touched my hair.

"Look at all that gray!" she said.

The joke jumped to my lips immediately. "Married life."

"Not to me."

"And that gray was there before *I* married you," Maura added.

I scanned the horizon, looking for a change of subject. "Any food around here?" I asked.

"There's an Indian place about a mile down the road," Julie said. "Do you mind a walk?"

In the chilled air her cheeks were what she always called "red rubber balls," firm and glossy and prominent when she smiled, which she did most of the time. Her dark brown hair had its own few isolated strands of gray, and though the perm she'd had the last time I'd seen her had long grown out, her hair still whorled to slightly above her shoulders. Her brown eyes were wide, the elongated shape of elm leaves.

Maura was starving quietly, politely. I wanted to make hunger the issue, bring it out in the open and let it dominate us. There was an Indian place a mile away, and we'd have to walk there and talk about other things for twenty minutes before we had the distracting props of forks and filled water glasses. Lots of time without interruption for me to exist simultaneously as husband and ex-husband.

"Indian is good with me," Maura said.

"Ditto," I said.

It wasn't as sunny as it had been downtown. Ropy clouds had moved in, and the sky was gray and yellow—like the evening skies of a steel-mill town. We walked at Julie's quick pace, and I looked at the houses as Julie asked Maura about her work, about the presentation she'd given at the conference that morning. No one was out, but every yard was raked free of leaves—signs of life. I tagged alongside. I watched.

And I saw it all boil down. I'd been wrong about showing off Maura to Julie. I hadn't brought her along only to let Julie know who had rebounded more successfully. I also wanted to show off Julie to Maura. No, not show off. Nothing that would imply possession. I wanted to make it conceivable—even self-evident—why I'd married this woman, why I'd stayed married to her for eight years. Was that a selfish interest? Did it matter if Maura understood what had defined my life for the decade before she appeared?

She certainly thought it mattered that *I* understood it. I'd had the idea to write about my marriage to Julie, and I'd been trying to figure out how to propose it to Maura—this notion that I should spend the first years of our new marriage rehashing my old, reliving loyalties and despair, revisiting memories of sex and disagreements and the robust certainty in the durability of our marriage. I didn't mention my idea until several months after that afternoon with Julie in Boston, and even then I thought for weeks about how to form my question. I dropped hints to pave the way and bolster my courage. When I finally asked Maura what she thought of the idea, she said, "I think you should either write the book or go into therapy."

It didn't sound like an insult.

"I can take that as a yes?" I said.

She shrugged, preferring, as I interpreted it, to let the options speak for themselves. I didn't push it.

But I understood that generosity filled her statement, that its real message was that she had little interest in my burying my past marriage as if it had never happened. Maybe she had some aims of her own, taking care not to be on the receiving end of any mistakes I might repeat. That seemed a fair enough reason to set my mind to figuring out what had happened. Figuring out who I'd been, who Julie had been, what *we* had been, and what in the world our marriage really was. It had been odd in many ways, but in more significant other ways it had been as normal—that is, as complex, mysterious, and utterly inexplicable—as any other marriage I knew of.

The truth was, I'd been analyzing for a long time, in between passages of anger, annoyance, impatience, lingering affection, and nostalgia. And, to be honest, love. One reason I was going to have lunch with my wife and my ex-wife in November 1993 was to push that analysis along, to test some waters. It had always been the nature of my relationship with Julie that she would raise questions for me—about her, about my own identities as a husband and as a man, about the foundations and expectations of marriage itself. She didn't do it pedantically, or even really consciously, that I could tell. She just acted. And sometimes I followed along, curious and excited about a direction I never would have taken by myself. Sometimes I continued alone, spurred on and spurred away by her energy and restlessness. There were moments, in the midst of our marriage and in the aftermath, when I had no idea what questions to ask about my life with her, about why it was happening and where it was going. She often didn't seem to know, either. And other moments we spent in utter confidence that we were married as couples were supposed to be married, with a healthy mix of dependence and independence, with a sharing of risks and responsibilities, with the willingness to avoid the dregs of too many marriages that we'd grown up watching. It was a strange combination over the course of our years together, half the one sensation and half the other. I suppose it started out, as most romances do, with a lot more certainty than questions. Then, as they do for anyone who is overwhelmed by the unexpected, the proportions shifted.

COMING TOGETHER

THE FIRST TIME I TOUCHED JULIE IT WAS A SHARP KICK TO THE groin. My big toe went into her crotch, deep into the folds of her sweatpants, and even deeper into softer territory. I had meant to kick her, but not so hard. "Oops," I whispered, "sorry." She ignored my apology and kept her fists up, continuing to circle me. Her eyes were locked onto my face, her long dark hair touched with sweat at the ends. I circled, too, but my concentration was gone. I barely stepped back in time to avoid Julie's kick to my stomach.

"Step *into* the kick!" our karate instructor, Carmine, yelled. "Stop, stop." He walked out onto the mat. Julie and I stopped, letting our arms hang down at our sides. "Step into any attack, but to the side," he explained to me. "Watch. Julie, a front snap kick right here," he said, tapping himself in the stomach. Julie put her fists back up and snapped a kick with her right foot. Carmine stepped forward with his left foot, turning his hips enough to get out of the way, and grabbed Julie's leg at the ankle and the knee. He held it firmly while she hopped around on one foot, trying not to lose her balance. "In here," Carmine said to me, "you've got her all tied up. She can't hit you from this angle, and you can run her around the mat on one leg." He took a couple steps to demonstrate, and Julie bounced backward and forward again, her arms flailing, the toes of her free foot grasping at the mat. Finally, he set her leg down slowly, like a lever, and she stood up straight, shaking her head enough for drops of sweat to fling away from her hair. Carmine looked long at me, as if to say, "Understand?" I bowed shallowly. *"Domo arigato,"* I whispered. *Thank you.*

"Hajime!" he yelled, walking off the mat backward. *Begin!* And so we began again, circling, occasionally risking a punch or another kick. But we were both fairly new at karate—I a green belt, Julie a white. She was the only woman in the class, completely different from guys like Bill, who spent fifteen minutes before every class methodically banging his forehead on the wooden bleachers to toughen his skull. Julie didn't bother with the traditional white karate uniform. She came to class in a faded red t-shirt with small ragged holes around the seams, and washed-out navy blue sweatpants with a crotch that sagged to her knees. I didn't know how she could walk in them, much less kick.

We sparred, but nothing was natural yet for either of us. Our moves were forced, woefully telegraphed. If either of us had been any better at blocking than we were at attacking, we would be doing the same thing Carmine did, catching punches and kicks, tossing the attacker around. But we weren't, and at last Carmine waved his hand to stop us. There was no clear winner, just two panting fighters with much to learn.

IT WAS January 1980. I was twenty-one, a college junior majoring in engineering because I'd been good at math and science. Julie was a sophomore, an art major. She was unattached, except for an old boyfriend in Boston who was or had been serious enough to have his picture on the wall of her bedroom at home—something I learned months later, before my first visit to her parents' house. I asked what I should expect. And she told me, laughing, that she'd already called her mom and told her to sweep the room clean of all signs of Jimmy.

But in late January and early February she focused her attention on me, catching me before class, asking if I might be able to stay after and show her some of the moves she'd need to know to get promoted to green belt herself. I stayed. Sometimes we went to the indoor track and jogged slowly, talking. The track circled four tennis courts, and we ducked missed shots. Then, during the first week of February, in the gym lobby after we'd showered and were going our separate ways, she asked me out on our first date. She said she'd been talking to her mom.

"I told her there was a cute guy in my karate class, and she said I should throw him down, pin him, and ask him for a date."

"Who's the guy?" I asked.

She laughed.

"I thought we could go on a bike ride."

"It's February. This is Ohio."

"We're having a thaw. It's supposed to be warm all weekend."

The snow had melted that week. I'd been out walking as much as I could, letting my coat hang open, listening to the birds being fooled into thinking spring was a month early. I had plenty of antsiness in my own bones.

"All right," I said. "If we leave early, make a day of it."

I arrived at her apartment at eight o'clock. Julie was different than I'd seen her in the afternoons—as sluggish as the dark, drawn-curtained apartment itself. I thought: *So this is what she looks like in the morning, this is what I would see every day if we were married.* Her face had the slight puffiness of someone recently sunburned. Her limbs didn't move in the arcing smoothness of karate class but swung reluctantly from her hips and shoulders like sandbags. It was cute. I loitered in the living room while she banged between the bathroom and her bedroom. Then she trudged to the refrigerator and pulled out a couple of fist-sized objects wrapped in aluminum foil and tossed them in her backpack.

"Chicken," she explained.

She had offered to bring lunch.

"How far are we going?" she asked.

"To hell and back?"

"It won't take long to get there."

We headed north. First through Dayton's empty downtown, then up a strangely sparse Main Street past empty fast-food restaurants and closed auto dealers and grocery stores. Then through the suburbs, and finally past the last housing development and into farmland. In the balmy, mistimed warmth of the morning, a tepid breeze coming up behind us from Kentucky, the miles clicked off like city blocks. We glided quietly up Route 48, past muddy cornfields. We could talk only if the person in front twisted around and threw back a quick comment: an observation about a brick silo or a collapsing barn, an exclamation about the great openness. I watched Julie wake up, saw her stretch her eyelids and wiggle on the seat to loosen her muscles. When she was in front, I watched her legs. She was wearing green corduroys, dirty white canvas sneakers. I could hear the chain on her ten-speed whirr lazily, hear it climb and descend the sprockets as she shifted gears. We went through Shiloh and Englewood and Ludlow Falls, rolled right through them and emerged again into the landscape of empty cornfields. We rode parallel to the skinny Stillwater River, crossing it south of Pleasant Hill. Out on the open road, cars full of families passed us, fathers steering wide across the center line to give us room, mothers sizing up the distance between us and the headlong rush of their right front fenders. Tires hummed against the pavement.

By noon we'd made forty miles. That was enough. We turned east on Route 36, figuring we'd start easing our way back south. First, though, we coasted through the bricky downtown of Piqua, looking for a spot to sit comfortably and have our picnic. What we found were the front steps of the Piqua Memorial Hospital, a low-slung, two-story building painted sea-foam green. It seemed deserted, as if everyone were either too sick or too well. We were well. Our legs tingled, the heels of our palms throbbed pleasantly, the cool concrete felt stable under our butts.

Julie gave me a paper towel and then one of the aluminum-foiled chicken pieces. I unwrapped it, and a pink thigh and leg lay in a small pool of blood.

Julie opened hers and laughed embarrassedly.

"I didn't mean for them to be *rare*," she said. "I thought they were done." She looked over at mine. "You don't have to eat that."

"No, no, it looks good. I'm hungry," I assured her. "I'll just . . . chew around the bloody parts."

"Oh my god," she said. "I didn't get these in the oven until after midnight. I sort of forgot about them. Then I was falling asleep waiting for them to get done. I guess I was too tired to let them cook as long as they should have."

"It's okay. This will fill me up and quench my thirst at the same time."

"I'm really a better cook than this," she said. "I just had to go on this stupid *date* last night." She looked at me as if unsure whether she should have mentioned it. "It was stupid," she repeated. "I only went to be polite. Boring! And before we left I had to run back into my apartment to get my gloves, and when I came back out the car smelled *awful*. He'd farted."

I nodded. "Bad date."

"Pretty," she agreed.

"Appetizing, too," I said.

I was starving and ate what I could of the chicken. Then I wrapped the rest in its aluminum foil, and that was the end of lunch. We hadn't brought anything else. I thought of hot soup in the hospital's cafeteria, but the clouds that we'd seen off in the distant west all morning were suddenly coagulating above us. The pleasant sweat I'd worked up turned to a chill. The wind was cooler. Searching for more food was going to cost us too much time.

"You happen to catch the weather last night while you were cooking?" I asked Julie.

"Uh-uh."

"Me either. But I'm thinking those might be winter clouds."

She stared hard at the sky.

"I thought it was supposed to be warm all day," she said. "We're having a thaw."

If there was a snowstorm moving in, I wasn't interested in being stranded in a ditch or riding up a dirt driveway to a farmhouse and being greeted by a Doberman. My parents' house was on the north side of Dayton, eight or ten miles closer than our apartments. When I'd talked to my mom the night before, she said she was going to make lasagne. We might not even get there if the weather turned too bad, but we had a better chance than getting all the way back to our places. I proposed it to Julie as a saner stopping point.

"I don't know about dropping in on your parents," she said. She had never met them.

"My mom makes lasagne like some people lay cement," I said. "By the yard."

I walked over to my bike and took the map from my pack. When I unfolded it, its center snapped toward me like a sail. I brought it back to the steps.

"We can go down Sixty-six straight out of town here, so we won't have to backtrack to Forty-eight. It's not going to be as pleasant a ride, since we have to hit Dixie Highway, which runs right along the interstate, but it'll be shorter."

"We're going to have more trucks that way," she pointed out. She looked skyward again. "Is it good lasagne?"

"Primo," I said.

We loaded up, then Julie paused.

"You know that date I went on last night? I think he asked me out only because he wanted me to ask him to the Turnabout Dance next week. I didn't."

"Did he ask you to reimburse him for dinner and the movie?"

"I don't like dances," she explained. "So I don't want to ask *you* to go to it either."

"Uh-huh."

"But!" She was clenching her teeth and raising her eyebrows, as if the danger in front of her weren't a storm but the need to finish the

explanation she'd started. "I wanted to ask you if you'd like to go out to dinner instead. My treat."

"With cooked food? In a restaurant?" I asked.

"Yes, cooked food." She sighed.

"Then . . . I'd love not to go to the dance with you." I swung my leg over my bike and pushed off. "I'll even make it worth your while right now," I said, "by being the windbreak for our first mile out of town."

"But not," she called after me, the breaker of wind!"

We began with a burst of energy—like kids racing to the end of the block—and then escaped the town and hit the wind that had nothing to stop it except a monumental oak tree next to the road every quarter-mile.

We rode hard but slow, the landscape looking as level as it had coming north but making us pedal as if the bearings had seized up in our wheels. Our eyes teared from the dropping temperature. Drivers slowed as they passed, looking concerned and on the verge of offering to toss our bikes in their trunks and give us a ride home. But no one stopped—maybe because we looked too determined. We pushed downward on our pedals, needing almost our full weight sometimes, leaning forward and still feeling their resistance, like planks of wood being pushed under water.

Five miles out, drops of rain began to pop on my shoulders and burst darkly on the asphalt until the road was coated. But it was only a tease, the rain quitting after two minutes. Still, the clouds had dropped lower, and we rode into a mist that collected on my forehead and dripped over my eyebrows. How easy it would have been for our thin tires to slide on the wet asphalt and throw us under a semi. Or for a car going sixty to wallop our back tires and send us rolling over the hood and the roof and bouncing off the trunk. I knew a guy who once got clipped by an old man who was on his way to the hospital because he'd been having fainting spells. He insisted he drive because his wife was too tired. That was the kind of people who were out on two-lanes in lousy weather.

Car tires hissed over the wet road, throwing more mist up into our faces. An eighteen-wheeler rose up behind us like a battleship. I ducked.

"Shit!" Julie yelled.

I glanced back.

"Why are we out here?" she yelled. Her voice sounded like a whisper.

"Lasagne!" I screamed. "We're riding for lasagne!"

She held up a hand. I could see the red of her fingers.

Then the rain started again, not quitting this time, and we fell into a pattern, yelling "Lasagne!" every quarter mile. When one of us wanted to pass the other to take a turn as windbreak, we yelled "Lasagne!"

I worried that we'd be rescued.

I THOUGHT OF the first time I fell in love—the only time before Julie. Anne was an officer's kid who lived up the hill from us in the cinder-block sprawl of air force base housing eight miles north of Las Vegas. I began by walking to her house almost every evening. I'd pass barely a tree, just lawn after lawn of grass that survived the desert summers only by the grace of sprinklers. Then we'd walk together, through the streets of the housing complex. Our friends, when we happened upon them, started backing away from us whenever we were together, as if the rules stipulated that any couple holding hands had to have plenty of space to allow their love to grow unbothered. "Hi, Dan and Anne," they'd say as we joined them in the dusk underneath a streetlight. They would all face us, as if we and they were sitting on opposite sides of a booth. Did everyone sense the fragility of love, walking carefully around it to let it solidify in peace? Or was it the mystery that struck all of us, the sense that love was unknowable except by the people in it, and to get too close was presumptuous? Something about asking those questions in the desert— an ungraspable landscape for me, the Midwesterner living away from thick, deeply ridged tree trunks for the first time, away from the winter snows—gave the inquiries an extra weight. I liked to walk down the streets on the edge of the housing area, within sight of the chainlink fence that divided government property from civilian. On the far side of that fence, desert stretched clear across the valley. All year round, my friends and I rode our dirt bikes straight out for miles and miles, toward and past Sunrise Mountain and the other craggy, brown dirt hills, only occasionally having to steer around a cactus or an especially deep gully. It was open, bare, empty land, stark land in which to have a first love. And yet the starkness made me feel as if I were discovering something essential about love—that there is nothing around to support it, that it must exist in and by itself. Maybe, I thought then and years later when I was falling in love with Julie, isolation was precisely what love needed in order to grow.

IT KEPT RAINING. Each drop felt as if it were part slush, as if soon it would be snow that would cling to our handlebars and make us guess where the edge of the road might be. I wanted to have every burden of the afternoon exert its weight upon both of us, wanted to tie our experiences together for safety and companionship—all exactly the opposite of the morning, when it felt as if we were riding inside gliders. I wanted to take advantage of the privacy we had within such open space. I wanted to talk. I yelled to Julie, "My parents had a first date something like this!"

She wanted to talk, too. "Tell me!" she said.

"It was in January!" I craned my head backward. "Cold! Lots of snow!"

"Good start!" she said.

"They'd been hanging out together for a couple of months in some bar in Chicago! Can you hear me okay?!"

She held up a hand.

"My dad was in the navy, Great Lakes Naval Base up there in Illinois! Mom lived at home with her parents, liked to drive down to these bars where the navy guys hung out! Mostly this one bar, where she and my dad danced to Elvis!"

"Wait a minute!" Julie yelled. She sped up and pushed by me. "My turn in front. You can talk straight ahead."

I yelled forward: "They finally went on a real date by themselves! Borrowed a car and drove up to Wisconsin to go *sledding!* Only thing was, they didn't bring a sled!"

I waited for a laugh or a question, but none came. It felt liberating to scream a story. I wanted both to pare it down to its bare essentials and to elaborate on it, make it last longer.

"So they found this sled on the hill, some abandoned one, all rusty and broken up! And they climbed on it *together!*"

She yelled back: "Romantic!"

"But halfway down the hill, they hit a huge rock because they couldn't steer, and nearly got killed!"

"Really?!"

"Almost! Or at least my mom! The sled broke apart, and one of the runners went up her butt!"

"What!" Julie yelled, swerving dangerously.

"Right in! Rip! Blood all over the snow! An ambulance had to come and take her to the hospital! And my dad . . ."

I paused as three cars passed, listening to the Doppler effect with each of them. *Sssswwwwooooosh! Sssswwwwooooosh! Sssswwwwooooosh!*

"My dad had to go to her *parents'* house, carrying her bloody clothes, and tell them their daughter was in the *hospital!*"

"That's awful!"

"It was the first time he met them! And there was an article in the paper the next day, 'Woman Pierced by Sled'!"

"Ha!"

"It turned out okay, I guess!" I yelled. "My dad went to visit her in the hospital every day for two weeks, and ten months later they got married!"

"Happy ending, anyway!"

"Guess my dad figured: You impale a girl on a sled, you ought to at least marry her!"

"Good story! Except for the blood and the pain"—Julie shifted her weight on her bike seat—"it's romantic! Do you think they fell in love in the hospital?!"

"Maybe on the hill, right before impact!"

We rode for two hours, maybe three. Then Julie pulled onto the head of a farm's long driveway and stopped.

"Short break," she said when I slid in next to her. The rain had decreased to a sprinkle, but small flakes of snow had begun to mix in. The clouds looked even darker in the southwest, where the wind was coming from.

"What time do you think it is?" she asked. "And how much farther?"

"We're going right by the airport," I said, pointing to a plane with a red TWA tail descending in the distance. "However far that is, we've got another six or eight miles on the other side of it. It must be four, four-thirty by now."

"It feels like we've been riding forever." She filled her lungs, then exhaled. She said, "You sure you still want to go out to dinner with me next week? This might be a sign of something, you know."

"That you're bad luck?"

She shrugged her shoulders cutely, asking me to tease her.

I thought I ought to kiss her instead. But I was shy, and I stood and watched her spin her right pedal around with her toe and then settle the ball of her foot on it. I could have leaned over anyway, but there were three or four feet between us, and I wasn't sure I could angle my bike that far without falling over completely. I felt senti-mental and suddenly earnest, like a soldier in a war movie falling in love rapidly because of the tenuousness of his existence. Or like my parents.

I *should* have kissed her, but I teased instead. "You could be a real danger to me," I said. "I've put my life on the line to be out here with you."

"Carmine would say to stay focused," she answered, "to empty your mind. He wouldn't even notice this rain."

"Carmine would have checked the weather report before getting on his bike."

"Carmine's very careful," she said.

My handlebars had gotten cold through their thin cloth tape. We sat poised, watching a half dozen cars whiz past, then waited for a semi that was rising over the horizon. Everybody's lights were on.

"Is that story about your parents true?"

"Gospel, start to finish."

"It doesn't make me want to get back on this hard seat."

"I saw you squirming."

ANY CONNECTION Julie and I were making so far was oblique, the two of us crashing our forearms together in karate class but not yet our lips, our hands, our full bodies. But in the midst of the storm we were crashing side by side against something bigger, and I began to understand that this was much of what it meant to attach yourself to someone. This was the thrill of having a partner who would take part in whatever you took part in, who would thrill to the same joys and challenges you did. I didn't know what Julie was thinking, though whenever we switched positions I could see the same resolution on her face and in her hunched shoulders that I felt in my own. We rode and rode, pushing harder. It took hours, and then it began to get dark, so it was probably five o'clock. We grimaced at each other and some-times burst out laughing or tilted back our heads and screamed "Fuck!" at the clouds. But mostly we were silent with a concentration more intense than that of karate class. Later—weeks later, when winter had settled in again and the bike ride felt like some distant mania—Julie told me, "The only way I got up some of those hills was by repeating 'Lasagne, lasagne, lasagne' to myself." And later still, when we knew each other better, she added that when even the lasagne, in all its cheesy heat, lost its full power of motivation, she made it up the hills only by promising herself, "If I make it up this hill I'll marry Dan."

I had fantasized in the same way, but I was astonished to hear her admit to something so romantic.

"I wasn't really serious," she said. "I mean, it was our first time out. But I guess on some level I knew."

The suburbs. They rose out of the horizon like a shoreline. First a few gas stations, then a subdivision. I knew where we were, how many miles we had left to go. I picked up the pace, took shortcuts through housing areas I knew well because I used to deliver prescriptions for a pharmacy in them. Then we were in the last couple of blocks, going down a narrow, busy road that dipped into even blacker darkness, and then down a small hill into my parents' subdivision. Up their street, hit the bottom of the driveway already cleared of slush by my dad, and into the garage. There, in the dim yellow of the electric light, Julie's face was red and chapped, her hair blown back and in tangles, her eyes puffy.

"I can't believe I look like this the first time I meet your parents," she whispered.

But with warm food waiting on the table and coziness that would inevitably make everything we'd experienced during the day fade into a hazy unreality, I wanted Julie to appear as physical and beautiful as a rainstorm. I wanted my parents to think I'd brought home a woman as unique as a mermaid.

I HAD LOTS of ideas about marriage. It lasted. It was stable, safe, even a refuge, though I couldn't have said from what. No one in my family would have spoken so sentimentally about the institution, but implications floated around me like unspoken values. And it didn't end with my family. Nearly every adult I knew when I was a kid was married. Had been forever. Would be forever. Kids abounded—five in our family, six in the next-door-neighbors', eleven in the family down the block—proof of every couple's devotion to some venture bigger than themselves. Those were conservative neighborhoods that I grew up in, air force bases where people seemed to take all pledges of allegiance seriously. Then there was the Catholic church—pledgers extraordinaire.

The church called marriage a "sanctuary." I liked it, felt enclosed by it. I liked, too, the term for the public announcement of a proposed marriage, banns of holy matrimony, which I heard as *bands*. It made me think of restraints, but in a good way. An enwrapment.

What, though, did one escape by being married? There were the obvious—loneliness and childlessness—awareness of which came from sermons or novels or movies, or simply from my own imagination. If there were more subtle things, I didn't see them by looking around me. All those marriages. Most of the adults I knew already had escaped whatever was to be escaped.

Or they'd become priests. I knew plenty of those. They didn't enact, but they still articulated the concepts of marital happiness and durability. *Then the Lord God said, "It is not good that man should be alone; I will make him a helper fit for him."*

It would have been hard to escape the church and its philosophies even if I had known enough to want to. My brothers and sisters and I went to Catholic schools when we lived near them; I did heavy time as an altar boy and went to mass regularly well into college. My dad's family came from Irish Catholic stock, hard-line enough for his father to pound the reality of their heritage into my dad's brother Bill as late as the early sixties. At the breakfast table, Bill had been wondering aloud over the newspaper why the Irish couldn't stop killing each other. My grandfather set his spoon down slowly and said, "I'm only going to tell you this once: They ain't all Irish. Half of them bastards are Protestant."

Yet on the other side was my mother, who was Protestant.

My mom recalls my dad's proposal like this: "He said, 'Ya wanna get married?' I said, 'Sure.' He said, 'You know, the kids have to be raised Catholic.' "

Mom showed some resistance after she got married, going to both

Protestant and Catholic services. Gradually, as the Catholic kids came along, she cut back to the ten o'clock mass. Too much cooking and diaper changing and dressing of kids. Even when outnumbered, though, even when ushering us through the rituals of baptism and first communion and confirmation and monthly trips to confession on Saturday evenings, she had her limits. She didn't convert, which would have been the easy thing to do, especially since she's always said that it's not the specifics of dogma she goes to absorb but a broader spirituality. "One religion is the same as any damn other," is the way she puts it. Dressed in a black-and-white dress, black-and-white pumps, and round black clip-on earrings trimmed in gold, or some other outfit as respectful and elegant, she sat patiently in the pew each week while the rest of us filed forward for communion. She played on our Catholic team, supported it, even managed it, but wasn't a part of it. Her *essence* was something other than Catholic, and it was to that essence I looked as if through a window, outside the religion. It hinted at a place where not everything was sacramental and bathed in darkness and incense. A place where marriage, as I imagined it any-way, was not always described—formally, seriously, even porten-tously—in terms like banns.

And then even within the Catholic church, some of that sobriety started to lift. It was the early seventies, and I was in high school. Suddenly at mass there were a half-dozen acoustic guitars, a snare drum, and a tall woman in the choir belting out "I Don't Know How to Love Him." Things began to rock, which brought with it a sense—created not only through the music but also through the pragmatic sermons that couldn't help but be about Vietnam and race riots and women's liberation—that Sunday morning was somehow connected to our lives the rest of the week.

Church became, in other words, social—as much about relationships as about the individual soul. Besides Sunday morning itself, the kids had Wednesday night CCD classes and the Catholic Youth Center with its basketball court and Universal weight machines. For the adults, there were potlucks and discussion groups. And there was a mysterious retreat called Marriage Encounter that got advertised like a weekend party but which I understood was serious and disciplined. Couples who went through the program came back swearing by its ability to rejuice their relationships. They pasted small red-and-yellow decals to the insides of their car windows like inspection stickers or Grateful Dead logos.

My parents never went to Marriage Encounter. Maybe it was too Catholic for my mom, though I don't think it was something only Catholics did. Maybe they didn't feel they needed it, or didn't want to be cooped up for a weekend and forced to "share" with other couples. They seemed to encounter their marriage fine every day without extra help, so it made sense to me that they didn't have to go. But I was still intrigued by what happened during those retreats, what sorts of subjects got talked about. Since marriages in my family seemed to run on automatic (not always smoothly, but at least without long pauses for "taking stock"), I had trouble imagining how one would temporarily put the brakes on. How one would step outside the routine, and what one would take stock of. I asked Anne to ask her parents, because they had gone, and they had the decal of proof in the left rear window of their VW bus. Finances, she said. Who does the dishes. Lots of talk about raising kids.

"My parents have all that stuff worked out," I told her, and I repeated a shtick they liked to perform. "My mom says, 'He's still telling me what to do and I'm still telling him where to go,' and my dad answers, 'I say wash the dishes, she says go to hell. I say clean the house, she says go to hell.' "

Because Marriage Encounter pitched itself as "a journey into intimacy," I assumed that Anne's parents simply didn't tell her about the details that I imagined were most responsible for the promised "enrichment." Anne's parents had always been one of the most "enriched" couples I knew—the habitual touching of each other's arms or shoulders, the easy and interesting conversations between them. Maybe they hadn't needed the weekend, and were merely intrigued by it as I was. Maybe they wanted to take their marriage to even richer levels. Maybe they needed a vacation. Though I never knew how the experience might have changed them, their attendance implied that even the best marriages required work and attention. That was the admission I heard the church itself making, too, through the very existence of the program. The traditional description of marriage as a "vocation to holiness" suddenly connoted not only divine calling but also the more earthly idea of vocation as labor—and the consequent implication, as with all work, that the effort might fail.

WHATEVER I HAD learned about marriage by the time I reached my twenties, I wound up convinced of at least this: that engagements should be long—in proportion to the marriages that would follow. Maybe this idea came in part from falling in love with Anne so young (she was fourteen, I was sixteen) that our engagement would *have* to be long. But the empirical evidence of my parents' own terse engagement flatly contradicted my irrational belief. So, in fact, did the other marriage I knew well, the other marriage that defined for me what marriage "was": that of my mother's parents. It was a fifty-year union, jump-started by an engagement as brief and traumatic as my parents'.

My grandfather Jack Matthews was twenty-eight when his first wife died in childbirth. He lived in western Kentucky, a hundred miles from a city of any consequence. Much of his family had already moved north to the big city of Waukegan, Illinois. And in the weeks after his wife's death those relatives worked on him to make the move, too, to let them help raise his daughter. He hated cities, but had no real idea, either, of what else to do. The loss of his home miserably compounding the loss of his wife, he went.

In Waukegan, he got a third-floor apartment and a job as a bus driver for the Waukegan–North Chicago Transit Authority. On the second floor of his apartment building lived Sylvia Fanta, a secretary in the office of a downtown Waukegan lawyer. They met—on the stairs, in the lobby, on the sidewalk out front: she dressed up for work wearing a long wool coat; he in his bus-driver's uniform, or in slacks and a stiff-collared shirt when he took his daughter for a walk. Even in tragedy he had funny stories, and Sylvia heard some of these bubble to the surface. She listened for them, but didn't stop him from wallowing in his deserved grief. Patient and generous, she understood that with time and help—her help—Jack Matthews could become again what she imagined to be his old cheery self, and maybe better, with his youthful enthusiasm tempered by early pain. She began doing his laundry, helping him with the baby, taking the responsibility away from his cousins. He accepted. They knew each other six months before they got married.

JULIE AND I knew each other thirty-four months before we got married. Our relationship probably seemed like a model of inertia to other members of my family, though only because Julie and I waited a year and a half before going public. *We* knew almost immediately. Two weeks after the bike ride we were in a pizza joint writing names for our kids on a napkin.

But there is engaged, and there is engaged. One of the great blessings for my family is that marriage is a social act, and that the participants far outnumber the bride and groom. "We didn't know!" they would have protested if we skipped a step and rolled right into the wedding itself. "You couldn't have been engaged!"

"But we've been planning the wedding ourselves," I would have argued.

"We didn't know!"

In the years to come, Julie and I would both do all we could to avoid mere "correctness" in our marriage, but at the time I hadn't discovered which correctnesses I could or wanted to live with. I had a vague discomfort with many of them—including the ritual of getting engaged. But I had little idea of how to escape the cliché of it myself. One possibility would have been to have been born into a different family and live in a different time and place. If that was too much to ask, how, then, to get engaged correctly? If you bought the ring with a rock that hovered half an inch above the bride's finger, where would it all stop?

I got no sense from Julie that she'd want or expect intricacy or grandeur. She hated surprise parties, a fact I extrapolated out to mean that she would be no more appreciative of a surprise proposal. On the other hand, it felt dangerous to assume she was thinking along the lines I was, and would be happy with a handshake.

Elaborate proposals were taking place all around me. Once at the airport, walking from the plane into the terminal, I saw a man in a tux get down on his knee and surprise the woman in front of me. We all stopped. The woman hefted her suit bag high over her shoulder and looked confused. The man pulled a ring from his pocket, held it forward in his palm like a bird's egg. "I love you, Dixie," he proclaimed. Finally, the woman burst into tears. She couldn't speak to accept or decline, but she let him stand up and hold her head against his chest. The man looked relieved. I moved on to the baggage claim.

When I described the scene to Julie, I wondered if she really meant it when she said, "Please don't ever do anything like that to me."

The next day I asked a friend who was planning to get married soon if he had proposed. He and his fiancée had been dating since their sophomore year in high school; neither had ever gone out with anyone else. No two people could have been more sure—in their own eyes or in the eyes of everyone who knew them—of one day winding up married. He hedged, wanting to keep it a secret between the two of them, but finally he admitted sketchily to the whole formal thing, on his knee with a ring.

And soon after that, when Julie and I went to a swanky country club for the wedding of my old roommate, the pressure built more. "You're next!" people said to us all night, though we weren't officially engaged. Money had been poured into the wedding like a construction project. We didn't want one like that, but I drank a lot and in that environment the conventionality was surprisingly powerful. People seemed to love the small rituals—the toasts, the bouquet and the garter, the dollar-dances—and for most of the night I found myself caught up in them, too. I began to think: Weren't these the elements of future stories, the moments that served as markers of one's entrance into the culture of marriage? Weren't these the things you could tell your kids, as my friend would be able to tell his kids about proposing to their mother, as my mom had told me about being proposed to by my dad? Did I really want to miss out on that? Julie and I danced so much that I sweated the liquor out of my system, and then the rituals got oppressive. We slipped out of the bright, noisy ballroom and strolled quietly to the empty, isolated sixteenth green, where we made love. Then we went back and danced some more.

If I was going to do anything, I knew it had to involve a ring. No one was ever so crass as to ask Julie where her ring was, and she certainly never hinted to me that she expected to have one already. But a ring, sooner or later, would have to enter the picture.

The ads said I ought to drop two months' salary on one, and I had no doubt some people like my old roommate, who'd gotten a job as a salesman in his wife's father's chemical company, did. I was thinking a week's salary, and I was happy when I found a way to spend even less.

Julie's grandmother had willed her a ring. A silver band with six diamonds. Julie didn't wear it because it was too small, but she kept it in a small plastic bag in the top drawer of her dresser, with her socks. I knew I couldn't simply take it and present it to her. But I lifted it anyway one evening while she was in the bathroom. The next day I took it to the mall, where a jeweler reset the diamonds in a gold band for me. After I picked it up, I carried it in my backpack until I could decide my next move.

Rigid formality was out. So was slickness—like dropping the ring into her drink and letting her discover it among the ice cubes. She didn't drink, for one thing. And nothing too public. No proposals on billboards, for instance, or over the radio as a DJ played my requested song. Anything premeditated, in fact, felt antithetical to our whole relationship, which I liked to think, at the risk of her thinking that I was taking her for granted, had already moved into a kind of long-married casualness. I put the ring in my backpack and decided to play it by ear.

I finally proposed because I got worried she'd notice her ring missing. This fear struck me the first evening I had the ring back, and I lay in bed thinking about it most of the night. Julie was with me, and I woke up every hour or so and looked over at her left hand, which was curled softly near her chin. I tried to visualize ways of slipping the ring onto her finger so that she'd wake up with it already on.

"It appeared magically!" I'd say in the morning. "It must mean we have to get married!"

Then it was light and we both had to get up. I'd missed my chance. I was going to have to propose while she was awake.

Julie had an early class. I let her take a shower first. While she was in the bathroom I pulled on my robe and slipped the ring into the pocket.

The robe was old, brown terrycloth with lots of threads pulled loose. Julie claimed it was sexy, but it wasn't very warm, because it came to just above my knees, and the sleeves were three-quarter length. I sat on the bed and pulled it as tightly around me as I could, waiting.

She came out of the bathroom dressed, and when she sat on the edge of the bed to put on her shoes, I bent down in front of her. There was old shag carpet in my room, and my bare knee dug into it uncomfortably. She looked at me quizzically.

I had thought I might be funny or witty, spoofing the scene as I was creating it, but from my perspective on the floor I felt a seriousness overtake me. "Julie," I began, "I really love you." I had thought out my opening line during the night, but a follow-up had never come clearly to me. What I knew was that pacing was everything, and I didn't want to rush into the request for marriage. Julie was still groggy, and I wanted her to realize gradually what was going on, to see a smile of joy appear on her face. I moved into a history of our relationship, and then into an argument for why we were well matched. I mentioned the bike ride, and then the lovemaking on the sixteenth green. I explained that we both wanted to travel, to do exciting things with our lives, to continue karate.

My knee hurt. I pulled the ring from my pocket and held it out to her. I had an image of the man in the airport, and my hand looked the same as his, the ring lying there like a small bird's egg. I concluded with words that sounded as familiar as his, words that I imagined flowing out of the mouths of twenty billion men dressed in gray suits and togas and plaid cowboy shirts and denim overalls and nylon running outfits and bearskins—men of all history. "Will you marry me?"

"These are my grandmother's diamonds!" Julie said.

For a moment I didn't know whether to hear it as an accusation.

"They're beautiful!" she said. She kissed me, and then she let me put the ring on her finger. She said that of course—of course!—she would marry me.

She had to go. She had an early class, and though she offered to skip it, I could tell she didn't want to.

"Go," I told her.

As soon as she left I began thinking how I could have done the whole thing better, how I should have made more of a production of it, the way my friends had. I could have at least brushed my teeth! I could have pulled on a pair of sweatpants and a t-shirt! To make up for my casualness, I immediately began planning a postproposal celebration—an expensive dinner that night, maybe give her another piece of jewelry. Did I have time to go to the mall that afternoon and find a complementary necklace or bracelet? Did anyone give bracelets for engagements, or were those reserved for going steady in high school?

I took a shower and revised the entire morning. By the time I finished shampooing I was much more concise in my proposal, and I spoke it aloud to take pleasure in the greater effectiveness of it, but quietly enough so that no one would hear me over the running water.

Then I composed an invitation for dinner that night and tried to re-
call my checking account balance to see whether there might be flow-
ers involved in the extended proceedings. There probably wouldn't be.

When I got out of the shower the phone was ringing. Julie wanted
to tell me how much she loved me, how romantic and perfect the proposal had been. And what a surprise! She had rushed home and got
her roommate out of the shower so she could show her the ring and
repeat for her everything I said.

"You didn't tell her I was wearing an old ratty robe, did you?" I
asked.

"Of course," she said. "That was the cute part."

WE THOUGHT ABOUT getting married in the chapel on campus, but
it was Catholic. Julie was Jewish, though her family had never been
observant. "Still," she said apologetically, "I don't know that I can ask
my parents to walk in and come face to face with the Virgin Mary."
Also, the priest had side-stepped our request to have a rabbi offici-
ate with him, telling us, "We can talk about that as we go along."
Instead, we moved the planning to Boston and put Julie's mother in
charge. She found a nondenominational chapel used only for weddings. She sent us a brochure: a classic white chapel set on a small hill
amidst woods that would be orange and red and yellow in mid-
October, the time for which we told her to book it. She asked around
some more and found a justice of the peace who would be glad to
marry us. As a bonus, he was a retired Jewish cantor.

By October 1982 it would be nearly three years. The pace had
been good, and except for a three-day spell of cold feet in January (I'd
run across a line in a story—"One day you realize the person you've
been living with for fifty years disgusts you"—that stopped me in my
tracks and made me wonder whether that was the inevitable end of

any relationship), I felt confident and excited about the wedding. We'd get everybody out to Boston, where none of my family had been. We'd show them the U.S.S. *Constitution* and try to get tickets to a Celtics game at Boston Garden. We'd let them bond with Julie's family, forge the ties that would bind them forever through us. Julie's dad and my dad both were gregarious and funny. They'd love each other. We'd have the wedding of the year.

THEN MY BROTHER Steve beat us to the punch. He was nineteen, as was his girlfriend, whom he had knocked up. Of course, no one put it like that, and maybe it's not fair to do so now. But there's something solid about such language—despite its dicey assumptions about who was the instigator and who was the instigated—and solidity is what I remember as missing at the time. I got my reports secondhand, a day or two after my parents did. I had recently graduated, Julie was in her last semester, and we were both living across town, out of the daily ebb and flow of my family's household life. What I heard was "Kim's pregnant." No mention of how so, which, I don't know why, was my question. Did I want to know the gory details—in Steve's car? in the house? with or without protection? I did. I craved them, tried to imagine the circumstances of his carelessness. It wasn't the fact that it *could* happen that shocked me, but the fact that it *did* happen. Who'd be so sloppy? And why? That was the heart of it for me.

The baby, even before his arrival, was not spectral or dreamlike but instantly real, without hesitation a part of the family, as if he had been poured out of a cereal box. Seven months away from his first appearance, he was already a sun, a hub, an axis around which we were all flung into orbit.

My dad got the news first. In the middle of a cold February, Steve took him to Clancy's Pub. He told him over a pitcher of beer, not saying that he was going to be a father but that my dad was going to be a grandfather. A smooth rhetorical decision, playing to his audience's weakness. My dad had not yet been a grandfather. Steve said the old man smiled, told him he didn't have to get married if he wasn't ready for it. There was no anger, not a raised voice. The two of them drank soberly but not unhappily, then went home and told my mom she was going to be a grandmother. She cried—elated.

Steve had been on a five- or six-year streak of difficulty with my parents, and sometimes with the law. He and I couldn't have been going in more different directions. Still, rather than making his relationship with my parents worse, this pregnancy lifted Steve above it. I couldn't figure it out.

Maybe it was the stress of the circumstances—similar to the stress under which my grandparents and my parents fell in love. But this was altogether different and did not seem to be the kind of stress that would meld a couple together responsibly. It wasn't necessarily going to pressure-cook their feelings into mature love, though it sure might splatter them all over the kitchen wall.

Recently, Steve and I were sitting around remembering how this all had played out.

"You were such a holy man," he said. "Some kind of right-wing moralist."

I was shocked. Where had he gotten this idea?

"I believed in love!" I told him, and I had.

I was a liberal romantic. Love led off my value system like a premise, everything following from it. If two people were in love and wanted to get married, they *should.* That was the *reason* for getting married, as I saw it. There was no other good reason. I knew I'd be hard pressed to live in any country where marriages were prearranged or dictated by money or tribal politics.

"I didn't object to your marriage because you and Kim were young," I said. "I objected because you were stubborn. Everyone was stubborn!"

"How?"

"It wasn't even you," I tried to explain. "It was the culture that taught people to become completely irrational at the idea of a baby. I rolled my eyes not at you and everyone else who came happily to your wedding, but at Western civilization."

"You sure seemed to be a lot more personal than that," he said.

IN THE YEAR we got married, I spent a lot of time comparing Julie and myself to other couples. Sometimes it was to figure out where we might be going wrong but more often it was to gather evidence that we were well ahead of everyone else, that whatever might seem odd was really the inevitable consequence of blazing trails that no one else had the guts or foresight to blaze. Or the luck. It was a judgmental view of others' lives, but I held on to it because, I thought, it was the standard by which I evaluated my own situation. I was *ready* for marriage, and if pressed on what that meant I would have listed the essentials: a sense of independence, combined with a willingness to give up some of yourself. I'd arrived at this idea by looking at marriages in real life and in books. I didn't study them too hard, but I felt observant nonetheless, and it seemed easy enough to pinpoint where men, especially, went wrong in their marriages and how I could step around those mistakes. It all boiled down to generosity, which I also thought of fuzzily as flexibility. And there were ways to search that out, rather than having it forced upon you. Generosity forced upon you was sure, sooner or later, to dry up.

Steve hadn't been completely unprepared for marriage. After high school, he had gotten a job in a tool-and-die shop and was working there full-time and more, because the shop was jumping. Steve would be able to support Kim and their kid. That was something. And I liked Kim—a pretty girl with a quick laugh and a mellow twang in her voice. She seemed on the ball.

But those two things didn't add up to enough. They didn't, for instance, guarantee that once Steve got married, especially under duress, he would inevitably take his place in the long line of good marriages. That's what I saw people expecting. Out of habit, I even caught myself considering it, though not hoping for it, because his success would lessen the reputation of my own marriage. In all matters relating to Steve's wedding, I was the family skeptic, insisting that it was merely a way to save face. Everyone else seemed to see it as a moment at which Steve and Kim would automatically be awarded unforeseen strength to face their troubles. A blessing. It was a concept I couldn't fathom, and no one else seemed to fathom anything I said about it. At least Steve and Kim didn't. They would get married on March 6, twenty-four days away.

"I've decided I love her," Steve said when he told me about the imminent wedding. I pointed out that bravery was a lousy substitute for smarts.

"And you don't *decide* you love someone," I added.

"I love her."

"That doesn't mean you have to get married."

"Dad told me the same thing. I *want* to get married. I think I'm ready"—he paused—"to have a family. Kim's a family person."

"Are you talking yourself into that?"

He shook his head, claimed that he'd been thinking marriage for a long time, maybe years, as crazy as that sounded.

He laughed. "Those old married guys at work have been telling me ever since I started there that I need to get married."

"Maybe they're miserable and want you to be part of the group."

He shook his head. "No. They keep saying, 'Man, marriage is the greatest. The only way to be really happy.' " He paused. "Of course, they also think it's a way to be more sane. They see me come in late with red eyes every morning, and they say, 'Dude, you *have* to get married before you kill yourself.' "

"And they don't think it's stupid to get married because Kim's pregnant?"

"They don't know yet. I'm sure they'll think it's the right thing to do."

"Everyone else seems to."

He shrugged, then sat up straighter, took on a bit of formality, said, "We'd like you to be in the wedding."

"I DON'T THINK there should *be* a goddamned wedding, much less want to be in it."

"But you said yes," Julie replied.

"I said yes. I'm petty and I disagree with it, but I'm not going to boycott the wedding."

"That," she said, "I'm glad of."

BENEATH MY pessimism I tried to harbor a small conviction that I might be wrong, a nugget of faith in Steve and Kim's wisdom—a willingness, even, to give myself over to mystery. The feeling was small, though, and didn't compete well with my satisfaction in knowing the sad way it would all play out.

The wedding and reception materialized out of a tidal wave of strategies and arrangements. And on the wedding night we filed into the church as planned, a party of a dozen.

Julie was the photographer. "She's with the program," my dad kept saying. She crouched in the aisles in her black pants and white silk blouse, two cameras slung around her neck. I most decidedly was not with the program. I stood straight and unsmiling, befuddled by the way the minister talked chummily to the young couple as if their lives together lay smooth before them like a carpet. The word *obligation* kept pounding in my head. Who would want to be obliged to love someone? One ought to be responsible about getting married, not get married for the sake of being responsible. The difference seemed significant to me, borne out in small details: Julie and I had reserved our chapel and reception hall a year ahead; were already on the verge of choosing the stuffed chicken or the fish! Tiny details, unimportant in the grand scheme, but details that gave me a sense of control and satisfaction. Details that represented for me a larger and more careful understanding of the transition from bachelor to husband.

"No way it'll last," I predicted to my mom after it was all over and we watched the DJ unhook his equipment. "I give it two years. Max." I'd made this prediction before, and she'd ignored it, thinking perhaps that the wedding itself would open my eyes, that I'd learn to live more by faith than futilitarian logic. But now that they were actually married and I was insisting on the last discouraging word of the night, she looked sadly at me as if I'd insulted her. I would've taken my words back, if I'd had any doubt about being right.

QUITE POSSIBLY Julie and I were altruistic. Idealistic, even. While Steve and Kim were under the gun to make plans, Julie and I were hashing out things of our own. Babies weren't involved. "Maybe way down the line with the babies," I'd say to Julie. "I have *no* interest now," she'd reply. Nor did we want anything *like* babies—houses, cars, commitments to eat Sunday dinner at the folks' house. The other commitment we were making was to something far outside that labyrinth. Far outside Marriage. Far, in fact, outside Dayton, Ohio.

We'd joined the Peace Corps. Or had applied. The process took months, and by February, we'd filled out a half-dozen sets of paperwork and had one interview. We had to do more of each every few weeks, until July, when a fat manila envelope landed outside my door. Our acceptance letter, and a dozen brochures on how our lives were going to change.

And a location: the West Indies.

"Is the Caribbean poor?" Julie asked me. "My parents go there every year on vacation."

"I haven't been," I said. "But I doubt that we're going to work as lifeguards."

I was going to teach math, and Julie, the letter told us, was designated an SAV—Special Assignment Volunteer. It sounded mysterious and vaguely military. The bureaucratic truth, we'd find out, was that the Peace Corps simply didn't know what to do with her. She had a bachelor's degree in commercial art—not a qualification heavily in demand in the Peace Corps universe. Math teachers, though, were scarce and desired enough that the Peace Corps would make special arrangements for a married one—even if that person had never taught math in his life and was actually an engineer, like me.

I teased Julie, calling her "Sav" or "Savage," but not too much. She was worried about being a tag-along housewife rather than having an identity of her own, and I tried to assure her that it would work out.

"You could advertise nutrition," I suggested. "Do brochures or posters."

"I hope I can do something practical like that," she said.

We called Washington several times, digging for more solid possibilities, but the Peace Corps bureaucrats would only assure us that a job would be found; Julie's skills would be put to good use.

Uncertainty or not, we were amazed each time we looked at the map of the West Indies—minuscule dots like a handful of gravel flung into the water. We hoped for an island near South America.

And we felt good. This was the presentation of our selves to the world, the free giving of the energy that we had as a couple. People called us "gutsy" and "noble." Wanting to seem confident but not overly proud, I didn't agree with them outright, but I didn't disagree with them, either. I shrugged modestly, simultaneously denying and confirming gutsiness and nobility. And I liked to mention that my college roommate had joined the CIA. Because that comparison, I knew, was part of the point. The CIA, law school, engineering jobs, graphic designer positions, accounting careers—the choices our college friends were making, the gravitational pull on freshly minted B.A.s and B.S.s in the first years of the Reagan administration.

SO WE'D LEAVE in late October—in-processing in Miami, six weeks' training in Jamaica, then our two-year assignment. Before that, though, the wedding.

And before the wedding, there was a small detail Julie and I had been debating. I'd given her a hard time, sometimes jokingly and sometimes seriously. But then there we were, at the courthouse in Boston, to get our license. We finally had to conclude it.

Behind a wooden counter stood a woman with frosted hair and a flower-print blouse. She pushed an ochre form toward us, then glided her ballpoint pen down the side of the page, slashing small blue x's at every blank we were to fill in, explaining each item. We nodded. Then, she reached the last two blanks, labeled "Name After Marriage," one for bride and one for groom.

"Here you write in what your names will be after you get married, your married names."

"Anything?" I asked.

"Whatever your names are going to be after you get married." She was all business, like a tax officer.

Julie went first: current name, address, date of marriage. She hesitated at the "Name After Marriage" blank, pursing her lips as if organizing the answer to an essay question.

"You want me to spell it for you?" I asked.

"E – L –," she started reciting.

"R – O –," I said louder than her.

She laughed, then elbowed my gut. "I gotta think."

But she was only stalling, teasing. She'd been thinking, she knew "absolutely positively" how she wanted her name to be written on that paper. For weeks she'd been explaining that she saw little reason to change her name. Twenty-two years, never a problem. She meant to hold on to *Elman* like an old but solid car.

"You want to have to convince the life-insurance agent that it's really you who ought to collect on my policy when I croak?" I asked. "You want to do the registering when we stay at motels?"

"Other people's problems," she said, waving her hand impatiently. "Besides, *you* could change."

"Oh, oh. 'Okay, Dad,' " I said, practicing how I'd break the news, " 'I've changed my name to Elman. Oh, I've had a vasectomy, too.' " I hovered closer. "R – O – C . . ." I whispered.

She printed, slowly, as meticulously as a second-grader: J – U – L – I – E M – A – R – A E – L – M – A – N

"And?" I asked.

She laughed again, hiding the pen from me as if I'd try to scratch out what she'd written.

"And?"

"What if I leave it at that?"

"You could."

"Or," she said, holding the tip of the pen over the tail end of her name, "I could add a little. . . ." She made writing motions, an inch above the paper.

"You could do that, too."

All summer she'd been planning this compromise—stitching our names together with a hyphen. I thought it was reasonable and was happy when she finally wrote it in the space. Then she stared: *Julie Mara Elman-Roche.*

"It's official," I said. "There it is in blue and ochre."

"Hmm," she said slowly, taking the paper by one corner and extending her arm as if she were going to drop the sheet in a waste can. She tried not to smile. "I could still change my mind. But . . . I won't."

She put the paper back on the counter and handed me the pen. I answered the easy questions: current name, address, date of marriage. I didn't want to play the same game, but at the crucial blank I paused anyway. Julie insisted I pick whatever I was comfortable with. It was the hundredth or so time I'd heard that.

"Preferences?"

She smiled, declining the opportunity to sway me one way or the other. "I think it'd be great if you hyphenated, but . . ."

Other possibilities came to my mind: White, Jones, Richards. Names that had nothing to do with me, or with us. I could see marriage as an escape, a new beginning, one of those few opportunities when we get to re-identify ourselves. Where could I go with that? Japanese words from karate hung before me: *shuto* (knife-hand); *uraken* (back-fist); *kiai* (life force); *nekoashi* (cat stance); *hiji-ate* (elbow-smash).

Exotic to be sure, but what were the implications of *choosing* to change one's name to "Elbow-Smash"?

I couldn't say for sure whether at that moment I really wanted to change, but the possibility made me feel a surge of love for Julie, which in turn increased my desire to dive in, to hell with what I left behind. I *could* join her family. Buck the expectations I felt but never heard outright from my dad, who took, I thought, an exaggerated pride in the family name. Best yet, as of two weeks before, Steve and Kim had a son to carry on the family name—Robert Ryan Roche. He took some of the pressure off me.

The last thing Julie expected was that I'd stitch my name to hers as she'd stitched hers to mine. She hadn't asked me to do it, hadn't argued the idea beyond saying that it would be "neat." Oddly, the fact that she *didn't* prod made me want to do it all the more. My choice would be a shock—to Julie, to her family, to my friends. I felt like an Affirmative Action proponent, and also as if right in front of me, on that piece of paper, was nothing less than the opportunity to become the greatest son-in-law in history.

And riding high on the waves of unselfishness, I felt the undertow: Oh my god, then what? There were two sides to this, it occurred to me. No one would give Julie's hyphenated name two looks, but where would it leave me? I wondered (it wasn't a new thought) who was taking the real risk here. I *wanted* to do this together, this ritual, this statement. But where was the equity really? Julie was hardly diving into this marriage. She seemed more to be easing in, her hyphen like a safety rope. It was cynical, I know, totting up amounts of "sacrifice." I stared at the clerk's profile; she was crouching to riffle through folders in a file cabinet. Her chin hung softly when she looked downward.

I wanted to think about it. I *had* thought about it, but suddenly not enough. This was the long haul, and whatever I put down in that instant wasn't going to change the immediate future. The wedding was that weekend. No threat of a switch there. Julie wasn't holding a gun to my head. She wasn't even asking. My choice, she had said. Whatever I felt comfortable with. I felt comfortable thinking about it. So I wrote my name, *my* name—D – A – N – I – E – L M – I – C – H – A – E – L R – O – C – H – E—and she squeezed my arm lightly.

MY FAMILY flew out two days before the wedding. Faneuil Hall. The harbor and the aquarium. The *Constitution.* I didn't have to entertain them. And while they were out on Friday afternoon Julie and I drove thirty miles to the town of Sharon, where the JP who was going to marry us lived. His license was good only in his own county, so he had to marry us there. He did it in the living room, bunches of family pictures hanging on the walls, his kind wife sitting on the piano bench watching. She made us lemonade. Julie and I stood in the middle of the carpet, in jeans and t-shirts, and the JP did the bare essentials—no introduction, no sermon, no reading of Kahlil Gibran (which he would do the following night)—only the vows. We repeated after him, then slipped the rings onto each other's fingers. He pronounced us husband and wife, and his wife clapped. It took two minutes.

"That's it?" Julie asked. "We're married?"

"Officially, but we won't tell anybody that tomorrow night."

He signed our marriage license and dated it October 15, 1982. Everyone would attend the "wedding" on October 16, and, assume, year after year, that that was our anniversary. On the drive back, we didn't feel any different, only as if we'd checked off another task, like confirming with the caterer.

"You know, your parents still aren't going to let us sleep together in their house tonight," I said.

She laughed. "Well, I guess I wouldn't *want* to," she said.

At the house, Julie's mom had all the "big ceremony" preparations well in hand. Everyone could be loose, and was. We had the rehearsal dinner in a dark wood-paneled restaurant with deep red tablecloths. We were lingering over a few beers afterward when Steve decided he ought to give me the talk.

"Well, you're the old married man," I said. After seven months, he and Kim were hanging in there. They seemed pleased with the way they'd surprised even themselves. I wasn't afraid to admit things were going better than I'd hoped, and I'd been trying to do so with some grace. A month before, I'd asked Steve to be my best man. This talk was his duty.

"Well, you have to be the man of the house now," he said, letting his voice drop but unable to wipe his smile away. "You know, keep the wife in line, let her wait on you."

"Yeah, yeah," I said. "Tell me the good stuff. Get to the sex."

"Hey, you're getting *married,*" he said. "No sex."

"Fat lot of help you are."

"Hey, if you had to wait until you're married before you have sex," said my sister Kathy, who had been listening in, "Steve wouldn't be married today."

We stayed late, but didn't feel the effects the next day. Everyone got dressed on time. Everyone stayed in the caravan out to the chapel without getting lost. The JP showed up, did his reading, and repeated our vows from the day before, but with more drama and seriousness of tone. And once again, he pronounced us husband and wife. My grandmother said the wedding was the most beautiful she'd ever been to. I believed her.

At the reception I collected cash. We'd informed our guests through the polite channels that one uses to communicate these things (that is, we let our parents spread the word), that money was all we could use. No dish towels. No sheets. No frying pans, woks, or picture frames. No *weight.* We were leaving the country in a week.

And so, in the basement of the Tudor-style hotel, guests slid envelopes of money into my hand. Most of the guests seemed to be older Jewish men, friends of my new in-laws. Like actors at a wrap party, Julie and I circulated among the older folks, showing off our rings and collecting envelopes. By the end of the evening, when we rode upstairs in the elevator to our awaiting room, the right pocket of my jacket hung as low as if I'd been carrying a brick. We counted the cash the next day—more than three thousand dollars.

"Not a bad take," I told her.

The money made her nervous, and she insisted we get it into the bank as soon as possible. But she agreed that it would help us get off on the right foot.

STARTS

WE PLAYED A GAME. HOW LONG WOULD ONE OF US WOULD STICK around if the other one became a vegetable? Julie was always too honest, relegating me to a nursing home while she went out and got married again or stayed single and lived it up.

"But it wouldn't be *you* lying there!" she explained.

"Who would it be?"

"I mean I'd take *care* of you, pay the medical bills or whatever. But you wouldn't be the same person I married."

"I'm me," I said. "Even when I'm unconscious and drooling."

She exhaled in exasperation.

"You're twenty-two years old," I told her gently. "You don't know anything about devotion."

I, of course, swore I'd never abandon her.

THE MARRIAGES in my family live on like sea turtles: over half a century for each set of grandparents; forty years and counting for my parents; decades upon decades for aunts, uncles, cousins. An almost perfect record, in fact, until an aunt and uncle got divorced about the time I got married. But they didn't bring down the average; by then they already had twenty-five years in the can.

Not that the bumps weren't visible and ominous. When my parents hit a rough spot, they fought in a way that felt strangely threatening in a home that was usually noisy. They became as quiet as housecats. Once during my childhood they refused to talk to each other for two full weeks. We kids relayed messages: whispering to Mom that Dad was going golfing, telling Dad that he had to pick up three gallons of milk on the way home.

Within a few days, though, the silence took on the odor of burlesque. It was the classic absurdity of stubbornness. "This is ridiculous," my mom would whisper to me as she pulled pans from the oven and stirred things in pots on the stove. My dad drew long and carefully timed sighs, as if deeply pained—dragging himself to the table to eat the dinner that he tried to pretend he wished Mom hadn't prepared. But always hanging over the unraveling tension was an understanding that sooner or later the game would end, that Mom and Dad's simultaneous voices would once again join the cacophony of all the kids.

My mom's parents, on the other hand, bickered all the time. My sister Kathy was their best imitator. She went into her routine each time we were getting ready to go visit my grandparents. My grandfather's grumbling when he had to stop the car so my grandmother could browse a garage sale; the haggling over whether Grandma should go out with her friends while Grandpa stayed home. But there was a rhythm and snap to this interplay, as if it was what gave their marriage spark. I saw it as an intentionally scratched veneer over the kind of interdependence and comfort you see in couples who have come to know each other nearly as intimately as they know themselves. It was the mutually agreed upon give-and-take of a symbiotic pair. It was the way they got on. When I got married, I took comfort that my grandparents' marriage had, so far, lasted forty-two years. I didn't think too hard at the time about how much it had coughed and sputtered along.

My other grandparents' marriage was so wonderful it hardly seems possible to write about it honestly. To hear my grandmother tell it, anyway. And there's nothing in my own memories to make me think she's wrong. She admits, when I ask, that there were "a few hard times." The Depression, for instance. For four years my grandfather didn't work. But "he was always happy," my grandmother says. "I used to wonder sometimes, how can he be so happy, when we owe these bills? But he'd say, 'Oh it'll be all right, everything will work out.' And it always did." Even when I press her for some cataclysm or treacherous woe, she continues to say, "No, we were always happy." She is ninety-four, twenty-five years a widow, and still talks about her marriage like a newlywed. With an optimism. An unwavering confidence in "just being together."

A WEEK'S honeymoon in Maine (October, the off season, just us and the lobsters), then to Miami for three days of orientation and shots. The one for diphtheria left me flu-ish and in bed, which in turn left Julie to answer every one of the other seventy-six astonished volunteers: "You two got married when?"

We weren't the babies of the group, though. A half-dozen other people were in their early twenties, fresh out of college. There was even another pair of newlyweds, but they'd been married eight months instead of our eight days. Old-timers. The rest of the group was as varied as a church congregation: a thirty-year-old dentist, a forty-five-year-old corn farmer, a couple in their fifties (a dietician and a science teacher), a seventy-nine-year-old nurse. The idea of this variety excited us, as if our diversity were proof of the worthiness of our cause.

When my queasiness and nausea from the shot subsided enough to let me mingle in the hotel with everyone else, I could feel the antsiness. We all wanted to get to Jamaica. We wanted to dive into our six weeks of training, learning everything we could about Caribbean culture and survival techniques (disinfecting water, growing vegetables in the volcanic dirt, learning a little local patois). We wanted to get to work.

"I know this feeling," I told Julie. "I felt it a month ago, wanting to get married. It's like, 'Let's get on with it. Let it roll.'"

JULIE AND I fell in with Diane and Les, another married couple, in their fifties. They were from Los Angeles. Diane looked like Julie's mother—taller, blonder, but with the same elegance and sharp beauty. Les was six inches shorter than she. They had an almost nervous worry about what they were getting themselves into. It didn't strike me as strange—we all were stepping into some unknown. Les was an economist planning to advise local businesses, but Diane was an SAV, like Julie. Each day Julie and Diane tried to figure out what they were going to be doing, and they took turns badgering the trainers for news from Washington or from the Peace Corps offices in the West Indies. There never was any.

The four of us sat in a row on the plane to Kingston, taking turns leaning our faces into the small, scratched windows. We were amazed at the cobalt blue water, the fact that we were flying over Cuba, the lushness of Jamaica as we began to descend. We filed off the plane together, and, after customs, walked two by two out the front door of the tiny terminal into a crowd of little kids who stared at us silently. There were thirty or forty of them lining the sidewalk, none more than twelve, all with dark faces, close-cropped hair, white eyes. It was like a movie. We nodded and smiled. They didn't.

"They here all the time," said the Jamaican man who drove us to our hotel. "Watch the people coming to visit."

"We're not just visiting," I said.

"Same, same."

THE PEACE CORPS training center was in the tiny village of Sligoville, atop a mountain overlooking Kingston. Julie and I got prime accommodations, right in Sligoville. From the training center you could look down on the wide expanse of Kingston and the stunningly blue water beyond. You could watch thin clouds drift in from the west, deposit their rain, then move on, leaving rainbows in their wake. It all happened below you. Julie and I were billeted with a host family named Watt, whose large, airy house was a quarter-mile from the training center. Other volunteers, including Les and Diane, were billeted in a village halfway down the mountain and had to take taxis up and down. We took the taxis often enough ourselves, when we wanted to go into Kingston, and the experience made us doubly glad we didn't have to take them every day. They were Toyota Corollas that carried as many people as could fit into them. Once, on a Saturday morning, we squeezed nineteen in our car. Ten were stacked like lumber across the backseat, and Julie and another woman sat between the driver and the stickshift.

Mr. and Mrs. Watt had a twenty-year-old son named Roger, and a twin teenage boy and girl who spent the weekdays down in Spanish Town with relatives so they could go to school.

We had the guest room. It was at the front of the house, a big room with white sheers billowing in the tropical breeze. A large bed with a white brocade spread. Luxurious for a couple of volunteers.

Mrs. Watt hovered over us as my mom would have, making us big meals, washing our clothes, teasing Julie because she didn't press her jeans, asking us for days on end about the details of our wedding and how we met. "You kicked her?" she kept asking me.

"It was karate class. I was supposed to."

"You kicked her?"

"He kicked me," Julie said. "I don't know why I married him."

Mrs. Watt was the postmistress in Sligoville. Besides distributing mail, she also liked to distribute news. Everything we told her, I was sure, would make the rounds of Sligoville society. I was worried about being known as a wife-beater.

"She tried to kick me first," I explained.

If doting Mrs. Watt was interested in us, Mr. Watt was the opposite. He was tiny but sturdy, gnarled like a thin-trunked tree. He was maybe fifty-five or sixty, though it was hard to tell, and he never said anything that gave me much hint. No stories of his life, the things he might have lived through. He didn't talk much, or even smile. It was a week before he said anything of consequence to me. I'd been taking a bath every morning, but it wasn't as if I was using much water. Turning the spigot on all the way resulted in a thin stream, about like squirting water out between your teeth. It would have taken an hour to fill the tub. So a bath involved a lot of splashing. To wash your hair you had to get on your hands and knees and stick your butt up in the air. It took forever, and both Julie and I had been doing it each morning. Also, the water was cold.

"Water has to come up from Spanish Town," Mr. Watt said simply as he walked through the kitchen at breakfast-time one morning. Until that moment, I hadn't even realized that the large tank out in the side yard was a water tank, and that it wasn't self-filling. In fact, a water truck chugged up the mountain every couple of weeks with a resupply. If you ran out before then, you were out.

I felt awful.

I wanted to talk more with Mr. Watt, wanted to take my place, even temporarily, as one of the men in the house, one of the two husbands. But I didn't know how. His silence led me to fear that it was Mrs. Watt, twice his size and ten times as outgoing, who had talked him into renting out a room to Peace Corps volunteers, and he was going along with it for the money. I soon discovered, though, that he did have a more gregarious side.

Mr. Watt owned a shop. Sort of a general store, with a bar and some stools where you could sit and drink a Red Stripe. The shop was nothing fancy, and his stock was almost too small to qualify it as a store. Some canned goods. The beer. Some ginger cakes the size of hockey pucks and about as dense. The whole thing was made of plywood. It sat fifty feet from the house, at the edge of his property, right where a kid might put a lemonade stand.

It became a habit at the end of a day of training for a half-dozen or so volunteers to fill the stools and talk politics. It was only then that I saw Mr. Watt laugh and even offer his own views of the current government. He had the raspy voice of a smoker and seemed to like the role of wise bartender—liked, even, to be teased by those volunteers who could do it unself-consciously. I couldn't tease like that, and after one beer I usually bought a ginger cake and took it back to my room, where Julie had already gone to rest.

IN TRAINING we didn't learn any patois, but we gardened—modestly. Pairs of volunteers were assigned small plots and given bok choy seeds. Bok choy was cabbage that would grow fast enough to provide us a crop before the six weeks was up. We hiked out to the gardens on the first day, gathered rocks that were in the way of our planting, and heaved them down the hill. We put the seeds in the ground, carried water to them in buckets, then waited. Each day we went to check on the progress of our plants.

We talked for days on end about the economic realities and dreams of the Caribbean peoples. Or, anyway, of the United States' interpretation of those realities and dreams. The year before, Reagan had signed the Caribbean Basin Initiative, a huge project to pour hundreds of millions of dollars of aid into the economies of these tiny countries. There was constant talk about the Peace Corps' relationship to CBI. We volunteers spent hours arguing about where we fit into the "big picture." But after two weeks of training, even the diehard debaters were visibly restless and eager to move on to something more tangible. We wanted to get our hands dirty. We were ready to work. We'd listened to endless lectures on the role of women in matriarchal cultures. We'd done exercises meant to reveal our strengths and weaknesses in relating to other people. We'd tended our bok choy. A few gardens were flourishing, but mine and Julie's looked pitiful from the start and the plants never got any bigger. We finally dug them up and let our plot lie fallow. I took a stick and drew some smoothly curvy lines in the dirt from the stakes at one end to the stakes at the other. It was my Zen garden.

IT WASN'T without reason that Zen was on my mind. Even with Mr. Watt's silence and the idyllic nature of our environment, things weren't quiet. There was a little rum shop about fifty feet from our bedroom window. Like Mr. Watt's store, this rum shop was small and thin-walled. The music from its jukebox poured out its windows like fumes. As far as I could tell, the machine had only one volume setting: *high*. Our first night in the Watts' house, the music played from seven o'clock until midnight.

For that night it was "local color." Then it began to make us crazy. I peered out our bedroom window. Only a few men hung out in that rum shop. I could see their vague silhouettes. Sometimes they were playing dominoes, other times leaning back on the legs of their chairs. I thought of going over and asking them to turn it down. But Julie didn't want me to, and I had the vague impression that they were rivals of Mr. Watt's. When I asked him at breakfast one morning if the music kept him awake, he looked blankly over his fried eggs. "Slept fine," he said. And the jukebox fired up every night after that.

Relief came at midnight, when, as if they had a curfew, the men mercifully cut the sound and went home. The relief was short-lived, though it should have lasted four hours, until the dozens of roosters in town began crowing. In between the music and the roosters, however, were the dogs.

The Watts had six of them—scrawny, indeterminate short-haired types. Yappers and yelpers. The Watts kept them inside the iron fence that enclosed their small yard. What room the dogs had to run in was like a racetrack, a ten-foot-wide swath around the house, though with a few bushes as obstacles. But they rarely ran. They slept all day, and at night stayed right outside our window, barking unrelentingly at the dark, empty road.

We gave up hope of sleeping, took comfort in sleep when it did come, and several times a night I stumbled to the window to yell "Shut the fuck up!" just to hear something different. Julie was worried that someone would hear me, but no one ever said the next morning that they had.

BOGWALK WAS a tiny town five miles down the mountain. It was there, after three weeks of noise, that Julie insisted we walk. Not in the middle of the sleepless night, but on an afternoon the trainers had given us off. We needed a moment alone, to hear ourselves think, to remember that we were, technically, on a honeymoon. On the north coast of Jamaica, in Ocho Rios, other honeymooners were lounging in the light spray from spectacular waterfalls, drinks with small parasols in their hands. And more honeymooners were over in Montego Bay, sitting in chaise lounges, smelling of coconut oil. More still were in Puerto Rico and the Virgin Islands, and spread out across the very islands we and our fellow volunteers would be arriving at soon—Barbados, St. Lucia, St. Martin, St. Vincent, Antigua, Anguilla. But frustrated as I was, I didn't envy them. Theirs seemed like a moment away from the grind with little to show for it when they got home. Nothing about Julie's and my present situation was quite how I'd imagined it—the sleepless nights, the boredom, the lack of a job for Julie—but I wouldn't have traded places with any one-weeker I could imagine, either. Comparing rocks. Comparing the number of tiers on their cakes. Comparing who'd gotten the most straw picnic baskets as gifts.

The road was level for a mile, then descended. We walked in silence for a long time—the only sound the flip of my sandals. We passed small shacks sitting alone in open patches of grass. Bananas grew in thick stands of trees on either side of the road. A small short-haired mutt with its ribs showing approached us cautiously, but when Julie tried to pet it, it ran away. The farther out we walked, the more we became able to see possibilities that hadn't been clear in Sligoville; the Peace Corps' rigid weight began to lift off us. In one crazy moment, I suggested that as soon as we finished our two years, we ought to walk across America. "Leave from Boston and take a year to do it," I said.

Julie didn't hesitate. She grasped the idea as if it were an ejection seat out of Sligoville. "Excellent!" she said. At the time it didn't seem pie-in-the-sky. Why should it have? A month before, we'd been living in a nondescript suburban apartment and riding city buses to work every day. Nine-to-five. Now we were on an isolated road in a jungle, the two of us together and cut free from every predictable experience our friends in Ohio were living at that very moment. "We should make a list of our goals," Julie added, "put that at the top."

"And what else?"

"I want to live in Australia."

I didn't want to live in Australia—I'd had desert before in Las Vegas—but I was willing to bargain.

"Okay, a year in Australia if we can do a year in Europe."

"Australia's more adventurous," she said, "but all right."

"I want a banana." I walked toward the closest tree. Bananas grow on trees with their tail ends pointed upward, the opposite of how I'd always seen them in the stores. "How ripe do you think they need to be before they're safe to eat?"

"They're green, and probably hard as rocks," Julie said.

Suddenly we heard someone coming up behind us. We were at a

bend in the road where we couldn't see fifty feet ahead or behind. It was a Jamaican man, carrying a machete.

Julie slowed down, pretending that she was thinking about stopping to pick her own banana. "Let's let him pass," she whispered.

He nodded slightly when he went by, looking us up and down. I thought he was going to keep going without a word, but then he said, "Cubans?" His machete hung from his loose fingers like a riding crop, bouncing gently off his leg.

"Massachusetts," Julie said. "American."

"Brother and sister in Boston," he said, pointing to himself. He pointed his machete at the sky and said, "Rain soon come." Then he picked up his speed again, rounded another bend, and was out of sight.

When it began to sprinkle ten minutes later, I turned my face to the cleansing water. Then the rain increased, and we ran for it. We found a tiny shack—a plywood shed smaller than Mr. Watt's—thirty yards off the road. We got inside just as a great sheet of water broke out of the sky. The rain made the asphalt steam.

The shack must've been a shelter for banana harvesters, a place for this kind of occasion. We stood in it like homeowners. The water thundered against the corrugated zinc roof, then after fifteen minutes it quit and dripped lazily off the banana leaves. The sun came back out, but we stayed put, not wanting to lose the moment. We didn't talk, merely stood in the doorway with our arms around each other's waists. It was our most peaceful moment so far in Jamaica, and the idea occurred to me that we could stay in the shack for the night, get a good sleep. We could live there, I found myself fantasizing, get to know the locals and survive on the bananas and breadfruit and guavas. Buy a machete and keep clear the area around the shack. Watch the clouds move in every afternoon and then watch the sun reclaim the landscape. *This* was the escape we'd been thinking about all those months in Dayton, the dream of what we had been sure we wanted. No Peace Corps bureaucracy. The freedom of living simply. Now that we were in the midst of it, it seemed clear why we had imagined it. We could stay, I thought, stay and really live on our own, part of no group except the one we chose. The temptation was so strong, the romance so close and tactile that when we finally did step out into the wet grass, I think we were driven only by one fear: that the Watts would rustle up a search party, releasing their dogs from the yard to come look for us.

MAYBE THAT moment of freedom was most responsible for making Julie realize she was losing her independence. "Slipping away," she put it. But probably it wasn't only that moment. It had been, she explained, coming on for a long time.

"I've felt my dependency on you growing ever since we met," she said. She'd been thinking about it for a couple of days after our walk, and finally brought it up.

"Okay," I said. I waited, resisted with great effort the need to say the obvious—that we'd agreed to a mutual dependency. We had gotten married.

"I was thinking about being on that walk," Julie said. "It bothers me that I wouldn't have gone alone. If you weren't there . . . I feel more afraid now than when we met, less inclined to do things by myself."

"It was safe out there," I said.

"With you. Maybe it would've been anyway. But I don't think I would have found out."

"Maybe *I* wouldn't have gone alone," I said, though I knew I would have. She knew, too, and rolled her eyes at me. "Dependency is not a bad thing," I added. "I'm dependent on you in lots of ways."

"Like what?"

"Like feeding off your energy. Like being motivated even to apply to the Peace Corps."

"It was your idea," she said.

"Originally, maybe. But I'm not sure I would have done it on my own. Also, I rely on you in social situations. You know how to talk to people, you're genuinely interested in them."

"You're not?"

"You're a lot better at showing it, and I rely on that. Maybe I take advantage of it, letting you do the work."

"You're getting better at talking to people," she said. "You just have to *enunciate*. You've got to quit mumbling if you're going to be a teacher!"

"Thanks for the advice."

"It's just that I feel my sense of self-confidence eroding. I'm not saying it's *your* fault. It's probably my own more than anything. In school everything seemed so cut and dried. I got grades, I got attention and praise. Now, I guess, I have to learn to satisfy myself and be satisfied with my own work. I can't rely on friends for that, because I don't feel like I've gotten close to anyone here. I think that's one of the disadvantages of being married—the two of us tend to stick together and don't venture out and start new relationships."

"We could do that more," I said. I proposed it as a goal, like living in Australia.

She was quiet for a minute.

"I guess I'm frustrated. It's not like I can take off by myself. There's no escape when I need it."

I ran my hand through my hair. I didn't disagree with anything she said, but I wasn't sure how to respond. I didn't have any solutions, and it seemed that it would've been inappropriate to offer them even if I had. She was letting off steam. That much I understood, and that much I could help her with. Be a sounding board. I wanted to show her that I empathized, that we were a team whose problems and privileges ought to be shared equally. In truth, though, I knew our situations weren't at all the same. In Jamaica I could go off on my own, simply because I was a man, and she couldn't—or couldn't nearly as easily—simply because she was a woman. There wasn't much I could do about that.

"I know you're feeling frustrated," I finally said. "I am, too. But, you know, we don't have that much longer in Jamaica. The island we end up living on will probably be a lot better. Not nearly as dirty or dangerous."

It didn't seem to comfort her.

"It's not the environment," she said. "It's me. I don't want to allow myself to be *controlled* by what's around me."

I knew she meant me, too, but I chose to think—for as long as I could, which wasn't very long—that she didn't.

"I depend on you to talk to Mr. Watt for me," I said, snuggling up to her, lightening the conversation. I smiled, kissed her ear to show her I was on her side. "If you want," I whispered, "you could go down and buy us a ginger cake."

BY THE END of our six weeks everyone's general impatience with the routine had turned into loathing. At the airport, instead of the wide-eyed amazement of our arrival, there was a rush to get checked in and on the plane. When the plane's wheels left the ground, the seventy-six of us cheered. As soon as we hit cruising altitude, we began drinking.

WE WENT as a group to Barbados, where we were officially sworn in as Peace Corps volunteers, and the clock started on our two years. On a sunny yard outside the Peace Corps Centre, we raised our right hands and promised to uphold the constitution of the United States, and then we went back to the hotel and started drinking again. The next day, in sixes and sevens and eights, we rode in mini-buses to the airport and took flights to the islands where our jobs awaited us. For Julie and me, it was Antigua. For all the lectures we'd sat through, the two of us knew almost nothing in particular about this island, expect that it used to make its money from sugar and now did from tourism, and that only one year earlier it had gained full independence from Britain. It'd been a colony since 1632.

We were billeted with a local family again, a sweet older professional couple. Their house was luxurious compared to the Watts', but still our first order of business was our own place, and some privacy. We found it within a few days: a shotgun house on the west end of the capital, St. Johns. It was long and thin but had big rooms dotted with small pieces of furniture. And it had a small yard where we could grow vegetables.

AT TWENTY-FOUR (Julie had crocheted me a washcloth for my birthday a few weeks earlier) I was willing to believe that sleeping together is the essence of marriage. What better defines its routine or houses its pleasures? I would change my mind about this in later years, and then change it back again, but at the time I didn't have any desire beyond spending the night peacefully with my wife. I wanted a big, soft bed where we could rest quietly or passionately or some of each. We'd been in the same bed every night since we got married, but few nights had been peaceful. Consequently, little of that time felt like ours, like our own intimate world. We arrived in Antigua with the hope that we could create a retreat.

But on the first night we heard the rats. Lying in bed, we listened to them line up at one end of the attic and race to the other. There was a short pause, then they ran back.

"Fuckin'-a," I whispered.

"There is *no* way I'm going to sleep," Julie said.

She did, and I did, but only for brief moments at a time, like sentinels catching a few on the sly. The next morning we took our first trip to the hardware store. We loaded up on rat poison. It came in a box full of blue chunks, like badly dyed dog food. We hauled two chairs into the bedroom and positioned them under the square attic door. When Julie gave the word, I pushed up the plywood cover with the end of a broom, and she flung scoops of poison into the dark.

She heaved a third of the box up there.

"Throw more," I told her.

"My god," she said after I'd let the door slam shut. "If they die up there, they're going to start stinking."

I read the box. "It doesn't say, but I think they go outside to die. The poison is supposed to make them thirsty."

Maybe it did. But they ran through their thirst, like football players. Each night they thumped in mad scrambles. It was impossible to tell how many were up there. Sometimes it sounded like a few, sometimes dozens.

We bought more poison. And more. It made no difference though, and we began to feel a nostalgia for the drab but clean apartment we'd had back in Dayton. Sometimes we'd lie in bed laughing, but there was very little real humor in it.

So little, in fact, that we couldn't muster even an ironic chuckle when we had to deal with the daytime critters. One day we unthinkingly left some chicken scraps on the counter and came home to find maggots dripping off the shelves. We spent days cleaning and eating out.

I couldn't have said that the situation was as desperate outside the house as it was in, but it had little of the substance we'd been expecting and hoping for. My teaching job wasn't going to start for weeks, and the director of the school couldn't or wouldn't tell me exactly what I'd be teaching. Apparently, it would involve math, engineering, physics, and drafting. But the students—sixteen- and seventeen-year-old boys who'd dropped out of school and then come back to get a technical education—"weren't exactly top notch." The school trained electricians, automotive mechanics, and appliance repairmen. I had no idea what they'd need to know about physics.

Julie's job was even more mysterious. The Peace Corps office arranged a position for her at the tourist bureau, but on the Monday morning she showed up, the boss wasn't there. The secretary told her to come back the following Monday. She did, waited two hours to see the boss, and asked what she would be doing. "Come back in a week," the boss said. "You can work in the office if you want to. Don't let us chase you out!"

"She said she didn't have anything for me to do," Julie explained when she got home. "I offered to write up a proposal for projects, but she didn't seem interested." When her visit the third week didn't produce any more enthusiasm, Julie searched for positions on her own: at a nursery school and at Nelson's Dockyard, a historic hotel complex on the south side of the island, where a local photographer had a studio. She was forcing herself to be self-motivated, to make the best of her own situation. "Digging deep," she called it. And she found work at both those places; she proposed the idea of establishing a fund-raising program for the nursery, and of photographing historical documents for the archives at Nelson's Dockyard. After a week, though, the Peace Corps office put the nix on both sites. The first didn't sufficiently use her art talents, and the second threw her into the dangerous company of wealthy tourists.

So we had time. We went to the beach—a ten-minute walk from our house. It was usually empty, and the ocean floor was like slate, smooth and hard and clean. You could see the bottom no matter how far out you swam. Occasionally a French woman showed up and sunbathed topless, and Julie watched me watching her. We tanned and read books and then met other volunteers at outdoor bars to drink daiquiris. It was a rare routine for newlyweds—spending nearly twenty-four hours a day together. We supposed it was good. We weren't threatening to kill each other. Still, we had trouble remembering why we were there.

Weeks went by. Most of the time we were crazy with boredom and antsiness. We got better and better tanned. We tried to settle in, adopt the slow attitude of the island, quit taking the Peace Corps so seriously. One volunteer who'd been on the island for a year admitted he'd spent his first eight months doing nothing but going to the beach.

"My job took that long to come through," he said.

"Eight months?" Julie asked, horrified.

"Hey, live it up. Have a two-year honeymoon!"

"I don't want a two-year honeymoon," she said. "That's not why we came here. I want pressure, stimulation."

We took heart in the volunteers who had it, the ones whose jobs had clicked into place: Debbie, the special-ed teacher; Don, the carpenter; Sarah, the nurse. But they seemed to be the exceptions rather than the rule, and their accomplishments often got washed over by the gripe sessions that sprouted up among the rest of us.

Alone, Julie and I found ourselves drifting into long talks about

"Early Termination"—Peace Corps lingo for quitting. ETing, they called it. This wasn't the army; you could leave if you wanted to. Highly discouraged, of course, but the only thing standing between you and a flight home was a formal request and the stool sample you had to provide for your exit physical.

Sometimes it seemed a half-dozen of us all were looking at each other, daring someone else to go first, to set the precedent. At the same time we looked at each other in exactly the opposite way, hoping to find examples of strength and determination. Julie and I did both with each other. Could we pull each other through this? Throw enough encouragement the other person's way to keep him or her going? As December dragged on, though, questions of purpose came to hang heavy over us. What were we accomplishing? Whom were we helping?

Once in a while it felt as if the balance might shift for the better. Christmas was a good day. I gave Julie two bandanas, some notebook paper, and two oranges; she gave me a *Life* magazine and another crocheted washcloth. And on New Year's Eve, at about one o'clock, when we'd already hit the sack, a husband and wife dressed as clowns showed up on our front porch to bless the house. At least that's what we thought they were doing. They were drunk, and between their heavy local dialects and their slurred speech, we got only about a fourth of what they said. The man was beating a drum, and the woman was playing a harmonica. Julie took their pictures, and they performed even more vigorously. We humored them for an hour, then finally coaxed them on their way with some vodka and spare change. We tried to interpret their "blessings" as a good sign.

And then Fred and Edie ET'ed. It was obvious and a shock at the same time, especially to Julie and me, because they were the other married couple on the island. They were in their late forties and had left good jobs in Seattle in midcareer, as much to be completely to-gether as to be altruistic. Their own sense of romance, in fact, had come to outshine mine and Julie's. But it had its limits, or they sim-ply knew themselves better, and when it became all too clear that their jobs in Antigua weren't going to pan out, they admitted that neither of them had the inclination to spend excess time at the beach. They outprocessed, wished us luck, and flew back to Seattle.

Statistics started surfacing, ones we'd heard before but which the Peace Corps didn't like to publicize: Over the years, fifty percent of the volunteers in the Eastern Caribbean had ET'd.

In truth, we asked ourselves what we were accomplishing not only as volunteers but as a married couple. Though they hadn't said as much, I read into Fred and Edie's departure a fear that two years of slugging it out with a Washington bureaucracy was going to carry over into more personal areas where they didn't want it to. Maybe it was subconscious, a second-nature knowledge of how far they could push the marital envelope. Find that place where stress from outside begins to rip at internal seams. Successfully married couples, I think, adjust in reaction to such forces, and come to learn what they can stand, or are willing to risk.

Julie and I were learning those boundaries. Our first date—the bike ride—had convinced us early on that our boundaries might be pretty far out there. Nothing up to our actual arrival in Jamaica had contradicted that conviction. But now it seemed worth looking seri-ously at where those boundaries lay.

We waited a week after Fred and Edie left, then another. We de-layed our decision by talking it to death, backward and forward over the same ground, ironically, at the pace at which everything else on the island seemed to get done, or not get done.

Finally, one night we took some of Julie's notebook paper and began making notes. We filled up the left side of a page with reasons for staying in the Peace Corps. We put down everything, the minutest pros. Julie had been cutting other volunteers' hair. Who would do it if we left? Then we filled up the right side of the page with reasons for leaving. The list flowed over onto the back of the page. Then, to make sure we were articulating exactly what we wanted, we began writing it all out in sentences, paragraphs, pages. We wrote for an hour, maybe two, and when we'd finished, we had twelve pages. Almost all of it was an argument for leaving as fast as we could.

We let the matter sit for a day, but the day after that we took it to the island's Peace Corps office. The director was a gray-haired bureaucrat in her seventies who'd been stationed in Antigua for two decades and was generally resented because she had a car and a color TV. We handed her the sheets, then laid out our case for her verbally, going through the reasons methodically, trying to appear both devastated and yet confident that we knew exactly what we were doing.

She listened sternly, her fingers forming a steeple under her chin. Silence hung between us when we finished. Then she leaned over her desk and sighed.

"You're so young," she said, "and you've failed." She seemed intentionally dramatic. It was reverse psychology.

"Knowing what you want or don't want is not failure," I said.

She looked past us and through her open door. "I think it is."

She let the sheets of notebook paper lie on her desk without looking at them. A breeze blew under the top one and shifted it a few inches.

The next day we borrowed two mayonnaise jars from our friend Dave for our stool samples. We carried them across town to the clinic, and our clean bill of health was issued later that afternoon. We packed, and by the end of the week had our tickets in hand.

During our rounds of good-byes, nobody used the word *failure*. I was waiting for it. Other things came instead, some of them good, like admiration and solemn handshakes, and some of them not so good. When we told one volunteer, a teacher named Siobhan, she involuntarily took a step back, then wouldn't close that extra space between us. In the same way, there was a gap in the language where nothing was filling the slot that *failure* had briefly occupied. What could replace it, or be more accurate? Bad luck? Tough breaks? Lousy fit? Julie and I were tired of thinking about it. We'd think about it later, but for the moment it was a mishmash, inarticulable, any effort at trying to figure it out a sure route to self-pity.

We had a five-hour layover in Miami. Every step we took on American soil felt light, as if we were constantly riding on the airport's smooth inter-terminal transport. We chowed at McDonald's, our immersion back into American culture complete. I wanted to carry Julie over a threshold, signify that *this* was the beginning of our marriage, that we'd had a false start. We'd get on track, figure out a more sensible move. From Miami we flew into Boston, where there was a snowstorm. We had no winter clothes, and inside the terminal men in parkas sneered at us. Julie's dad drove us home and got us some take-out Chinese. I walked around the house and ran my hands across furniture that had the strangeness but familiarity of something that's been in storage for ten years. While we were gone, our wedding pictures had come—bound in soft, tooled leather. The album was sturdy and vivid, but the event seemed distant and in the immediate past at the same time. I was disoriented for a full day.

DRIVING

I FIND IT HARD TO THINK OF MARRIAGE—OF LOVE AT ALL—
without thinking of how it is dynamic, slippery, constantly in mo-
tion. Even when it seems immovable and immutable—like the long-
spun marriages of my grandparents—it is as active as an atom. And
so the process of "settling down" into a love or marriage has always
seemed to me misnamed. It's not settling down, but finding a pattern
of movement. And sometimes the pattern doesn't come at all, and an
entire marriage is spent groping for it—a more random, anxious
movement.

ONCE WE WERE back in the States, my marriage to Julie took off behind the wheel of a five-year-old orange VW Rabbit. We withdrew

some of our savings from our Boston bank and—after huddling together in earnest adult consultation outside the hearing range of the used-car dealer—bought our first joint property. We paid thirty-five hundred dollars cash.

We drove the Rabbit to Dayton, where our stuff was stored in my parents' basement, and decided what to do next. Letting our fingers hover over the smooth pages of a new road atlas, we picked Denver almost at random. We had loose and casual criteria of where we wanted to live: a big city, mountains nearby, an art scene, and enough industry to make my prospects for landing an engineering job as solid as our Rabbit. In the end, Denver won out over Seattle and Portland because it was only a two-day drive rather than four.

In mid-February we packed the car most of the way up its boxy windows and lashed our ten-speeds to the roof rack.

"Everything we own is in there," Julie said. "Not one book, frying pan, or pair of pants left over. It's perfect."

We scraped a thin layer of frost off the windows, and I slid into the driver's seat—Julie couldn't drive a standard. We cranked the defroster to high and left Dayton in the fleecy smoke of our exhaust. On I-70 across Indiana and Illinois, I could see us as if I were looking down from a passing semi: my fingers drumming on the top of the steering wheel to Bruce Springsteen and Jackson Browne; Julie and me singing along with the muffled music, the speakers in the back buried under piles of clothes; Julie passing me an apple or a peanut-butter-and-jelly sandwich from a lunch my mom had packed for us.

We weren't making any turns, just humming over interstate—Kansas City the first day and Denver the second. Five or six hours out of Dayton, deep into flat, empty Illinois, we quit singing and simply rode. Driving had already become monotonous, the highlights our stops for gas and food.

We hadn't been asking ourselves where we wanted to live so much as how we wanted to live. Released from the boundaries of a college campus and then from the inertia of the Peace Corps, location and lifestyle—the where and the how—seemed intertwined, mutually dependent. If we could define the method, the location would flow out of that like water from a hose. It didn't take us any time to decide that Dayton—the stale scene of my parents—was most certainly the wrong place.

I'D SAVED six thousand dollars in my nine months as an engineer, and the Peace Corps had given us three hundred and fifty dollars apiece for each month we'd served—another fourteen hundred. We had enough money to heighten our sense of opportunity.

Behind the wheel, I felt more in control than I had in months, my arms resting outward and at an angle as if on a dancing partner's shoulders. My father came inevitably to mind—the image of the back of his crew-cut head and his broad shoulders as he steered us toward another vacation in the aqua Dodge sedan with the push-button transmission, or the brown Plymouth Fury station wagon. Cars that were always filled with the smoke of his blueberry Tiparillos.

We stopped at a cheap motel off the interstate in Kansas City, and Julie insisted we unload everything.

"Just take your camera equipment and overnight bag in," I pleaded. "Our room's right there. We'll leave the curtain open."

She was already hauling things through the room's propped-open metal door.

"Can we at least take a walk?" I asked. "We've spent twelve hours scrunched up in a compact car with the seats pulled all the way forward!"

The car was half empty when I began hauling boxes in with her. But I let the tension go. Back in the room after dinner, the day's tiredness hit me and I felt drugged, but we made love in the excitement of being away on our own.

THE NEXT DAY: a western Kansas snowstorm. When the snow was at its heaviest, the driver's-side windshield wiper began flopping like a broken arm. It swung to the left, swishing away a layer of wet snow, but could barely control itself to return in the other direction. I opened the window, caught the wiper, heaved it back to the right. Julie pulled on her coat, then held the wheel while I squirmed into mine. We rode like this for a hundred miles, me leaning out the window to catch the wiper arm and swing it again to the right. My back was cramping, and each time the wiper landed in my hand I expected it to stay there, detached from the car and useless.

At the Colorado border, finally, the snow quit. I sat upright; we closed the windows and cranked the heat. Julie had piled blankets and pillows on top of herself, refusing to come out from under them until it was warmer.

"We're home free now," I told her. "Dead ahead to Denver, and clear skies all the way."

Then we got behind an eighteen-wheeler plowing along at thirty, its box of a trailer buffeted side to side, its rear tires throwing up a wall of slushy snow taller than our car.

"Son of a bitch," I told Julie. "I'm going to try to pass him."

"Try?"

"We've got one more good wipe."

I saw Julie clench the armrest, saw her knees and ankles lock. She stared straight ahead.

A hundred feet behind the truck I eased down on the gas pedal, wanting to reach passing speed before we hit the snow. When we pulled even with the back end of the trailer, the windshield was covered. The snow was heavier and wetter, and I began to realize that it might be too much for the wipers. They could strain and go nowhere, their tiny motor whirring helplessly, leaving us as blind in front of the truck as we were beside it—unable to stop without being crushed from behind. I glanced at the handle for the window, memorized its exact location.

"Dan," I heard Julie say stiffly.

I was completely blind, aligning the steering wheel with a spot on the dashboard, holding it steady. I heard the truck but couldn't see it, and I glanced left to judge our location by the shoulder, but the snow was without detail. My right hand was poised above the wiper lever, and I snapped it down. The small motor kicked in and the black blades hesitated. The motor sounded like an old dog trying to rouse himself from a long nap. Then suddenly the wipers flung upward, cutting underneath the snow and letting it tumble loosely back onto the windshield. But a good heap got heaved off the side by the left wiper, which followed it over the edge and dangled like a tree limb snapped in an ice storm.

One wipe it was. I gunned the engine and almost skidded past the semi. But out in front I could see well enough to put a half-mile between us, and then rolled down the window and stretched out again with the scraper.

Twenty miles down the road, we got off and hit a gas station. The attendant took out a socket wrench and tightened the nut that held the wiper arm.

"That'll fix it," he said.

"That's it?" Julie asked.

The attendant shrugged. When she looked at me, so did I.

IN DENVER we found a furnished apartment we could lease month-to-month until we found something better. I spent my time doing sit-ups. "Fat married man," I joked to Julie, but actually I was in good shape—six-one, one hundred eighty-five pounds. I had read in a book on karate that a Japanese actively seeking enlightenment will say that he is "training his stomach." By bringing the stomach muscles to a state of perfection, he is able to control not only the movements of his hands and feet but also his breathing. I wasn't doing karate in Denver, so I concentrated on training my stomach, with the expectation that the control, the enlightenment, would begin to flow. I levered my torso up and down on the brown shag carpet, my bare toes hooked under the plaid couch. The skin stretched taut over my spine was scratched red by the roughness of the old carpet, and my tailbone was rubbed so raw that a scab formed on it.

I WAS A married man in a suburban apartment—it was a strange existence compared to what we'd planned. There was something depressing about our scene, but the oddness wasn't local. It was almost as if we were in Denver on the lam, running not from a crime but from something that felt more embarrassing and uncontrollable. We were trying to get some distance from our early setbacks. Julie and I had been married five months, and our history was already weighing on us.

We had the urge to get outside of ourselves, outside of *us*. We sent dozens of letters: cream-colored, eighty-percent-cotton, textured envelopes with our resumés folded inside. But in the aluminum mailbox that we opened with a small key was only an occasional circular from a discount store, once in a while a letter postmarked Ohio. My mom sent cards containing crisp ten-dollar bills, scribbling in explanation: "My mother used to send your father and me ten dollars once a month when we were first married. At the end of some months that's all we had to buy groceries." The ten was gravy for Julie and me—we were hitting the restaurants several times a week just to escape the apartment—but we didn't send it back, didn't tell her not to send any more.

It wasn't merely joblessness or the need to rethink what kind of life I might lead that made me feel adrift. I was a husband now, expected to practice without fail the intricacies of marriage. It was an isolating feeling, but one that filled me with a mixture of fear and pleasure—like being put in a room alone to take a test.

Odd, then, how confident I felt. Even while winging it, I assumed—as my parents had assumed before me—that since I'd grown up within a marriage that worked I'd intuitively know how to work my own. My parents never spoke about what it takes to be married successfully, but hadn't the rules leaked into my system like common sense?

I sometimes wondered what things I'd learned that I was then putting into practice. What kept coming back wasn't anything from my parents' marriage but a cloudy image I'd once heard a marriage counselor describe on the radio. He'd told of a new bride who complained because her husband refused to sit on the couch with her, holding hands and eating popcorn, as they'd done when they were dating. I thought of the lonely wife, and I understood where my empathy was supposed to lie.

JULIE COLD-CALLED design studios, photography studios, any likely candidates in the Yellow Pages. She introduced herself to the people whose names she'd gotten in Dayton. I chauffeured her to interviews. She was quiet on the rides, her thin black portfolio flat across her ironed skirt, her eyes straight ahead, on the road. Other times she was nervous and worried that we were going to get lost.

"I read the map," I would say. "I know where I'm going."

"I'm sorry, I'm nervous." She looked out her side window.

While she was in the studios, I roamed the sidewalks, scanned magazines at the drugstore, treated myself to a chocolate cookie that I wouldn't need to tell her about. The waiting filled me with hope for her chances and anxiety over my own search.

"You know, I used to come home every evening and bitch about my first engineering job," I sometimes reminded Julie.

"It was a crummy job," she said. "You sat at a desk all day and solved equations. You can get something better here."

It would have felt too much like quitting to come right out and say that I no longer wanted to be an engineer, even if I explained that I'd prefer to try my hand at something else. The only "something else" I really wanted was "writing," which I was qualified for on the basis of spending occasional hours working on a story, and by having completed one twenty-five-page story that I'd handwritten neatly and presented to Julie in January for her twenty-third birthday.

The story had a solid moral about self-sacrifice, with an ending that spoke of being true to oneself—conflicting qualities I'd always admired. I didn't know how to say so to Julie, but I wasn't in much of a self-sacrificing mood. She was different. As the weeks went on without her landing a full-time job, her confidence began to slacken and the idea of lowering her goals seemed to attract her. For a few days she circled ads in the paper that called for nurse's aides. "I need to prove myself," she argued. "Emptying bedpans. Gaining simple human respect, not admiration." She had an interview and even was offered a job in a center that had a geriatric ward, a psychotic ward, an intensive-care ward. She dropped the idea reluctantly, and then only when she added up the numbers and saw how far three-sixty an hour would get us. She was keeping a journal, and she showed me one entry that hinted that I wasn't handling the uncertainty with nearly as much fortitude. But then she was looking for a place to belong, a place to center herself; I had in mind getting the hell out of engineering.

> Maybe I'll go into medical technology. There seems to be a demand for that. Oh—I don't know. Confusing times, and to make matters worse, Dan has been a real "baby" all day. He's been in a rotten mood, he's barely talking, and he's quite unbearable at this time. He only went to 2 places this morning. AMF wasn't hiring, so they directed him to another company which is expanding and will be hiring. Hope he gets an offer—at least an interview. He's been pouting all day. I think he needs a job desperately. I think he's tired of aimless days. So am I.

The aimlessness, we kept telling ourselves (when I was talking), was a part of the risk-taking.

Julie was diligent about trying to bolster herself, and she tried to bolster me in the same way. "Things will work out," she'd repeat. But much of the time I heard her slogans as from a distance. With every letter I mailed out, every call I made to a secretary asking whether her company was hiring and whether she'd received my resumé, every visit I made to an employment office to fill out an application, my mood grew more rotten. I *was* a baby, and quite unbearable.

THE LEASE said no pets, but one day Julie woke under a heavier loneliness than usual and answered an ad in the paper for free kittens.

"We might as well have a kid," I told her.

"There's a little difference, I think," she said.

Weeks before, I'd talked her out of spending twenty-five of our rent dollars on a hamster. This time I didn't say anything.

Julie brought the kitten home in the middle of a snowstorm, stashed inside her coat like a whiskey bottle. She was a tiny black thing, six weeks old. She crawled all over us before sniffing out the apartment.

"I picked the one that came to me when I called," Julie explained. "She likes to be held."

Still green as a husband, I let this drag on our independence raise thoughts of fatherhood. I was only playing house—what responsibility is a cat?—but I had plenty of time for the game. We named her Flannery after my favorite writer, Flannery O'Connor.

Between us, we'd had only one real pet while growing up—a schnauzer that my sister had convinced my mom to let us get (but the dog lasted less than a year before my dad made us give it away). So on the first night with our cat we made a bed with a spare blanket on the couch, put a water dish next to it, and clicked the bedroom door shut. Flannery, of course, scratched at the door and cried.

"Leave her alone," I whispered. "She'll find her bed and go to sleep."

We lay still, trying to make the kitten think we weren't there anymore. An hour crept by, and she was still crying. Julie opened the door and carried Flan back to her bed, then ran down the hall and closed the bedroom door again. An hour later I did the same. Each time, Flannery sprang back out of her blankets like a toy.

"Maybe we should let her in," Julie finally suggested at three o'clock.

I was dead tired, and I couldn't decide whether I was angrier at the cat or at the cheapness of the hollow apartment doors. "You do, and she's going to expect to sleep with us every night."

The next night I stuffed a towel under the bedroom door to muffle the sound. But the cat had as much reserves as before.

"The neighbors are going to think we're torturing her," Julie said.

And when we gave up, removed the towel and opened the door, the kitten loped into the room and jumped to the foot of the bed, where it took her thirty seconds to curl up comfortably and fall asleep.

JULIE AND I carried Flannery in a paper bag to the schoolyard three blocks away. Or at least until we were out of sight of the apartment complex. Then I lifted her out of the bag and pressed her against my chest. We walked on the gravelly shoulder of the road, and each time a car went by, the cat tried to climb to the top of my head.

At the football field, we set her on the fifty-yard line so she could run around and get some outdoor exercise. The grass was winter-yellow and soggy from the snows that kept hitting Denver then melting completely away. The immensity of her surroundings intimidated the cat, though, and she crouched near our feet. But we went there every few days, easing the cat into the grocery bag, rolling the top shut, and hustling across the parking lot and down the street like kidnappers. We felt sure that soon she would get acclimated to the outdoors and romp across the field like a dog, coming back when we whistled. Though it didn't happen, we didn't stop taking her out. We didn't have much else to do.

In some ways, I felt like Flannery. Even in the center of Denver, the landscape made me feel exposed and barren, and I looked for protective things to hunch against. The Rockies weren't working. We could see them from the west end of our parking lot, but they didn't excite me the way I'd thought they would. I avoided them most of the time, looking east or keeping my head down as if not wanting to make eye contact with something unapproachably monumental.

Trying to be responsible, to make our job searches primary, Julie and I made only one quick foray into Rocky Mountain National Park. We had been fighting beforehand: Julie urging me to send out more resumés, to be more cheerful in my pursuit; me wanting nothing more than a day off, time to think about something besides how diligently she was selling herself.

On the drive to the park I'd been stonily silent, taking the curves faster than I knew Julie wanted me to. She pressed herself against the seat and didn't say anything. In the park, I pulled to the side of the road, close to the guardrail, by a sheer drop. We got out into the cold wind and hunched our shoulders under our light coats. We'd underdressed, not thinking how the temperature would drop as we got higher. Julie wore a bright blue windbreaker over a sweater. Her hair whipped across her face, and the balls of her cheeks turned red almost instantly. Her camera hung on a strap around her neck, and before we'd had time to gaze at the scene she had me pose with it, and then made me take her picture in the same spot—as if we could leave then if we wanted and look at the mountains back in the warmth of our apartment.

I wanted both of us to break out of whatever was straining our relationship, to get Julie out of the depression that hung on despite her strength, to convince us both to enjoy the world into which we'd ascended. I stood by the railing throwing chunks of snow over the ledge, trying to start an avalanche.

"Look at the goddamn mountains," I said. "There they are."

"You look at the goddamn mountains," she answered.

SOMETIMES WE went two days without talking. "We're still not talking," Julie would say on the phone to her mother in Boston. Low enough to be polite but loud enough for me to hear if I was paying attention. Because there were no other voices in the apartment, I always was.

Many days I justified my silence by writing. I was working on a story called "The Marriage Ad."

"It's going well," I'd report to Julie, and she'd tell me she couldn't wait to read it. But I wanted to hold on to it until it was done, until I could prove to her that I'd accomplished something and had a chance of excusing myself from the job search by making it as a writer.

SOMETIMES WE broke the spells by going bowling. The closest alley was smoky and packed with regulars, but the atmosphere gave me a sense of community, something bigger than the two of us and our cat. Once, three teenage girls in the lane next to us kept asking me how to keep score.

"They sure *bowl* as if they ought to know how to keep score," Julie whispered, smiling. "I think they want your attention."

"Maybe I should give them more of it."

It felt good to laugh with the crash of balls against pins and the ringing bells and the jabber of everyone in the joint. The louder the better. I swigged from my bottle of Coors.

ONE NIGHT I made up a list of the ingredients I needed for the week's meals, and Julie checked off seventeen items that she labeled "extra and extravagant." Then she asked me not to put salt in any of the meals I was making.

I looked at her.

"*Not* putting in one teaspoon of salt isn't going to drastically change a recipe," she said.

The issue wasn't only salt. It was control. At the Safeway, we marched up and down the aisles silently, until in the checkout line Julie pointed out that if she were single she could live any way she wanted.

WHEN SHE FINALLY got some freelance work in Boulder, thirty miles away, Julie had to learn to drive the Rabbit. A young guy named Ken, who had a studio through which he piped soft rock music, hired her to lay out catalogs and brochures. She'd have to go up two or three days a week. So we went for short practice drives in the evening, and after a week Julie got in the car alone with a confidence that surprised me. She puttered away through the slushy spring snow that seemed always to be melting from the night before.

In April the snow was finally gone. I watched Julie drive away one morning, went back inside and ate breakfast, then got on my bike and began riding after her. I had the idea that I could ride all the way to Boulder, and then, if she wasn't ready to leave when I got there, ride all the way back. Thirty miles each way. Even a one-way trip would be longer than any ride I'd done since she and I had gone to Piqua on our first date three years before. I'd been sitting inside all winter and felt ready to break out. If I didn't get out into the Colorado land-scape soon, I was going to be stuck in the ruts of suburban life like the other renters in our apartment complex.

I fought the wind, and I knew right away that sixty miles was crazy. I cut it down to thirty—fifteen out to Golden and back. The wind was coming in from the west, flailing as if it had skied down the mountains and couldn't stop at the bottom. I was on my blue Schwinn Traveller, a ten-speed that needed oil. The sun was out, the air thin. There wasn't much traffic on Route 72, and there were no towns or places to stop for supplies (candy bars, Cokes, anything that would give me bursts of energy). The farther I got from the edges of Denver's suburbs, the farther away Boulder felt. I worked hard to make it to Golden, and then I turned around and let the wind do some of the work for me.

Even the shortened trip felt like a small success, and with the wind in my face and later at my back I thought that the key to everything—our individual lives, our marriage, our happiness—was movement, forging ahead. Julie got mad at me because I didn't want to analyze why we had left the Peace Corps. I wanted to live for the future, and I pointed out to her that the future wasn't dragging me down like the past was her. She pinched herself daily to see whether we really had quit and were back in the States, no different from any other couple we knew, and worse off than most who had started out on safer roads. I had no desire to dwell on that. On days when I wasn't being a baby, I preached patience, and wanted to throw some optimism into the mix, as well. Those were the qualities, a year before, that made me confident I could do a hitch in the Peace Corps in the first place, and I could still feel them deep within me despite the fact that it had been Julie and not I who had clung to them most diligently in Jamaica and Antigua. They hadn't been practical then, I told myself, just as, I thought with gratification, it made little sense to pedal all the way to Boulder simply because I'd originally thought I might.

I knew that Julie would tell me I couldn't compare a bike ride to our Peace Corps stint. But I didn't want to ruin the freshness and trust in life that I got from being out alone in the sun and dry air, and I wasn't going to bring up the comparison for her. The whole subject was still hard to talk about, and so we didn't talk about a lot of it.

She didn't say aloud, for instance, that she blamed me for leading her away from the Peace Corps, but I suspected she had such thoughts. I had them myself. She might have stuck it out if she'd been alone. Instead, she'd trusted my logical reasoning. It had been I who had written out those twelve pages, laying down in ink an attack against her intuitions. Her regrets now, I suspected, were regrets of not trusting those intuitions more. And fighting for them.

I couldn't bring myself to admit that the worst conflict of those months hadn't been so much between us and the Peace Corps as it had been between her and me. I couldn't admit being wrong, and I hoped I could relieve myself of feeling any need to if I now acted differently. I desperately wanted optimism and patience to work in Denver—to prove to myself my own strength, and to let Julie see it against her own pessimism and impatience. Selfish reasons, partly. But not completely. I was also thinking of us as a couple. We didn't have to answer to anybody else. We'd have no red tape and no cultural differences to blame if we quit this time.

ON AN EARLY-JUNE evening, the sun already set, I walked into the living room naked. I stopped in front of the chair where Julie sat and clenched my stomach muscles.

"I'm going outside."

She looked me up and down. "I dare you."

"You dare me?"

She laughed nervously, nodding.

"You don't believe I'll do it?"

She stood up and held the cat over her shoulder. Her eyes were wide, and without hesitation she turned from skeptic into cheerleader.

"Do it," she said, laughing.

I opened the door and strode the few steps through the red-wallpapered hallway and then down the stairs. If I met someone, I decided, I would keep walking. Julie trailed behind me, grasping the wall to keep herself from collapsing from laughter. I'd walk right on by and let her do the explaining.

"I'm going out the front door," I said over my shoulder. I glanced quickly through the door's mullioned windows—my warped, naked reflection shone back at me—and didn't see anyone in the lot, an emptiness that allowed me not to pause or seem hesitant.

"Go all the way to the street and back," Julie said between her laughs.

The air was cooler than in the apartment. I could feel goosebumps rising and my balls pulling up close to me. I felt broad against the night, my chest and shoulders a wall over which the air flowed. My thighs felt thick and solid, my feet long and husky. I walked away from the building and into the dimness of the parking lot, between two clunker Chevies that were always parked near the door. I walked out into the open lane that a neighbor's car, its headlights glowing, could ease into at any second. Turning left at the middle of the lot, I glanced over at the three levels of apartment windows and knew that anyone who looked out right then would see me unmistakably, my skin yellow in the streetlight. I tried not to flinch when my heel hit a sharp rock. Julie's laughter was nonstop, buttery and diluted in the moistness of the night air.

From forty yards away I looked back at her once and waved. Then I looked to the western horizon, squinting to make out the tops of the mountains. I could see the stars, and when I stared hard enough at the dark below them I saw where the ragged, blue-black tops of the peaks began. I felt closer to them than ever, standing bare against the same night sky. When I reached the end of the lot, my toes on the pavement of the street itself, the mountains loomed closer than the apartment building, closer than Julie. I stood—shoulders pulled back, stomach tucked in, feet pointing northwest and southwest—and looked at them.

The suburbs hunkered around me. The pavement under my feet was connected to the pavement over which I could hear tires humming in the distance. That in turn was connected to pavement that stretched to other towns, states, countries. At the end of my parking lot, I had all options open to me. But even the next block felt worlds away, the humming as if from boats I could never swim to. My isolation gave me both comfort and worry. The night air chilled me.

Julie hissed at me through her laughter to come back in. I counted the peaks I could see. Then I spun slowly, felt the cool breeze dripping off the mountains bathe my back and buttocks and calves. I could see Julie over the dewy tops of the cars, small and helpless in the doorway, and I felt our reputation as a couple on my bare shoulders. It was a good weight, and I liked the feeling of control. If anyone saw me, I'd be happy for it, happy for Julie and me to be thought of as the couple who would pull such a stunt. She was growing more panicky—it had been a good three minutes, the odds that a car would pull into the lot increasing exponentially—but her panic only made me want to assure her that I knew what I was doing. I walked back between the Chevies, back through the door to the red-carpeted lobby, back up the stairs and into the apartment. But there I felt the claustrophobia once again, as completely as I had the freedom of the outside air.

I TOOK MY energy from those brief moments of control. It was a dangerous energy, because it depended on taking control away from Julie. I wondered about how to share control, whether it was even possible.

Julie's own sense of control seemed deeper, longer lasting than my own. Often it was hidden under her depression, under her anxiety about finding the "right place" and the "right job." But over and over again, when she had gotten tired of feeling useless, that control rose up and shocked me, as if her spine were an I-beam.

While Julie zeroed her energies in on getting a job, I concentrated on being a good husband. I knew I could fall back on being domestic. I thought I had a talent for marriage, an understanding of the unconditional support and trust that all of the books claim is ideal. At least this was the way I let myself see it.

And in the end I got the chance to practice that support. When four months in Denver had passed and it was obvious that none of her freelance work was going to turn permanent, Julie called her old boss and asked what he thought about her coming back. He was enthusiastic, something no one else had been since we'd left Dayton. She hung up the phone and told me she thought we ought to move on this offer, not dig ourselves into a deeper hole. I reached over the table and picked up the car keys. If that was what she wanted, I wasn't going to argue. I was tired of acting, tired of not knowing whether I was being strong or weak.

"You drive," I said.

IMMERSION

I SOMETIMES RODE THE BUS OUT TO THE PHOTOGRAPHY STUDIO and let Julie pose me for catalog shots—modeling shorts, t-shirts, and sweaters for Dayton's big department stores. Once, for a brochure meant to illustrate a ball-bearing manufacturer's willingness to listen, she shot my ear. Another time I sat astride on a chair, my forearm draped over the chair's back, casually displaying my left hand. The Lutheran church was publishing a brochure on relationships, and my wedding-ringed finger was its synecdoche for a good one. Then there were the Sunday newspaper inserts, with their glossy ads. Whenever they were selling picture frames, Julie filled them with our wedding photos. Anyone in Dayton who looked closely enough saw us decked out in gown and tux, tiny representatives of an idyllic, archetypal marriage.

THE SMALL company where I'd worked before the Peace Corps wasn't as forthcoming with my old slot, though for two weeks my ex-boss strung me along with vague intimations that he was pulling some strings. I soon realized he was only being polite. But I had a puppyish gratitude for his gentle lies, and my resumés were stirring up zero action elsewhere. After six weeks, I drew up an alternate version of my resumé—one that didn't mention that I'd ever been an engineer. I got a job as the host at a brass-and-fern restaurant. My job thrilled Julie more than I expected it would. She didn't care so much about the money (hers was enough to support us), but I would now have a reason to get out of the house. It was movement and energy, a sign that I wasn't dead. I made a production out of the fact that, with me leaving before Julie got home and her being asleep when I snuck in at midnight or one, our honeymoon was finally over. I moaned, partly for fun and partly for the romance of it, but after a day or two the time apart didn't really seem unbearable or, to tell the truth, unwelcome. I assumed Julie felt the same.

I was saved, anyway, from having to test the limits of that separation. In November, out of the blue, came a real job offer, from a resumé I'd sent in June. It was engineering, but it was also money, benefits, eight-to-four. Still, I didn't quit the restaurant right away. There were concerns. For me, anyway, if not for Julie, who saw the engineering job as a gift one didn't pass up. At least not one in my situation, who was earning minimum wage and before that had not earned a buck for almost a full calendar year.

My first concern was the job itself: at Wright-Patterson Air Force

Base, in an office that managed sales of fighter planes to American allies. My duty, if I chose to accept it, would be to help sell F-5s to the Saudi Arabians. Not exactly the kind of cross-cultural experience I'd been hoping for. Closer, though, to my life experiences, even to my training. Eighteen years on air force bases had schooled me in things military. I knew the lingo, the values, the arguments for massive weaponry. It all boiled down to a plaque my dad hung on the living-room wall in every house we'd lived in. It was a paragraph each of us kids memorized, like a poem.

> War is an ugly thing, but not the ugliest of things. The decayed and degraded state of moral and patriotic feeling which thinks that nothing is worth war is much worse. The man who has nothing for which he is willing to fight, nothing he cares about more than his own personal safety, is a miserable creature who has no chance of being free, unless made and kept so by the exertions of better men than himself.

So my doubts about taking this job stemmed not from unfamiliarity with military philosophy, but from the fact that it wasn't my philosophy. Mine was the opposite. Reactive, sure, and not extensively thought through. But still, I initiated serious talks with Julie about morals, altruism, selling out. My old college roommate who had joined the CIA was living in Paris and would later do tours in Buenos Aires and Moscow, all the exposure to the world he could hope for. Julie nodded. She wasn't going to disagree about the big picture. She understood my reservations. She wouldn't have married me if I were a gung-ho mercenary. But, she carefully pointed out, not everything is black and white. There are complexities; it might not be impossible to sell fighter planes and still be ethical.

I teased more arguments out of her and voiced the ones I could think of myself, but I understood that I was going to take the job anyway. I was a husband out of work. Not work I *needed*, absolutely, not in the sense that we'd starve. But I liked to think that I had a choice. That I wasn't taking this job out of some protracted sense of a husband's duty as caretaker. Such expectations were the kind we wanted our marriage to undercut. Still, history has a tight grip, and it was a fact that every man in my family—my father, my uncles, my brother Steve—had been or was the bringer-home of the bacon. I felt that weight the way you feel a pattern of early heart trouble among your immediate ancestors.

"You'd better make a decision before they change their minds," Julie finally told me.

So I threw Concern Number One out the window, compromising what I liked to think of as my principles. Concern Number Two didn't stop me either in the end, though it was a more immediate worry and would have a much bigger impact on my daily life than would filling the Saudi skies with millions of dollars' worth of lethal American hardware. My second concern was the fact that my dad worked in the same office.

The same room, even. Granted, it was a room the size of of several C-5 hangars put together, divided by miles of cubicles constructed out of movable, six-foot-high walls. To get to his cubicle from mine, I'd have to walk past a wall of supervisors' offices and through a maze of copy machines. My dad had finished his thirty years in the service and was working at the base as a civilian. His uniform was gone, but the work—selling fighter planes to China, Pakistan, Israel—was essentially the same he'd been doing a few years before his retirement. He'd retired as a Chief Master Sergeant, but everyone still called him "Chief Roche." Everyone knew him, and, when I joined, knew of me through him.

"You Roche's son?" colonels would ask me.

THE PREVIOUS winter Julie and I had fit everything we owned into our VW Rabbit. Now we were renting an apartment in a complex called Georgetown Estates, with parquet floors, mullioned windows, and a population of young professionals. The tennis courts were thirty feet from our door. Our angst and guilt over knowing that this was exactly the kind of life we'd gone into the Peace Corps to avoid evaporated when we looked around the big, freshly painted rooms. We immediately had the urge to outfit them—floral-patterned sofas with lots of pillows, an oak dining-room set, new mattress and box springs. We had to start almost from scratch on the kitchen. If only we'd asked for wedding gifts instead of cash! We returned to one furniture store three times to look at a four-poster bed, deciding against it in the end only because of the red of its particular cherry. We got another cat.

This was the right thing at the right time, we told ourselves. Live fully where you are. Immerse yourself. We agreed, as much as we could, that the two huge projects we'd taken our cuts at so far simply weren't meant to be. I could accept this more easily than Julie, it seemed, who still let our Peace Corps history get her down. When I tried to explain the uselessness of regretting, she didn't want to hear it. I tried to shut up.

We went back to karate class. We went to my parents' house for dinner every few weeks, and had them over in between. We entertained friends, saw movies. To assure that we wouldn't get pulled too deep into yuppie-dom, I tried to continue some stories I'd begun in

Denver. But I had little energy, focus, or time in the evenings after work. Julie was better at such extracurricular activities, devoting part of many weekends to taking pictures on her own. She insisted on going alone, even though she still wasn't completely comfortable with the stickshift. She'd become tired of my driving her everywhere. She was worried about slowly but unmistakably slipping into a real dependency on me: barely being able to talk to people she didn't know, barely being able to fathom carrying out the most basic tasks like taking the car in for an oil change. She made no bones about her need to go out on these shoots alone, calling it a matter of her survival. When she didn't want to drive, which was most of the time early on, she took the bus. She went to a carnival, a river festival, a church festival, a doll show, a cat show, a rodeo, a medieval fair. She forced herself to take pictures of people she didn't know, not from a distance but walking right up and asking their permission. She said she went to each event with a knot in her stomach and came away from it electrified. And when she got the courage to drive, she went to Fantasy Farm, Americana Park, county fairs—as many as she could find within an hour or two of home. As winter set in, she began to believe that she ought to strive for that electricity constantly, that she had to get away from taking pictures of bedspreads and sets of kitchen knives.

"What are you thinking?" I asked her.

"I don't know. I guess I was thinking that it wouldn't be a bad idea to go back to school."

I looked around at the new furniture.

"Maybe not right away," she said. "I'm thinking about the next few years, what I want to do with myself, my career."

"Good stuff to think about," I said.

"If the Peace Corps taught me anything," she said, "it's that I need some structure. I can't have everything be random and uncertain. I can't go out every weekend and take pictures of whatever I find. It's not going to add up to anything. And I need to work with people who are doing what I want to be doing."

"Which means?"

"Nothing in particular. Yet."

But it came to mean something in particular within a couple weeks. Or at least Julie let me in on that particularity, which was that if she wanted a graduate program in photography, she'd have to leave Dayton for it. The closest good one—the one she wanted—was at Ohio University, in Athens, in the southeast corner of the state. She'd checked it out, talked with her old college photo teacher about it. He thought she ought to give it a try.

I knew what she meant about structure. I understood it, and neither the Peace Corps nor our months in Denver proved that I could forge my own framework either. But I saw things from the inside, and knew I was either stubborn and misguided or stubborn and self-aware. I hoped for the latter. Julie seemed to accord me that confidence. She spoke only of her own requirements, her own lessons, leaving me to articulate what I knew of myself if I wanted. In fact, I didn't want. I chose instead to think myself comfortable and on track without the kind of guidance she was speaking of. The evidence might have been to the contrary—my job at Wright-Patt, our accumulating possessions, the unfinished stories in my desk drawer—but these things were ephemeral, I told myself, and fine for the time being. There wasn't, at the moment, anything better to replace them—no other job, certainly, and no new and better stories getting written—but that didn't increase their worth. Nor did it make me think that replacements *wouldn't* come along sooner or later, and add more definition to my life. But I'd always been one to allow situations to develop in their own good time; Julie liked to forge ahead at speeds she determined.

And what about our philosophy of immersion, living in the moment? The moment was passing quickly. Or maybe its focus was shifting. Julie's graduate program would be for two years—plenty of time for its own immersion. The school was only three hours away, nothing compared to our other move. But then we tried to figure out how we might pay for this adventure. (Not "adventure," Julie pointed out. School. Work.) I could find a restaurant job in Athens, or maybe technical writing, if there were any companies there. I had no gumption for another engineering job. Chances were I'd make minimum wage or slightly more at whatever I did. We could sell the furniture, take a loss, and bank the cash to live off for a semester, anyway. If, that is, Julie got a teaching assistantship *and* a scholarship. The idea of us both going off to school together barely even came up. We'd never be able to afford it. Besides, I wasn't ready to be so confined.

It seems now that it must've been I who suggested the other option, after several weeks of letting the plausibility of the idea emerge. I can't imagine Julie making such a proposal, not then, and at least not seriously. Even as her conviction about school grew furiously ("I *know* this is the right thing; the Peace Corps wasn't but this is"), she wouldn't have asked for something so momentous. But I took it upon myself to volunteer. I could hold down the fort in Dayton, keep the apartment and my job, serve as our logistical and financial base. I'd be the supporter for two years. To keep the offer from seeming too generous or addled, I figured when the two years were up, Julie could get a job and put me through graduate school (by which time, I guessed, I'd be ready for it). It was a trade-off, both of us doing what we wanted and yet doing it as a team.

"You want to live apart?" she asked.

"It's been done before," I said.

It surprised me that I would have pointed to any long-distance marriage as a model of what ours could temporarily be, because the only long-distance marriage I knew of personally was that of my parents. I'd gotten married with the idea that Julie and I would start out differently from all of our friends, and that we'd end up someplace other than where our parents ended up. Yet halfway between our first anniversary and our second, we were living in Dayton, and discussing my mom and dad's marriage as one to emulate.

I'd grown up seeing them do it. The air force never quite got the idea that my dad's marriage had higher priority than national security. Four months of schooling in Montgomery, Alabama. Six weeks of jet-engine-repair training in San Antonio. TDYs—temporary duty yonder—to Utah, California, Alaska, and Omaha, Nebraska— usually only for a week, but sometimes twice a month. Then the big assignments: a year in Vietnam, a year in Thailand.

By 1983, my parents had been married twenty-six years. With luck, I figured, they'd slept in the same bed twenty of those years. Perhaps closer to eighteen. As far as I could tell, the missing six or eight years didn't have all that big an impact. My mom had no compunction, in fact, about saying she *liked* her time alone. She often looked forward to my dad's hitting the road again. Nothing against my dad, just the facts. During most of those years, "on her own" meant her and five of us kids, but that didn't seem to change her mind.

"I'd be glad to try living apart," Julie said. "If you think it's what you want to do."

"You don't have to agree to it so quickly," I said.

WE LET THE idea stew for the next month while Julie went on more and more photography expeditions: downtown Dayton on heavy shopping days; a gun-and-knife show at the armory; closed-for-the-winter King's Island amusement park. She stayed late at work printing stark black-and-white images, doing each one over and over until it had the richness and texture she wanted. She wrote her application essay, had me help her hone it. Then she sent everything in.

TO JULIE, the "randomness" of her work was like a roll of snapshots that don't mean anything as a whole, don't resonate internally. She was getting the same feeling from the randomness of her life, she told me—a snapshot of the Peace Corps, a snapshot of unemployment in Denver, a snapshot of her forty hours a week at the photography studio. Small pockets of structure, but nothing overall. Nothing pushing her forward.

What about the structure of our marriage, I wanted to know. Or its randomness? Was it as fractured and incoherent? Truthfully, I wanted it to be. What was the alternative? Dinner at six every night? Mowing the lawn every Saturday morning? Sex three times a week? (I'd been reading an *Esquire* article about couples married less than two years. "Julie," I pointed out, "we're way below average!" She didn't seem worried.) Two weeks' vacation? Sunday-night dinners with the folks?

If Julie wanted structure in her work, I had no objections. I admired her for it. And I thought our marriage ought to leave whatever room she needed for that. Because I wanted its structure to flow from the small to the large—wanted, that is, the small slices of our lives to define the whole pie. Small choices seeping back into the accommodating marriage, giving it shape. There were limits, of course, defined not by the rules of society but by our simple desire for particular limits. So off to Athens with her! As the days passed and we waited to hear from Ohio University, the upcoming two years of being a two-household family seemed inevitable—and right.

WHEN WORD did come from Athens in March, it was a thin letter, in stark contrast to the bulging envelope we'd gotten from the Peace Corps. The contents were equally flimsy: little explanation for the rejection, thanks for applying, wishes for success elsewhere, and a sentence about the portfolio being "inadequate," "weak." Julie took it hard. For an hour she read the letter over for clues, scoured it, partly in disbelief, partly in anger, but mostly in mystification. The lack of explanation bugged her most. If it hadn't been evening already, she would have called the department, asked somebody to say something more to her.

I had mixed emotions myself. First, disappointment. And second, though I thought I'd talked myself out of it, relief that I wouldn't have to send her off with love, a stiff upper lip, and the assurance of an adequate bank account. I told her of the first, not the second. When she couldn't look at the letter anymore, she left it half-unfolded on the kitchen table. I wanted to move it, to put dinner there instead, but she claimed she wasn't hungry. When it got fully dark outside I made us some sandwiches, set them on the table, and moved the letter to the counter. I left it up to her to put it away.

We sat down in front of our sandwiches. Julie hadn't cried, though earlier I half expected her to. Sitting at the table, though, what I had sensed as an undercurrent of tears turned visibly into a clear current of determination. Her jaw was set so that I didn't think she could eat her sandwich. She announced that she was going to Athens anyway, the hell with the letter. "I'm going to plead my case," she said. "I'm going to find out what I did wrong. Maybe I can redo my portfolio and submit it again."

She called first thing the next morning. The director of the photography department said he'd be glad to talk to her, could fit her in midmorning Thursday if she wanted to drive all the way over. She did. I took the day off and rode with her.

We parked downtown and wandered winding streets until we found the art building behind a hill.

"Give 'em hell," I said at the front door. "I'll meet you back here in an hour."

"Kiss," she said, pushing out her lips. I kissed her.

I WENT AND got a coffee, sat on the steps in front of a red-brick building, and tried to imagine this place as Julie's home but not mine. It was inviting—the red-brick paths leading from one red-brick building to another, the cobblestone main street with a mix of banks, old-women's clothing stores, and funky tiny shops with windows full of crystals and comic books. The pleasantness of the town made me forget the relief I'd felt at the sight of the rejection letter, and I began to want it desperately for her. To want it, as a matter of fact, for myself. Not directly, but *almost* directly, because it would be my wife here. This was the benefit of a long-distance marriage, this dual existence, twice the living at once. I wanted it for our marriage. The atypicality we'd felt as young husband and wife in the Peace Corps and for a short time after our return was history. Denver was receding into a vague blip at the edge of a radar screen. What remained strong for me, though, was the distinction of having been in both places. The distinction of simply being away from Dayton, from the conventionality we'd been grasping ever since we'd driven back the previous summer. Sitting on a step in a new town threw light on the ropes of conventionality that we were wrapping around ourselves. They weren't tied tight yet, but I could feel the scratchiness of hemp against my skin. I remembered the pleasure of having people think of us as different and original when we'd traipsed off to Antigua, then Denver. If Julie did no more than traipse to Athens, the rope was going to be a little looser.

SHE WAS WAITING in the sun by herself. Wearing a print skirt, long sweater, and lace-up boots, she'd tried to dress artily for this meeting. She was tapping the toe of her boot against a metal railing when I came around the corner.

"He didn't make any promises," she said, "but he didn't say absolutely no, either."

"He might let you in?"

"Maybe. He wants me to go to the gallery on the fifth floor and look at the student photography exhibit. Then I have to go back to his office after lunch and give him a critique."

"And that's how he'll make his decision? What did you talk about?"

"I told him about my situation. I told him how much I wanted to be in this program and what kind of work I want to do." She paused. "I don't know how I'm supposed to critique the work of students who are way ahead of me. This is a *thesis* show, people who are *graduating* this year."

"You can do it."

She kicked some more at the railing.

"You want to go look now, or you want to get some lunch first?" I asked.

"Look."

There were thirty or forty pictures in the gallery. A series of documentary photos about an Asian family settling into America. We walked through together, picture by picture. At each of the first dozen I asked her what she thought. "It's interesting," she answered. "It's hard to tell."

When we'd gone around the room once, we drifted apart and looked at the photographs separately. I could see Julie chewing her lower lip, trying to form an opinion.

She was dubious when we met back in the middle of the room. She spoke softly, scanning the walls slowly. "A lot of these aren't very good."

"You tell him that then."

"That his students' work is . . . blah?"

"Well, if it is." I was having trouble forming my own opinion, and I would have been ready to agree to their originality and artistic value if Julie had seen such qualities. So I joined her camp. "None of this knocks me over. Your pictures can outdo anything on these walls." I tried to be encouraging.

"You think?"

I nodded. "Absolutely."

She gnawed at her lower lip, took another look.

"The only thing at stake," she said, "is whether I get into grad school or not."

"Better not face the abyss hungry. Why don't we go get some lunch?"

She shrugged.

We got sandwiches at the student union and took them outside, to let the town's air flow over us as much as possible in case we weren't coming back. Neither of us said anything, but I was thinking about that possibility, and Julie looked like she was, too. Then again, maybe she was re-analyzing the photos, choosing the words to articulate what she thought. As we dug in, the director of the photography department walked by. He nodded softly at Julie, then at me. He was a big, burly white-haired man with a goatee. Julie had her mouth full, but nodded back.

"Shit," she whispered when he'd passed.

"He looks nice enough, for a man who holds your future in his hands."

"Don't joke about it," she said.

During her second meeting I went back to the gallery. The stuff hadn't improved, and I didn't think I was wrong to have said that Julie's own work could outshine it. In what hung on the walls, I began to recognize amateurish techniques, clichéd images, sometimes a kind of clunkiness. Julie *would* kick ass here. Why they hadn't seen that was beyond me. When the hour was up I went back out front to wait.

It was another half hour before she arrived. I tried not to look as if I was loitering, reading every flyer on the bulletin board with great attention. Ironically, one of them was from the Peace Corps, with cards to tear off and mail in for information. I took out a pen, sat down on a bench, and began filling out one of the cards. Julie arrived while I was doing it.

"I'm curious. Writing away for some info. I want to see if I've got what it takes."

She stared at me. She was trying not to smile.

"Interesting in joining me?" I asked.

"No," she said. She couldn't keep a straight face. She took my hand and made me stand up. Then she wrapped her arms around my neck.

"Jesus," I whispered.

She spoke into my neck. "He didn't like them either!"

"You're in?"

She nodded, bobbing up and down on her toes so that her whole body tottered against me.

WE SPENT the summer packing, but only Julie's bags. Supplies piled up in a corner of our bedroom—books, sheets and blankets, a new canvas travel bag. Whenever I looked at it, I got to thinking that I wouldn't mind having a little extra baggage myself. I was thinking metaphorically of my name, or rather of Julie's name.

I'd let the opportunity to hyphenate pass the year before, but since then I'd been growing more interested in the idea. My interest was partly aesthetic, the mellifluousness of *Elman-Roche*—completely different from the bluntness I'd heard all my life. It partly went along with my growing urge not only for us to distinguish ourselves as a couple, but for me to do so as a husband. I didn't know any guy who'd ever taken his wife's name. Partly, too, in a running dialogue I'd been having with myself since the wedding, I'd become convinced that it made little sense for one partner to change her name if the other wasn't willing to change his. One for all, all for one. There was some altruism in my act, but actually less than I might have suspected. I truly did think that fair was fair.

Julie would have been incredulous if I'd told her that her hyphenation also made me feel half a step behind her. When I watched her sign *Elman-Roche* on checks at the grocery store, an odd feeling of missed opportunity would arise. I'd been looking away when the starting gun went off, and Julie was gliding ahead, making the first turn while I was still loosening up. And she didn't even think of it as a race. Now she was going away for two years. Another step ahead. I told her I was ready to hyphenate.

"Ah, you finally want to be married to me," she said. "I'm kidding. I've always said it's your decision. Great! It's a great name!"

I knew that male progressiveness and sensitivity were rare enough to stand out whenever and wherever they came. And to call attention to my own desire to possess these qualities, even after I'd convinced myself that I was ready to change, gave me pause.

"People are going to think this is weird," I said. "My parents aren't going to like it. At least my dad isn't."

"So they don't like it. I think your mom is going to love it. When are you going to tell them?"

"On their deathbeds."

"Seriously."

"I don't want to make a big deal out of it," I said. "I was thinking afterward. Do it, then tell them it's done."

"Daniel, it *is* a big deal," she said.

"For me. For you, I hope. It may not be for everybody."

She shook her head slightly. "It's *your* name," she said more forcefully. "Other people can change theirs if they want, or they can keep it. Your name is your name."

Of course the issue wasn't as simple and pure as ownership, but neither was there anything complicated about the actual process of changing my name, so that's what I concentrated on. First I had to put a notice in the *Daily Court Reporter*, the county's legal paper. I made my entry without telling anyone but Julie, but the name I saw in the *Daily Court Reporter* the first time wasn't mine, anyway. They listed me as David rather than Daniel. So I published the notice again, waited four more weeks. And then in early July 1984, having raised no suspicions from the bill collectors or protests from any of my family and friends who might have been perusing the *Daily Court Reporter*, I had the green light.

"I think you should tell your parents before you do it," Julie said. She argued not for approval but for politeness. As the date got closer,

I'd had more and more of an urge to let out the news anyway. I hadn't told anyone other than a few married couples we hung out with, who'd approved wholeheartedly but without any risk to themselves. They'd already gone the more conventional route.

"If I do this, I want it to be on our territory," I told Julie. "Dinner here, or something like that."

"Call them," she said.

I reached for the phone. "This is about patriarchy, you know. I don't think he cares what I call myself, but he's going to be insulted because our kids aren't going to be named Roche." I punched in the numbers. My mom answered, and I invited them for dinner the next night. My dad was in the basement; she'd have to check. I held on.

"He didn't make much of a fuss when you hyphenated, because you're a woman," I said to Julie. "There's still that understanding in his mind that *my* name is the family name."

"He cares what you call yourself," Julie said. "That's why you have to tell him."

I knew what he was going to say, or hoped I did. It wouldn't be a critique, because his philosophy about his kids was pretty simple: When you're of age, you're on your own. This philosophy was not—is not—something that grew out of laziness or lack of love. I think it was more an expectation of self-sufficiency driven into him by his own parents, especially his mother, who raised four boys and expected them to fend for themselves.

I thought of recent instances when I'd told him I was doing things out of the ordinary: quitting my first engineering job and joining the Peace Corps, moving to Denver, staying behind in Dayton while Julie went off to Athens. Each time he'd appeared nonjudgmental: "You gotta do what you gotta do." Occasionally, for emphasis, he'd add, "Sometimes, that's the way life is." I was hoping he'd say the same again.

"Your father has a meeting," my mom said. "Can we come the next night?"

I'd planned on going to the courthouse the day after next. That night would be too late. I didn't want to wait anymore. So I decided to get it over with right then. There was no risk in telling Mom; in fact my change might actually be a compliment to her, a bonding moment. It never occurred to me that she might have laid some personal or emotional claim to the name Roche, any more than she, who had been going to mass for twenty-five years but refused to convert, had laid claim to Catholicism. As soon as I finished she held the receiver away from her mouth and yelled: "Dan's changing his name!"

"Subtle," I said.

She asked for details, and I gave her the quick rundown. Then she asked whether I wanted to tell Dad.

"I think you already did," I said.

"He's in the basement. I don't think he heard me."

"It's okay, I'll talk to him about it later."

After I hung up I thought he might call back, and hoped he wouldn't. Maybe he was waiting for me to call again, but I let myself become occupied with other tasks. And when I went to bed, I lay there and vaguely imagined all the ways my mom might have relayed the news to my dad, and how he might have reacted. But I didn't struggle to visualize every word, didn't *really* want to place myself in the midst of that conversation. I was happy to leave it hazy, to fall asleep satisfied that my mom had let both my dad and me—or at least me—off the hook.

THE NEXT DAY I decided to go with the momentum, to swing down to the courthouse during my lunch hour for a quick strike. Julie offered to go with me—"It *is* a ceremony, after all," she said, "and I am sort of part of it"—but I insisted she not bother. She was busy, would have to ride the bus all the way downtown, then hang out in a dank courthouse while people signed papers.

"I'll get it done, then we'll celebrate tonight," I said. "Dinner and a movie? An evening just for the Elman-Roches?"

At work I turned down a couple of lunch invitations and snuck out of the office at eleven-thirty. At the courthouse, I told the clerk what I wanted, and she pointed me toward the judge's office.

"Knock and go on in," she said.

The judge was an older man with dark horn-rimmed glasses that stuck out well beyond the sides of his head and bent down the tops of his ears. His black suit hung on him like a poncho. On his desk were a small American flag and an intricately carved wooden name-plate. He didn't stand when I came in, didn't look up while I stood in front of his desk. He was studying documents that I assumed were mine.

"Is your client here?" he asked.

"I'm my client."

He began reading. His voice was loud, echoing inside that bony body.

"The applicant wants to change his name from Daniel D – A – N – I – E – L Michael M – I – C – H – A – E – L Roche R – O – C – H – E to Daniel D – A – N – I – E – L Michael M – I – C – H – A – E – L Elman-Roche E – L – M – A – N – HYPHEN – R – O – C – H – E." He raised head slightly, his long nose blocked out his chin.

"Is that correct?"

"It's correct."

He signed the bottom of the sheet. "Approved. Take this to the court reporter."

Out in the hall, I delivered the signed paper to the clerk. "Go okay?" she asked.

"Fine."

"Good. That'll be ten dollars."

I slipped my lunch money out of my wallet. She gave me copies and explained how I could get more if I needed them. She wished me luck.

It was a hot day, and I walked across the concrete parking lot slowly, then sat in my car and let the tension leak from my muscles. I reread the document. After a preliminary sentence about my being a bona fide resident of Montgomery County, Ohio, and having "reasonable and proper cause" (who had asked?), was the simple sentence: "The Court orders applicant's name change to Daniel Michael Elman-Roche." They had left the *d* off *changed.* The copy was washed out and slanted—someone had put the original in the photocopy machine crooked.

I'd been wrong, I suddenly realized, not to insist that Julie come with me, wrong not to trust that she would read my mind better than I could read it and know that, despite what I said, I wanted her there. I sat in the hot car for twenty minutes and thought about how, in many ways, today *was* an extension of our wedding day—another public statement about our formal togetherness, our "oneness," and that there was something perverse about going it alone. I drew lines with my finger in the dust on the plastic that covered the speedometer. I was changed. I couldn't go back in the courthouse and return this new name. I'd have to jump through all the hoops again, another letter in the *Daily Court Reporter,* another month's wait, another "reasonable and proper cause."

How to mark the moment? I watched the judge walk out the front door of the courthouse and slowly down the steps. Should I invite him to join me for a drink? I thought of driving to see Julie, rushing in and presenting myself dramatically, sweeping her off her feet. I looked at my watch. I had to be back at work by one, but it wasn't so much the time that stopped me as the feeling that I wasn't really the actor in this scenario, I was the reactor. If Julie's hyphen had originally seemed like a safety rope easing her into the pool of marriage, mine seemed to be lifting me like a parasail. There was only air below me. I felt as if I were looking backward at the place I'd just stood—the place where my father still stood, and my brothers, uncles, and grandfathers. I was looking at them from Julie's perspective. I tried not to judge, tried not to hold against them the singularity of their names, their unquestioning acceptance of something they'd been handed like keys to a car.

I stopped at Rike's department store on the way back to work and bought a shirt. I didn't need one or even necessarily like the one I got. But I wanted to write one more check, use my old name one last time and have it count for something hard and fast. I signed with a flourish, inhaling deeply like a smoker swearing off on his last cigarette.

When I got to the office, the phone on my desk rang almost immediately.

"Is Dan Elll-mmmaannnn-Roche there?" Julie asked.

"You got him."

"I can't believe it."

"I accept your congratulations."

"Congratulations!"

I leaned back in my chair, trying hard for nonchalance and gallantry.

"How does it feel?" she wanted to know.

The moment of change had been tangible, and felt even more so once I heard Julie's voice. I wanted to be congratulated! But I hadn't congratulated Julie for her own change. So something about her enthusiasm seemed patronizing. She had done all she could not to dare me to hyphenate. She'd never pushed it, as if the choice were completely mine—all the way up to the moment I was at the courthouse alone. And maybe it had been—because for a man to keep his name subverted nothing, and therefore technically wouldn't be a statement either way. The only way I could make a statement would be to change, and in the eyes of a feminist like Julie, that change could only be positive. And so I felt deeply connected to her and immensely lonely at the same time. I had a split sense of being way ahead of everyone else and playing catch-up. A disappointing mixture! I wanted changing my name to make me cry, or laugh, or scream out in jubilation. I didn't want to take it in stride, sitting in my chair at the office with my ear to the phone.

"Like a kick in the nuts," I told her.

THE PROPER thing to do would have been to walk over to my dad's office and tell him it was officially done. But I didn't want to force a confrontation in public, or make it seem as if he had to respond to what was now done. Instead, I told JoAnn, a squat second lieutenant whose desk was next to mine. I didn't like her because she was a gossip and didn't know anything about airplanes. But if I dropped this information into her hands, she'd make it ripple around the office like waves.

"JoAnn," I said, shuffling papers on my desk after I hung up the phone. "Guess what I did at lunch today."

"Got a burger?"

"Close. I changed my name."

"You're no longer Dan?"

"Yes, but also no."

She leaned back in her chair, wary of being taken for a ride.

"I changed my *last* name," I said. "I hyphenated it, like Julie's."

She rocketed forward in her chair. "How? Where?"

I told her about the moronic judge, and the clerk, and the mistake in the *Daily Court Reporter.* And I waited for her to ask why. She didn't. In that way she was like every other woman I would tell in the future about hyphenating. As if the reasons were self-evident. What JoAnn wanted to know was the same thing that Julie had wanted to know: "How does it feel?"

I had some inkling of how it was going to feel in the coming months and years, some suspicion of what lay over the horizon. The fact that a hyphenated man suffers a constant stream of misapprehension and misaddressed mail. That he is often labeled "soft," accused of a crisis of masculine identity in the wake of feminism. It was as hard to answer JoAnn as it was Julie. I found myself dropping my voice and answering not quite her question, but more my own. "It was the right thing to do," I said. What a lofty claim! To take the edge off my self-righteousness, I quickly added that I was famished, though I didn't tell her I feared the feeling was actually nausea.

I went to the personnel office with my document from the courthouse. They'd change my paycheck and insurance forms. I went into my boss's office and told him, and my other coworkers. Over the next month, I tracked down everyone else who needed to know my name—driver's license bureau, Social Security Administration, credit card companies, the bank, magazine subscription services, the library. The hyphen inched through my wallet like a worm. And I got my explanation down to something sensible and direct. I could bring up the subject without seeing people's eyes glaze over with confusion.

If the buzz reached my dad's office, he didn't come over and acknowledge it. I heard later, from my mom, that someone in the office asked him whether I was adopted. He'd said, "No, he's my son." But I figured that he didn't know what to say to me, that maybe he'd find the words after he'd had a chance to think about it. And I didn't say anything myself. So after a couple of days, it felt too late to bring my name change up at all, and we never did. A year later, when I wasn't working in the office anymore or living in Dayton, he sent me a postcard from London, where he was on business. He addressed the card to Dan Roche. It could have been an honest mistake. My mom made the same mistake almost every time she sent me something for the next couple years. "Oh shoot," she always said. "I keep forgetting." I wouldn't hear anything about my father's thoughts on my hyphenation until years later, when I changed my name back. We wouldn't talk directly about that either, but my mom gave me the report: He didn't stop smiling for a week straight.

A MARRIAGE APART

IN JULIE'S CORNER OF THE STATE, IN THE SOUTHEAST, WHERE Athens sits in the foothills of the Appalachians, we hauled her stuff to the fourth floor of the graduate-student dorm. When she opened her door, the room stood before us tiny and austere, about the size of a walk-in closet. It barely widened out from the doorjambs, the windows were drapeless and blindless, and a metal-frame single bed took up most of the space. The floor was linoleum, the walls were sandy cinderblock, and the ceiling a discolored mosaic of sound-absorbing tiles. A black phone hung next to the door.

"Oh my god," Julie whispered.

We hit Woolworth's for lace curtains, a runner to fit the skinny floor, and a Norfolk pine. All afternoon we arranged and rearranged the contents of the room, trying to make it feel both spacious and cozy. It was like moving canned goods around in a cabinet.

"Give it a few days and it'll feel homey," I told her.

"This is the first place I've ever had completely for my own," she said. "I lived with my parents, with roommates. You." She nodded at the cinderblocks as if counting them. "I like it already."

I thought about staying the night, getting up at four to make the three-hour drive to work. But Julie would be awake for hours, nesting, and I knew I'd be in the way if I said I had to get to sleep early. The room was already *hers*, and she declined with a smile when I asked her if she wanted to inaugurate it, break in the bed before I left.

She walked me to the car.

"I may come back next weekend," I said.

"Okay."

"Or the one after that at the latest."

"Okay."

"A week or two apart at a time—nothing drastic. In short spurts like that the year will go quick, it'll be next summer before we know it."

"It'll be fine," she said.

"Enjoy yourself. It looks like fun."

She nodded. "Okay."

Almost as soon as I was gunning along the winding two-lane road back across southern Ohio, it struck me how good this reprieve could be. We hadn't cut ruts very deep yet—we were still a month shy of our second anniversary—but this could be like babying a new car, not putting too many miles on it too soon. I knew I was getting a break most husbands never saw, a chance to live a different rhythm. My dad had gotten a couple of these, as had his fellow soldiers, but only by being heaved into a war zone—a trade without much fairness to recommend it. My new situation was more like my mom's—but she'd had five children. I had none.

I was looking forward to reading in the evenings, taking a class or two myself, playing some ball, sticking it out at my job because the money was all right. This could be fine, I thought, for both of us. The freedom would be good, but that wasn't the main attraction for me. A scheme like this needed stability, and I was proud to be the one who'd supply it. I knew people might see me as the traditional husband bringing home money his wife could spend on buying clothes or getting her hair done. That didn't worry me. I felt a certain connection with the work my dad had done before he moved into his military office job. He grunted it out on the flight line, refueling planes and wielding wrenches on their bolts. His years in Vietnam and Thailand were well away from the "action." He spent them standing on humid runways, while the B-52s he'd serviced thundered off one after the other. It was pure support work.

Anyway, I wasn't sending Julie money to get her hair done. I viewed my role as more noble. She was working on the inside of her head, a worthwhile thing to pay for.

FOR THE FIRST month things were fine. I wasn't entirely alone. The cats were there, and for a while they were good company. Then they got fleas. I chased them around the apartment with a bottle of flea spray, and locked them in the bathroom while I loaded mothballs in the vacuum, then ran it over every inch of rug. When bumps starting raising around my ankles, I'd had it. I told Julie that to be completely fair, and to make our experiences as similar as possible (Why not separate-but-equal? I had begun to think), maybe we ought to get rid of the cats. It hadn't been my idea to get them in the first place, and now I was left to deal with the plague. I brought it up first as a joke: "Are you *sure* you can't keep these cats in your room?" But it went badly.

The next day she wrote me a letter.

> I think I have calmed down sufficiently to be able to speak about the cats. I was very upset after talking with you. I love those cats so much—they give so much joy and love to us—keep us company when we're lonely, yet ask for so little in return. But I can understand how you're inconvenienced, and since *you're* with them all the time, I guess I can see your point. I'd love to keep them, as you know. But if you feel that strongly about it, and since you're there and I'm here (not taking any responsibility for them), then do what you want. But you'd better be sure they're gone *before* I come back in November. Otherwise, I couldn't bear to say good-bye. If you do get rid of them, please take down the etching of the cats in the bathroom—I don't want to be reminded.

When she called that night I promised her that I would take care of them.

"You don't have to," she said.

"I will."

"Really?"

JULIE WAS elated over her new environment, and wrote of it in other letters. "I really feel okay about living alone in a room. I've adjusted fine! I miss you, but I am so excited!" And a few weeks later: "You can probably guess, I'm *very* happy here." And a few days after that, a reference to one of the actual reasons for her excitement: "Anyway, I love you a lot (and miss you, too). But remember—I definitely am becoming a stronger person while at school. I say that because I had some 'aggravation' today @ school w/ some fellow students and I didn't have you here to talk to or anyone to comfort me—I dealt with it alone—I suppose that's *good* for building character, right?"

She was also swamped. Almost every letter told of that. "I'm fine and excruciatingly busy." "Well, the mad dash is on—*lots* of work to do for the next three weeks. I'll be working like mad." "Literally, I have no time. It's unbelievable." And the inevitable result, fewer and fewer letters. "I am sorry if my letters sound so negative, quick, and uninformative. There's a definite time problem to be solved here." "Hello! Sorry for the delay in writing!" "Hi! quick letter before I 're-tire.' Today—I'm worn out."

I never seemed to be worn out, so I wrote long letters to fill the gaps. They were filled with details of how one cat was losing the hair on her belly or of my mundane daily encounters—a hilarious fat lady at the grocery store bending over to the bottom shelf and yelling, "Here's them pickles, Rodney!" With these small observations, I meant to give Julie a sense of how life was going on without her; I also hoped to build stories around them, so I put them in my journal as well as in the letters.

The voice I wanted in my letters was confident but willing to hint that I understood how easily things can get comfortable, how fast assumptions can solidify into beliefs. I wanted to make sure we were both seeing straight, that we understood how temporary my domestic role was, that we weren't out to set any ineradicable patterns.

Sometimes that tone broke down. Julie called one Tuesday evening and caught me depressed over not having seen her for two weeks, over a claustrophobia I felt every time I went to work. I didn't try to keep my chin up. I wanted some sympathy. I grunted replies, let silence hang on the wire like Spanish moss. It was a particularly bad moment, in which I elevated my depression to something that differentiated me from her, forced her—I hoped, vaguely and sluggishly—to remember my life as something different from hers.

"Do you want me to call you back tomorrow?" she finally asked.

"Yeah," I mumbled. "But I don't want to hang up now."

"Well, you don't *sound* like you want to talk."

"I want to be talked to." Another pause. "Okay, call me tomorrow."

I heard her take an in-breath, and I thought, *Here's a moment I'll be able to look back on: my first cop-out.* I believed in habits forming, in precedent. I imagined fortitude being chipped away, devotion beginning to melt.

"Call me tomorrow," I said.

She spoke warily. "Well, I *love* you." She left the words hanging out there.

I mumbled again, something that she might have heard as "Me, too."

I sat where I was for ten minutes, pursing my lips. Hundreds of crows were circling the massive maple tree outside my window, cawing and settling in for the night. The phone rang. I considered letting it ring; I didn't want to be talked out of my mood. I could tell her later I'd gone running to clear my head. I answered. It was a photographer friend of Julie's, a young guy with a thick ponytail whom I'd met several times and liked.

"Hi, Dan. This is your friend John from Athens, Ohio."

"Hi, John."

"I just wanted to call and see how you were doing." He paused. "I had a good day. I studied, sat in the sun. Then tonight I went downstairs with Julie and we ate s'mores. Do you know what s'mores are?"

"Yes, John."

"Anyway, that's about it, and Julie's here and she wants to say hi."

"Okay, John."

"Hi!"

"That's a dirty trick. But I'm glad you called back."

"I saw John downstairs and told him I'd talked to you and that I was going to call you tomorrow, and he said, 'Why not call him now?' "

"I'm glad you did."

"I can't talk long because this is John's phone, but I wanted to say that I love you very much."

"I don't know what I was thinking," I said.

"Don't worry about it. It's hard."

"I miss you." I moaned it but gave the sentence a sweep of cheerfulness, a signal that the depression had been crazy and fleeting.

"Tell me what you miss about me."

"What I miss about you. Should I start with body parts?"

"No." She laughed, then cupped her hand over the receiver and lowered her voice. "But if you drive down tonight . . ."

I toyed with the idea for a split second. Leave right then, be in Athens by eleven, drive back at four in the morning. It would be a show of my devotion to the marriage, an act far more dramatic than having a friend play go-between. But I couldn't, because I'd be saving myself from my own world simply by running into Julie's.

"Next weekend," I said.

"I can't wait."

"Tell John I love him."

When she did, he laughed like someone being tickled.

AS TIME went on, I realized that I had no interest in being a saint. On the other hand, how could I not convince myself that an emotional and intellectual connection—some beautiful resonance in the ether—rather than physicality led to closeness. I wasn't wrapping myself around Julie every night. No constant contact to keep the bond stable. It was something else, then, something—how could a Catholic boy not think like this?—purer. And so I began to see the romance in my marriage become like that of a prisoner, of an explorer setting out alone.

Because if there was one thing I understood about my own place in Julie's life, it was that it wasn't convenient. I was, in fact, often the height of inconvenience: showing up on a Friday night wanting to roll into her single bed for an hour or two and then lounge through the rest of the weekend. I'd try to cajole her into not going to the darkroom so early on Saturday morning, beg her to write more, call more, *think* about me more. I also understood that the distraction I tried to provide was not always unwelcome; sometimes she was clearly relieved to let herself take a breath, go out for a decent meal. Either way, each time I arrived I had before me the task of breaking into her attention, getting her to really know I was there. Even when she was willing to be courted again, she needed to be pulled away from her schoolwork—convinced to leave her camera in her room and skip the opportunities to photograph the dirt-bike races in Nelsonville, the Saturday-night bluegrass jam in Frost, or the young couple and their baby who were scraping by on welfare and whose lives Julie was documenting. (Her project involved photographing them several times a week for a year.)

When she wasn't willing—not every weekend, not by far—I had my fallback position, a strategy meant to protect both of us from the discomfort of direct confrontation. I pretended not to care that I was being shunned. I hung around her room reading a book, slouched on the bed against the wall or slung stomach-down with the thin pillows folded up and piled under my chest. I took walks along the railroad tracks or went for a run by the river. By Sunday she'd unfailingly notice me, and we might even have a few relaxed hours before I had to get in the car and drive home. Usually not enough for much besides a good dinner and maybe an early movie, but enough to keep the weekend from being a sour failure. Enough, that is, to convince us that the foundation of our marriage was still intact, that we still *had* a marriage.

SHE GREW her leg hair. She displayed her calf muscles for me one weekend—twisting around from the waist and clenching them as if she were looking at a new pair of shoes in the mirror.

"There's hair on them," I said.

"I'm going to let it grow," she proclaimed. "I haven't shaved in two weeks."

We were getting ready for bed, and when she climbed in she shoved the blanket aside and held her left leg in the air, giving a tight pull to several short black sprouts on her shin.

"Look. They're almost an inch long already." Her skin rose in bloodless bumps where the hairs were rooted.

I glanced over.

"I've been showing them off to everybody," she said.

I emptied my pockets, undressed slowly, then took my time squeezing into bed. She continued to hold her leg up as if in the middle of an abdominal exercise, curling her neck forward to get a closer look.

"You really like it?" I asked.

"I've never done anything like this before."

"It's only growing on the front of your leg. The back is almost completely bare."

I reached up and helped her cock her leg around to see the back of her calf.

"It'll grow in. I might shave it after a while, then let it grow again. It's supposed to come back fuller that way."

She didn't have a tan, and the dark hairs stood out berserkly, reminding me of an old man crossing his legs and revealing, between fallen sock and hiked pant leg, skin that hadn't seen the sun in years.

"Maybe if you had a tan," I said.

"You don't like it?"

"I'm just saying"—I picked my words carefully—"that it might look better if your legs were darker."

I looked up at the ceiling and breathed in deeply through my nose. In a moment, I could see Julie lower her leg and glance at her underarm, where she was also letting the hair grow. She was like a seventh-grade boy getting muscles, always discreetly squeezing his bicep. I turned on my side and let my arm hang down to the cool floor. Julie turned off the light and huddled against me. Growing leg hair was another thing she was doing without me, I thought later. I didn't really care about the hair, but about being left out.

IN DAYTON, I visited my mother, who was often alone when my dad traveled for work.

"I dropped your father off at the airport last night; he's in California all week."

"Miss him yet?"

"I was out for a drink with my girlfriends before his plane took off."

"You're sentimental," I said.

"He knew I had plans. Besides, I slowed down enough to let him get his luggage out of the trunk."

I asked her once how lonely she got when he was in Vietnam and Thailand—whole years apart. Did she miss him then?

"I just told him, 'Send me the checks!' " She laughed.

But he sent more than that. Every single day that he was in Vietnam and Thailand, my dad wrote home. In the long hot evenings, after twelve-hour shifts on the flight line, he composed letters on wispy airmail paper. A week later they'd arrive in our mailbox. When he was in Vietnam, he was a thirty-nine-year-old tech sergeant— crazily old to be away at war—and my mom was a thirty-two-year-old secretary raising five kids under the age of ten. What did their letters speak of? Fear? Boredom? Love? Anguish? In the midst of writing letters to my own wife I was curious about how it had been done before. I wanted some record of my parents' emotional whirls and waltzes. But when I asked my mom if I could read the letters, she told me she'd thrown them all away.

"You're kidding."

She shrugged. "I couldn't keep them forever."

"You didn't keep any?"

"Well, only the most romantic one."

She went upstairs to find it, stashed in the bottom drawer of her dresser like a love note. Thin, light blue paper. My dad's loopy handwriting. He'd clearly had a couple beers, and the monotonous days were wearing on him. "Hi, doll," it opened, and each paragraph (including the p.s.) told my mom how much he loved her. "A lucky son of a gun" he was, who captured her before anyone else did. He was lonely and bored, but knew he had little right to complain. She was the one with five kids and too many bills, and the checks the air force was depositing into her account were paltry. He was worried. It was a lovely letter, proof that they had been lonely. Here their feelings shone through my mom's wisecracks. But she always assured me that she "couldn't remember having very many problems when your father was away." Maybe in her years as a military wife she had taught herself early to be strong, independent, practical. And now I saw her dashing off for drinks, as happy and self-sufficient every day she was alone as she was on the days my dad was there. Maybe more. And that idea, when I thought about it in terms of my own marriage, did not give me comfort.

STILL, IN A WAY not unlike my mom's, I made up my mind to live with Julie's growing independence, to see it as a symbol of some positive thing larger than ourselves. When people asked how she was, I'd say, "She's growing hair on her legs." I always got a rise out of people, amused head-shaking at the harmless oddity of whatever expectation she was flouting next—and by implication whatever expectation I was flouting as a husband. But I didn't care what people thought, because all these things—the hair, her travels alone through southeastern Ohio to photograph dirt-bike racing and pumpkin festivals, the brochures on Australia she collected in hopes that we could blast ourselves there as soon as she graduated—seemed to me packed with their own subtle significances. They would add up gradually, until finally what would be revealed to everyone was a complete picture of . . . I wasn't sure what. A model marriage? One model, at least. What I did know was that all those bits kept people from assuming, at the very least, that Julie and I were on a normal or staid path as husband and wife. So I doled them out judiciously, which meant any time I wanted Julie's adventurous energy to be reflected back on me. I read to my mom the passage in one of Julie's letters about her dreams of Australia: "I think it's a desire to see the world and not fall into complacency and boredom and unconsciousness," she wrote. "Always have to be on my toes! Maybe I should consider some of the more dangerous occupations, like hit man (hit woman), or trapeze artist."

"I can see her as a hit man," my mom said. "In a good way."

And in between her busy-ness at school, Julie was getting up at six each morning, jogging to the gym, and working out on the Nautilus machines.

"What," my mom asked, "doesn't she do?"

BY FEBRUARY, the support role was seeming even more glory-less than I'd imagined. I went to work, then came home and watched the snow pile up against the green fence around the tennis court. I was doing some of the things I'd planned for my "freedom"—working out, taking night classes in literature, seeing movies with friends. And perhaps those would have been enough, if Julie's world hadn't been so full.

On the other side of the marriage was Julie's ever-richer life. Once she'd gotten the ball rolling in Athens, her world began filling up with her successes. One teacher told her she had "vision." In another class the teacher announced that students could pick up their final exams in his office, and that "if anyone's interested in looking at an excellent, A+++ final, please see Julie Elman-Roche's. Really, Julie, it was beautiful, just beautiful." She wrote to me that the class started clapping, and she held her hands up to her face to hide her blushing. "It's all too good, Dan!" she added. "Now I'm branded as 'star photographer'—ha ha ha. I don't want that kind of pressure!" But I'm sure she enjoyed the praise, as I would have enjoyed it. And I did enjoy it, as much as I could from a distance where it meant little to most people I could brag to. I bragged anyway.

I was proud of Julie, truly happy for her. But I yearned to be more a part of her success, to feel its grip and motivations. Its electricity. I tried, siphoned what I could from it. But there were always reminders that more than physical distance was keeping those parts of

Julie's life her own. One weekend in late spring, for example, she and I ran into the professor who'd made her critique the student show and then let her into the program. He'd been pushing Julie hard that first year, had conferred upon her some of her star status. She'd told me story upon story about their conversations, but I'd never actually met him until that spring weekend. In a letter a few days later, Julie reported his take on it. He'd called it a "turning point." "He said that to you, he was some sort of mythical figure," Julie wrote, "and to him, you were someone he heard about but who didn't exist, really. But on Saturday, we were all people doing our normal, everyday things, and he enjoyed our meeting."

It struck me as odd that he would relegate my existence to something so mysterious. Sometimes I forgot that other people saw the marriage differently than I did, that my presence in it was any less than what I knew in my own head. It wasn't an entirely pleasant reminder of how I fit (or didn't fit) into Julie's new world.

There was another moment, in another of her letters, a moment that spoke to me of Julie's own assumptions about where I belonged. She was writing about shooting portraits of her classmates, and added that she wanted to shoot mine, too, but that "you wouldn't be in your natural environment here!" Her statement was matter-of-fact, lacking any judgment. She'd photographed her friends in their apartments, in their work spaces, wherever they seemed at home. But if their natural environments were in Athens, then by extension so was hers. And mine wasn't. I was beginning to feel that Dayton wasn't my natural environment, either. Rather than a base for our marriage, our apartment had begun to feel like an escape for Julie, a dacha, while her real—her "natural"—home was in Athens. Each time I saw how intensely she lived there, I began to see less point in maintaining an outpost for her elsewhere. She rarely came to Dayton anyway. It was usually I who made the trip.

I told Julie I was thinking of applying to grad school myself, that maybe I wouldn't wait that extra year. I was beginning to feel ready, anxious even. She'd been offered a teaching assistantship for her second year, so I wouldn't have to support her anymore.

"Really?" she said. "Where are you going to apply?" I heard the caution in her voice.

"You wouldn't want me to come to Athens, would you?"

"Well. It would be . . . weird."

"You're honest, anyway," I said.

"No, no, it's not that. You know how busy I get during the school year."

I told her that what I really had in mind was Ohio State, in Columbus, only seventy miles from Athens rather than the hundred-fifty to Dayton. Its own world still, but a safe step closer to her.

"That would be great," she said. "I think you should do it. You'll get in, easy. And you're going to *love* it."

I SENT OUT my application, including a change-of-name form that I had to return to the courthouse to get so that OSU would believe that the undergraduate transcripts they'd receive were actually mine. I drove to Chicago on a Friday evening so I could take the GRE right away. I cranked out an essay that explained why I wanted to get out of engineering and become immersed in Western literature. With a couple of night classes in English under my belt, decent GRE scores, and some grand illusions, I somehow got accepted. I even got a teaching assistantship—a fourth of the money I was making as an engineer but enough to live on. That was fine.

In terms of my marriage, though, the logistics would be complicated. We both knew that. My program was two years. Unless Julie moved to Columbus when she finished, in another year, we'd be extending our separation to three years.

The prospect of a longer separation should have given us more pause than it did. What it gave us, instead, was a challenge at a moment when both of us were beginning to feel as if we could do anything.

Julie came home for the summer and worked at a bookstore up the street. During her free time she tanned and read. We went to lots of county fairs, where she photographed and I people-watched. We both knocked off work in early August and took a two-week train trip to Florida to visit Julie's grandmother. When we got back, we loaded up the car once more for a return move to Athens. Julie dreaded it for a while, remembering the insanity of the year before. But eventually the dread turned back into excitement, then longing. I started school in Columbus two weeks later, so I spent the time after she was gone getting rid of almost everything we'd acquired in the past year and a half. I sold the sofas and the dining table and chairs—Solid oak! Luxurious!—to newlyweds in the midst of their own householding mania, and amazingly got back almost the entire two grand we'd paid for them. The cats were a harder issue, but finally I gave them to some married friends who had a great big house and a love of animals. Julie knew it was coming and took it well, with the mixed emotions of a parent who's sending her kids off to boarding school.

PHANTOMS

IN COLUMBUS I MOVED INTO AN ASCETIC DORM ROOM OF MY own—but it was twice the size of Julie's and had a sixth-floor view of most of campus. The room was in fact meant to be a double, but not many graduate students wanted to live in the dorm. The cinder-block walls were mint green, and I had so much storage space that I organized my belongings into small piles so I wouldn't leave any cabinet, drawer, or closet completely empty. I could sit on my bed and see across campus into the open end of the horseshoe-shaped football stadium. During the fall I spent Saturday mornings watching crowds of people dressed in scarlet and gray stream in that direction.

I lined up a stack of new books along the windowsill, put my Crock-Pot on the floor next to my tiny refrigerator. There was a tan, metal-frame bed and a two-person desk, both of which I loved because they were solid and practical and I didn't own either of them.

Julie sent me an early letter ("I *swear* I'll write more this year!"), concluding "Give 'em hell, Danny! Love, Julie E-R," then took the bus up to visit the weekend before classes started and to get the car, which she'd need for photo shoots. She stayed one night, and I spent most of it rubbing her back, trying to get her to relax. Her teaching duties for the fall required her to give one lecture a week to an undergraduate photo class. She'd just given her first, which she didn't think had gone well.

To cheer her up, I told her about a purely accidental experience I'd had that day, which still had me thrilled. I'd signed up for a Spanish class and had gone to ask the professor if I could miss Friday meetings in order to be at another class I had to take. He was a tall, gray-haired man of about seventy, dressed completely in brown, who opened his office door with a cigarette in his mouth. He wasn't teaching the class, it turned out, but while he called the department office to find out who was, he invited me to sit down and offered me a cigarette. The walls of his office were lined floor-to-ceiling with books; papers and cigarette ashes were strewn across his desk. We got into an intense conversation, which went on long after the secretary called back, about the study of languages, foreign films, theaters in Columbus, Hemingway, *Moby-Dick*, the Spanish film festival coming to campus the next week, a TV movie made from a Faulkner novel. The view from his window was of the main library, and I sat feeling invigorated by his treatment of me as an equal—though I was mostly asking questions. I had barely studied any languages, hadn't read *Moby-Dick*, and couldn't have sworn that I'd ever seen a Spanish movie. Yet he invited me to come back if I had any trouble with Spanish;

sometimes a second explanation can help. Then he added, "Drop by, anyway—no matter what." I assured him I would.

"You have to," Julie said excitedly. "This is the kind of encounter that you have to take advantage of. You have to go see your teachers often, often, often. Pick their brains for all you can get."

I MET OTHER people quickly, and just as quickly made a name for myself as the wifeless husband. As the months went on and Julie failed to show up weekend after weekend (she was again driving around shooting, or in the darkroom), she earned a name for herself, too. My friends called her The Phantom.

On the phone and in my visits to Athens, though, Julie kept tabs on my reactions to school like an older sister. Who'd you meet? What did you learn today? How exciting were your classes? What *questions* did you ask? But not always. Just like the previous year, she was swamped with her own work—in the darkroom until midnight, writing papers, studying for the Spanish class she'd also squeezed into her schedule. "It was an *ungodly* busy weekend," she said when I called one Sunday night. She apologized for being unable to respond to what I had to tell her of my own weekend, barely able to hold the phone to her ear. Disappointed, I told her to call me in the morning.

We fell into a routine of talking twice a week, and I banked on them being good talks. I took guesses on the best times to call, and sometimes won. But it was dumb luck. Mornings she was often on her way out, and evenings she was either not home or completely exhausted. Or studying Spanish. Like the year before, it was going to be easier to throw a few books in my backpack and go work in her room, where I'd be sure to be present during moments when I might fit into her schedule.

In truth, I couldn't bring myself to mind the arrangement as much as I knew I should, or as much as I knew people expected I ought to. I'd come to accept the "necessities" of each of our situations, and knew that hers outweighed mine. We'd started off this whole grad school experiment with the assumption that I would do most of the sacrificing, that I'd take my turn first and then she would have the next go-round. The particulars of our arrangement had changed—I was no longer supporting us both—but the broad philosophy held steady. Or I thought it did. Or thought I wanted it to. There were moments when I began to reconsider that assumption, and I saw later that I should have done so more consistently. But I didn't then, for what I thought were good reasons—including a fear that my gnawing feeling of precariousness was more justified than I wanted it to be.

Still, it was a fall in which we began asking new questions of ourselves as a couple. Not the old ones of how we wanted to be married. We had been finding that out, had been living that experiment. A harder question began to form itself, began to force its way into our conversations bit by bit. It was a question some of my new friends in Columbus had the guts to ask, and one some of Julie's friends had laid on the line for her. Specifically: Why were we married?

I brought it up first in mid-October. It was our third anniversary, we hadn't seen each other in three weeks, and when I got off the bus in downtown Athens I wanted Julie to jump into my arms. She didn't, but I used the excuse of our anniversary to get her into bed early. "Rub my back," she said, and I did, to relax her before we made love. But she fell asleep under my hands, and when I woke up in the morning she was already out of bed and pulling on her clothes. She went to the darkroom until noon, and when she came back I told her I ought to leave if I was going to be intruding.

"I wasn't avoiding sex," she said. "I need to get used to you again."

"I don't know what that means."

She told me not to get mad, said she couldn't explain her feeling but that it was real. "We haven't seen each other in three weeks," she said. "There's got to be some readjustment period."

I looked out the window. What frustrated me most was the hard logic of her argument, there was really no answer possible. At least not one that wouldn't call into question her own self-knowledge. Rather than criticize that knowledge and her efforts at readjusting to me more quickly, I told her I had a "feeling" that we were going to split up, that with her living here and me living in Columbus, we'd inevitably go our separate ways.

I baited her, "Sometimes I don't see how it can work."

I stopped short of asking for guarantees that we'd stay together, or for a guarantee that she'd try harder to understand the insecurities I felt, watching her change before my eyes. I didn't believe in guarantees, saw them as weak substitutes for the actions that weren't happening. But I wanted her to make them anyway.

She didn't bite.

"I don't know what's going to happen in the future," she said. "I think we need to wait and see."

"That's it?"

She shook her head, not to disagree with me but to say that she had no better answers. I thought she could do better, and was afraid to let her not.

"We have *some* control over it," I said. "We have to think a *little* of the future."

But she wouldn't be budged, and for the rest of the day we maintained a polite silence. Then we slept in her single bed without touching each other—a feat that kept me half awake all night on the alert for any limbs crossing the center line. We slept like clenched fists, inevitably exhausted and slackened by morning, when we touched lightly, carefully, with intentions of forgiveness. But I had to catch the nine-thirty bus, and we had no time to find out where those intentions might lead. Three days later, though, on Wednesday evening, a guy in my dorm was driving to Athens for a dance, and I rode along. Julie and I had six hours together. We were in different mental states, embarrassed by our actions of the weekend. The questions weren't gone, but we laughed about the stony silence. We'd been ridiculous, immature, petty. That wasn't us, wasn't the kind of marriage we'd spent three years forming. At midnight we were in bed making love, celebrating our anniversary, and her body felt both familiar and completely new. Afterward I left her there, dozing and comfortable, and went to stand alone on the street, to wait for my ride home.

BUT THERE WAS no consistency to what felt good or bad between us. For every moment of fun there was a moment of despair. I held tight to my faith in an underlying solidity, a stable foundation of love and respect and shared history atop which the logistical details of our marriage could bubble. Julie gave me plenty of clues that she still felt the same—"Wish you were here," she wrote. "Hope you are surviving. Let's talk! I love you greatly. *Te quiero mucho.*" But more and more she didn't, and often what was bubbling seemed acidic, eating down into our foundation. A week after our brief rendezvous, the pleasure of that meeting felt distant, and I scribbled furiously in my journal.

> I just got off the phone with you, and whether it's conscious or unconscious, your "scheme" of alienating me so I won't feel bad when you go off on your own is pretty obvious. And it's also working. You put up a big wall and defy me to get past it. This time it's all because of this paper you've got to do, and I believe that that weight on your

shoulders is affecting you much more than it should, but that's not a full explanation of your closing up to me. I always try to attribute your coldness to the pressure you're under, but you're not under any more pressure than I am. You say you want to get rid of all that holds you back and not be dominated by strict plans for the future, but you'll never accomplish that simply by selling all the little things you own and going to travel around the world by yourself. The controls that you want to avoid so much are actually inside yourself, and you're not going to get rid of them unless you look there. You're letting those feelings inside of you dominate you, or at least you're using them as excuses to avoid things you don't want to be bothered with. Like me . . .

I quit in midsentence, my choleric wad shot. I put my journal away and never showed it to her.

IN LATE October, six weeks into my new life, Julie burst at the end of a letter into a reflection on what was happening to both of us.

The changes we're both experiencing, I'm sure, are tremendous. At least I know I've changed. I feel different. More "formed." Different. I'm sorry about "how I was" the other night when I spoke to you on the phone. I was dead tired. You know, this year apart has been very difficult. We're both busy, and we both are fairly (!) (very) independent. It's just been a strange year so far, that's all . . . We're both growing and thinking. It's all for the best—it's all positive!

She could say so easily at the time. She was still taking off. I felt proud and continued to brag about her to my family, to some friends in Columbus who were curious about her. But my feeling of being in a race only intensified. She seemed to work so much harder than I did, had payoffs that came so much more clearly. Offers for internships! Photographs in shows! I was reading and reading and reading, but what did I have to show for it? I needed to be writing, and for that I had to quit wasting so much time. I wasted time as if it were scrap paper. Too much socializing. Too much sleeping in. I played basketball every Saturday morning I was in town and thought I ought to quit that, because we played for hours and I was wiped out for the rest of the day. I wrote in my journal: "Julie's doing it for herself, you have to do it for yourself!" I was exhausted, with dark circles under my eyes. One guy asked me if I'd been hit.

OVER CHRISTMAS we analyzed me. I was too much of a thinker, not enough of a feeler. This is what the Peace Corps tests had told us, but now Julie looked at the more immediate empirical evidence. Specifically: I'd never gone back to see that Spanish professor. Specifically: One night at a coffee shop, we sat next to a young artsy couple with dyed black hair and thrift-shop clothes who were talking about the universe, philosophy, life. Their conversation was vague and pompous, but it went on for an hour while Julie and I each read a section of the newspaper, commented on the food, eavesdropped. When they left, Julie wanted to know why we couldn't ever talk like that. About art? Literature? Passionate things? Just talk about what touches you, whether it's profound or not. I told her that's easier said than done, when you're not a feeler. And I theorized that we probably didn't talk like that because we didn't have to, since we were married. If we were only friends, we could not see each other if we didn't have meaningful or satisfying conversations. Married, we could get lazy, rely on the *idea* that we were married rather than the act of being married. It went both ways, this idea of working hard at being married, I said.

She suggested I check into Gestalt therapy, which one of her professors had been talking to her about. Go to a counselor. Try something new, fresh, impulsive. She wanted to know whether I ever *really* got excited about anything. "Writing," I said. "I feel passion for that, but it's manifested internally." I didn't jump up and down as she did.

She was only trying to motivate me, she said, trying to make sure that we were both on the same track, that we wouldn't drift apart unconsciously. She told me again, as she had months before: "Go pick your teachers' brains! Claim your education!" She told me about her favorite photography book, by Chauncey Hare, favorite not simply because of the photographs but because of the dedication: "To those who are awakening to their own authority."

THE COUNSELOR I began seeing in mid-January was a tall, lanky, curly-headed man whom I often saw playing tennis on the indoor courts across the street from the dorm. His tennis racket was always leaned up against his desk when I went to visit him. He never acknowledged me outside his office, but inside we talked freely and in ways that weren't all that different from the motivational talk Julie had given me. The counselor was simply more laid back, quietly asking questions and then suggesting practical solutions to my problems. I told him I felt closed up, inhibited, too aware of every action I made. He told me to go to a grocery store across town and act completely different. Talk to people in the aisles, talk out loud to myself, crack jokes with the cashiers, then return to my "normal" world. Go to basketball games and scream. Find any occasion when it was "safe" to say what was on my mind, to operate not according to logic but according to my emotions. The sessions calmed me, and I reported good progress to Julie. "I'm glad you're 'opening up,'" she wrote back. "It takes a lot of effort though to keep doing it and to keep going. Keep plugging away. Day in and day out. Things will happen, you'll see."

I walked around with a heightened awareness of each moment of each day, trying not to let one melt into the other. Some of them stood out easily, like the one in February when I got a letter from Julie which she had neatly handwritten on small sheets of umber-colored paper.

> You know, something's been on my mind that I'd like to write to you about. I can't help thinking this way (and I don't want you to get mad or hurt, which I know you will), but I really like to live alone. I really do. I am so happy alone, I have discovered at school. I don't know what will happen when we start living together again. In a way, I don't want to live together while we're in school—it's just too distracting and I need my full concentration on my studies. I don't know if I want to live together this summer. Maybe you should just do your schooling at OSU and I'll do mine here. I know you're very excited and optimistic about living together, but quite honestly, I don't feel the same way. Major confession . . . It's hard to live apart, yes, but more and more I feel like I'm living apart from a stranger. I'm just finding it all very difficult these days—and for me to just live with you again is a lot for me to handle.
>
> I am being very honest with you. Please think about this to yourself before calling me or writing me and blowing up. I am not comfortable with these feelings, but they are very real. I just don't want to become a dependent, meek person again. And that usually happens in a very slow, unsuspecting manner—and before you know it—poof, it's happened.
>
> Well, so far this letter hasn't been much to smile about. I'm just

not sure that things can ever be the same, and I'm sure that I don't want to "pretend" that they will be the same. I'm mailing you this letter tonight. And I do know I will be hurting you, and I am sorry. I really don't know what else to say . . . But please wait before responding—and we can talk about it.

It was a great excuse to switch topics with my counselor. I told him flatly and out of the blue (we hadn't talked about my marriage before) that I was on the verge of divorce. He was kind, nodded toward a box of tissues in case I broke down, which I almost did, and he listened. But outside his office I refused to get morose. I refused to sulk. I went to a revival movie theater to see *Annie Hall* and found solace in Alvy's voice-over at the end about relationships being "totally irrational and crazy and absurd and . . . but, I guess we keep going through it because most of us need the eggs."

Julie called and tried to explain the "danger" she felt about becoming dependent on me again. I had no answer, except to say that I didn't understand what dependence she was scared of. What did I do for her? Take care of the car? Pay the bills? Fill out the tax forms? Cook dinner? She could do any of those.

I began to imagine my life without Julie, began to see that her departure would mean the baring of my own life to myself. Dependencies flowed both ways. Hers on me were trivial. Mine on her—which I could not express to her, partly because I didn't want to say them aloud and partly because I got no hint that she wanted to hear them—were manifested in letting her carry me along as the person I wanted to be. I admired her energy and focus, her talent and independence, and wanted them for myself. As her husband, I could assign those qualities to myself—not usefully but comfortingly.

Alone, my life, personality, and desires all would be different—or revealed to be different. I'd have to develop her qualities myself, an infinitely harder task than learning how to fix the car.

Julie told me that she'd read how Nietzsche broke his extremely strong friendship with Wagner in 1876 because the loyalty Nietzsche had felt gave way to an even stronger need for independence and his conclusion that their two strong egos could not coexist as equals.

In response I sent her a copy of Emerson's "Self-Reliance." She read it and hid her radio and headphones in her closet, trying to lower the level of noise in her life. "I agree with Emerson," she wrote back. "I am hearing myself think now, with no distractions to pull me away from my thoughts. It's a strange feeling."

It was strange for me, too, that when school ended in May I decided to stay in Columbus for an extra summer session. My staying delayed until mid-July any decision about whether I'd go to Athens. I toyed with other ideas. My friend Phil was willing to jump in the car with me and head to Mexico. Just say the word. Or I could go to Europe by myself. I looked into fares and itineraries, counted my money. In the meantime I took a writing course with a New York editor in town for the summer. She read my work and liked it, pouring out praise along with the other students in the class. I felt things clicking but wondered how I could trust such enthusiasm. Julie's thrill but discomfort over praise for her own work came back to me, and I tried to question all eagerness and ardency. I wanted a realistic view of things.

IN THE END, Julie moved out of the dorm and rented a trailer ten miles outside Athens for the summer. She sent me a black-and-white self-portrait of her sitting on her futon, her bare feet pulled up under her. The trailer walls were paneled and the two windows in the corner were covered with the lace sheers she'd had in her dorm room. They were billowing inward. She was wearing a black jumper, her arms and shoulders bare, and was holding the new cat she had gotten from the local shelter. She'd permed her hair so that it framed her face in gentle waves. She looked dead-on into the camera, no smile.

Once in a while she asked whether I thought we could live together. If I answered, "Sure!" I would seem not to have taken into account all the changes we'd undergone. So I told her we would have to relax and try it, that the more we worried, the harder it was going to be.

I thought most of the time that I was making a grave mistake. That I was being too nonchalant about our distance and so had begun to avoid the really hard work of staying close. For two years I felt I'd done that hard work—keeping the lines open—but suddenly it seemed wiser to back off. Self-preservation? For a week I didn't call or write. I half hoped she would, but was relieved when she didn't. When enough time had passed to show that I didn't *have* to call, I finally did but asked no intimate questions, assumed she didn't want my invasion.

She had her own sense of casualness, which she played up for other people. I wasn't sure how sincere it was, how much it might be for her own benefit. "My mom called Sunday," she wrote.

> We had a quickie talk. My mom keeps wanting to know when you're coming to Athens or when I'm going to Columbus. I said, "Oh, Dan's in school and then he's going to Europe." Big pause. We ended our conversation and the next day Mom called back. "What's going on?" she said. I answered, "What? What are you talking about?" "I

know something's going on." I said, no, no, everything's fine, etc. It's so strange dealing with parents when you're almost *30* . . .

She concluded:

> Things are moving ever so slowly for me here. I feel so lazy, neutral. I'm thinking seriously about talking to a counselor. I feel so trapped inside myself and I admire the patience you have with me. I love you. Lately I feel like such a nonperson—I haven't a clue of *who* I am. No idea. The search continues— Write soon. Send tax form. Do I need a new muffler?

I waited until almost mid-July before I finally discounted Europe. I had no money, and it would be crowded. Columbus was incredibly hot, and Mexico seemed like too much of the same. So I finished my writing class and thought about the unknowns that would face me if I did go to Athens. Was patience, a slow growing back together possible? Would it be so tense that I wouldn't get any work done? I had a nervous stomach all week, then I got completely looped along with everyone else on the last night of class. I let myself get morose and sad and reflective. And I woke up the next day and went to Athens.

BUGS. Julie's trailer sat at the edge of a cornfield and a cow pasture. At night it was noisy with bugs. I'd arrived with some optimism, which had been bolstered by the intense peacefulness of the scene. No other people lived within sight, there was little traffic on the rural road, and I imagined the next two months filled with good work. The trailer was long and thin, with dark faux-wood paneling. The living room held a metal kitchen table and three flowered vinyl chairs. A few cardboard boxes hunkered along the baseboards. Besides the cat, we had no one to talk to but each other. On the second day, Julie thought it was important to lay things on the line.

"I'm realizing how much I need solitude," she said, and "I don't know what's going to happen. I only know I want to be alone."

My optimism vanished. I'd fought my way back from the edge of divorce, often because I could be the strong one in the marriage. "I feel so low," Julie had written in April, then similarly in May. I'd given her the motivational talk, been there to listen. But what kind of talk was the right response to this? What solution was there? And what was the point of my being in Athens? To see whether we could do it? I knew we could, if we eased into it like roommates. But at that point, I was at a loss of how to act around Julie. I felt like ignoring her, and then wondered why it would be up to me to make things miserable. She tried to make them pleasant, friendly. In a letter several months earlier, she had written, "I love you dearly, my husband, lover, and most important, friend." At the time, I'd wondered whether friendship was most important, and what that said about the other two. In the trailer, I took friendly as an insult.

We kept passing each other in the narrow hallway as if pacing a corridor, waiting for something momentous to happen.

It was ninety-five degrees every day, with little breeze. I sat in the tiny bedroom I'd claimed as my "office," shirtless, sweating, trying to read or write. Every book made me feel heavy with the guilt of escape. What pulled me was the tension out in the hallway, in the rest of the trailer. I had nothing as vital as that to write about, and yet I was inarticulate in both places. I held a ball-point pen over heat-softened paper for hours at a time, and when Julie was home I sat nearly silent in her heat-softened presence for similar stretches. A half-dozen cows hung out at the near edge of the pasture, as close to the trailer as they could get, only twenty yards away. They and I often made eye contact through the dirty screen of the bedroom window. Sometimes I went out to stand by the wire fence with them, but they always floated away from me. I couldn't gain their trust, either.

Each morning Julie drove into town to work at school. Sometimes I went—to wander the streets and drink coffee at the deli, which was long and thin like our trailer and never crowded. Usually, though, the trailer seemed a better place to get work done. Then I'd discover again that it was too hot and too quiet. I didn't want the solitude that Julie craved. I'd had too much of it in the previous nine months. I hated it when she was gone—as much as I resented hearing the car pull onto the gravel each afternoon at four or five, signaling that I had to give up the privacy I'd suffered all day.

"It's so hard to get used to having another presence in my space," Julie would say. I'd reply angrily. I'd think of how I was trying to make it my space, too. "I feel like I have to apologize whenever I roll over and accidentally touch you in the middle of the night."

Lying in bed I felt most urgently how we'd forgotten how to talk to each other, how we no longer spoke of our marriage as something that might stretch over a lifetime, as something that had girth and the thickness of a galaxy. We were circles with impermeable borders, butting up against each other like coins, the heat not nearly high enough to melt us together. I'd never been so tired.

I should've left. I said as much to myself a half-dozen times a day. "I should leave." I said it to the cows when Julie wasn't there. I didn't say it to her, though, because she wouldn't have tried to talk me out of it. So I talked myself out of it. Where else would I go? Wouldn't I feel that we hadn't tried hard enough? I didn't know what purpose my presence was serving, what long-range goals I was shooting for, or even whether I ought to be thinking past the very moment in front of me. I knew that Julie could change her mind, that her resignation could lift. Or that I could be wasting two months of my life.

I was held easily by small signals. I trod lightly—letting her drive the car, choose the meals. I considered each potentially controversial remark that came to my mind, and decided whether it was worth uttering. Usually not. In this way, after the first jolts, the surface of our coexistence was smooth. Surprisingly, too, we had sex twice in the first week, in spite of Julie's daytime worries that she'd be hypocritical in making love to me after the talks we had about solitude and divorce. But they were her moves. I trod more lightly in bed than anyplace else.

AT TWO WEEKS, we tried to settle the relationship. We finished dinner one night and stayed in our seats. I was held there by fear and fatigue and—through all my anger and resentment—a love that felt submerged but still present.

I remember the hours passing. Darkness came, but the temperature and humidity didn't drop. I sweated. Did we love each other anymore? Was there any way we could live in that trailer together? Or anywhere? I straddled a flowered vinyl chair, my arms folded and resting on the top of the chair's back. Julie sat forward in her chair, slumped slightly, her legs straight out. Her kneecaps were small, damp bumps. We both stretched our necks, turned our heads slightly this way and that. No one risked a move any more dramatic or intrusive. The crickets piped up; some crows settled into the nearby trees.

"You want to play cards?" I suddenly blurted.

Surprisingly, she said yes. She hated games. We played gin, first one to five hundred.

"I'm thinking about learning to play an instrument," I told her. Julie had bought a mountain dulcimer, a quiet instrument she strummed lightly. She was teaching herself to play. "I'm thinking about the banjo."

"Oh god," she said, but she laughed. "I can't live with someone practicing banjo."

"Do you love me?" I asked.

"I do love you. I really do."

"Enough to let me play the banjo?"

She laughed again. "No! Pick the guitar, please. Or the dulcimer."

"I don't want to compete with you on the dulcimer."

"I think we can live together this summer," she said. "It hasn't been so bad, has it?"

"A barrel of laughs," I said, but I smiled. "What about your solitude?"

She chewed on her lip. "I want that, too," she said. "But I have to define it for myself. Maybe it doesn't have to mean that I'm single. I don't know what it means." She paused, then said, "I do love you. I know it doesn't look like it, but I do. We've gone through a *lot* together."

It wasn't the guarantee I'd been hoping for, but she wasn't wrong. We were both thinking of our adventures—that first bike ride, the Watts' dogs, the crummy times in Denver, the drama of living apart. There was more, too, that I didn't articulate at the moment but that I sensed: the possibility that we'd revealed our emptiness to each other, and that we were bound to each other not by knowing each other's strengths but by knowing each other's weaknesses and foibles—and that for either of us to break in someone else would be too much work. It was a harsh thought. But I remember the fear of it, my hesitancy to imagine myself capable of the same kind of resignation that my grandparents had.

"I don't *want* to get divorced," I said. "I don't like the idea. I don't even like the word." I was worried that I sounded panicked.

"We don't have to," she said. "I don't want to get divorced, either. Unless you take up the banjo."

"So, I'm . . . welcome here? Can I live here for the rest of the summer? Have some space of my own?"

"Yes. Yes, you can live here. I want you to live here."

"Don't you get crazy for noise sometimes?" I asked.

"I get enough noise," she said.

We sat quietly for a long time. Then we shut off the lights and went to bed. We didn't make love, but we lay there awake, our arms touching. The cat walked over us, then settled down at the end of the bed.

I hadn't cried over anything but movies since I was twelve, though I'd tried to force myself when I felt I should. I tried again, squeezing my eyes shut, then letting them open, feeling them start to water. I swallowed, sniffed, made all the noises of crying. But I didn't get any farther than that. Julie didn't say anything. Which was fine. I wanted the relaxation crying would bring, but I was beginning to feel that in my bones and skin anyway.

"I feel like a huge knot has been pulled out of the middle of a rope," Julie said softly.

I touched her hand to agree.

SWERVING

WHEN I THINK NOW OF WHY WE CAME BACK TOGETHER, OF HOW
we were able or willing to give ourselves over to each other again that
summer ("Had an *excellent* summer!" Julie wrote without irony after
I returned to Columbus), I thought not only of what I was learning
about my own marriage but also of what I was learning about other
marriages in my family. The information along those lines began to
come too fast and thick to ignore.

First, my brother Steve got married again. His marriage to Kim
had lasted only a few years, as I'd sourly predicted, and after the divorce he moved to California. He met someone out there. They dated
for two years, and then one day he called my parents to announce that
the two of them had gotten married.

"Big mistake," he says now. "It was infatuation, not love." It was also, he said, an attempt to provide a family life for someone who'd not had a good one growing up. "I thought if I could give her a better, more stable environment, I could save her," Steve said afterward. A generous intention, admirable. No go. The marriage lasted only a few months.

The "failure" disappointed Steve greatly, made him feel even worse about his ability to be married. It made me feel bad, too, and from where I sat I wasn't about to make pronouncements on any person's talents in choosing a partner wisely. I was beginning to understand the long odds of making the right choice. In my family, people had mostly beat those odds. But not always, and sometimes when they hadn't, they'd stayed married anyway. My mother's parents, I was starting to see, were one of those couples. They'd staked out their claim on romantic perpetuity early in my life, and their marriage had endured for fifty years. Now that marriage was finally swelling unhealthily as if infected, threatening to fall apart.

My grandmother getting up to light the oven in the middle of the night and then going back to bed, forgetting midsentence what she had been saying, turning on the shower in the middle of the day and then walking out the back door—the first signs of Alzheimer's. My grandfather, never a patient man to begin with, became so angry and lonely that he could barely contain himself. He lashed out relentlessly at my grandmother. But this turned out to be nothing new. He'd been yelling at her, I learned from my mother and my aunts, for half a century. Sometimes violently, beginning only months after their happy wedding in 1937. It changed everything between them.

Booze was a big part of it. My grandfather drank—not constantly but frequently—until 1968, when he collapsed one day at the bus station and had to have seven-eighths of his stomach removed. Liquor brought out a meanness that found its force in words.

My grandmother had her own quiet reasons for staying with him. "She didn't want us growing up without a father," my mom says now. "We told her over and over to leave him, and she'd say, 'No, maybe when you're all out of the house,' but she never did it then, either."

But in 1986, while my grandmother was losing her wits but still had a few good ones left, she did leave him. Moved across the lake to live with my aunt and uncle. My grandfather, in despair and confusion, called my mom in Ohio, who charged north to bring them back together. Their reconciliation took a week.

Why? Why not let my grandmother live out the rest of her life in relative peace, let my grandfather pay the price for his marital crimes? Was it simply because, despite all odds, Jack and Sylvia had made it fifty years? Was it that longevity had to be honored somehow, had to signal some unaccountable connection impossible to explain but too valuable to discount? Was it really romance, the impulse that had given everybody hope that my nineteen-year-old brother and his pregnant girlfriend could make a serious go of it? I didn't know, but the idea of reconciliation was weighing heavily on my mind. What *did* keep people together for a lifetime? What made them willing and able to forgive? Did Julie and I have this kind of forbearance? Should we? I wondered where our own marriage was at this point. Had we redefined any rules, broken down any obstacles, formed any new expectations? Had our devotion to each other changed?

What I knew was that we were a lot less naive. We understood the precariousness of a relationship and the chances we were taking by living apart. We were often invigorated to know exactly what sort of edge we were walking on, but our sense of precariousness came from something more basic than the fact that we were living apart. It was as much the fact that we were married at all. Almost everything we'd encountered or discovered in the past two years we would have encountered or discovered if we had been living in the same place. Those discoveries were matters not of logistics but of sharing and independence—the issues that gave real definition to the marriages in my family, and to those all around me. They were inevitable issues in any marriage, and whether or not one recognized them and dealt with them well seemed, to me, the key to how well one was married. Good marriages weren't just long ones, any more than a long life was a signal of how well a person had lived.

So we'd come back together, proven to ourselves in the last six weeks of the summer that we still could live together. We could still be in love—not in the abstract but in the jugglings of day-to-day life, feeding from each other, serving each other as windbreaks. When I was honest about it, and when I felt confident enough about our relationship—as I did after that summer—to articulate what kept us going, I had to say it wasn't security and love by themselves, but those things mixed, ironically, with risk. Danger.

But I didn't want danger without security. One made the other possible. And bearable.

JULIE TOOK an extra year in Athens while I did my second year in Columbus. She moved into town, rented a small apartment. I shared a house with Phil, a poet, and Karl, a psych major whom Phil had roped into playing basketball with us. Both were more or less unattached, and we liked to think of our place as a hip bachelor pad. But mostly we worked, hung out and talked for an hour before going to bed every night, played wiffleball in the backyard. Fairly domestic. Every second or third Friday afternoon I disappeared to Athens until Sunday night.

Julie came up to Columbus once early on, but she was around so little that only Phil got to meet her. She'd wanted to photograph "something exciting, different, something really photographable." So she spent almost all of the weekend at a strip joint called The Garden. She was the only woman in the place except for the rug dancers, whom she talked to between their shows. She photographed them getting dressed, putting on makeup, smoking cigarettes backstage, performing their ten-minute routines. She photographed the bored workers who took money for the shows, and the lap-dance cubicles, and the video monitors in nearly every corner that played continuous loops of hard-core movies. She got some good pictures.

"HOPE YOUR libido is holding up okay," Julie wrote several weeks after returning to Athens. We'd talked the night before, joked about whether we'd get through the year okay. Or at least whether I would. I told her the hardest thing about this long-distance arrangement was sleeping alone. The response I wanted was that the hot, bare-skinned summer nights had changed her mind, reminded her of the early years when we never spent a night apart, made her sentimental, too . . . or horny.

"You must want sex more than we have it," she said to me once that fall. Who was I to disagree?

"Are you projecting or empathizing?" I asked.

"You mean today?"

The answer could have been either, or both. Sometimes—mostly when she had been funneling her energies into her work—Julie felt "sexless." Everything was intellectual, or emotional. The only body part she needed was a gut, for feeling. Other times, specifically the previous spring, she swung to the opposite extreme, to the point of questioning the wisdom of fidelity. It was a thought-experiment that she never acted on but which contributed as much as anything to my despair and frustration, to my certainty that the marriage was unsavable. She'd been wondering, flatly, why she couldn't sleep with anyone she wanted to. I'd made up my mind the year before to live with her growing independence, and I'd been trying to outgrow jealousy. I could look back and laugh (uncomfortably, but still) at how foolish I'd been about her old boyfriends, but I couldn't raise the bar that high—personal growth or not.

"You *have* come a long way," Julie often told me. "Remember the time in the Peace Corps when I wanted to go to the library with another guy, and you said, 'No, absolutely not.' You got very upset."

"It was an all-day trip into Kingston," I reminded her.

"We were *friends*," she said.

Having given her "permission" to go off and live alone, though, there had to be limits—impossible to set until we'd reached them. Of course there were our vows, which we'd intended in good faith to keep. Idealistically, though, I wanted to think that everything, at some level and in certain situations, was open to question. Wasn't that part of the healthy danger of marriage? I wanted to think so, but I couldn't really buy it. I was no free-lover, and I came down finally on the side of solidity of trust over personal development at any cost—or at least at my cost. Maybe my arguments had some impact. Maybe she came to her own conclusions. In any case, her "phase" (as she later called it) passed without incident. Almost. There had been one guy, she told me later, though I knew at the time, and she'd been infatuated. I met him once that spring in the lobby of a movie theater in Athens. He was with his girlfriend but there was an awkwardness all around, a surprise on his face that said I was the Phantom Husband suddenly shown up to complicate things. Nothing happened, Julie assured me. Some tension, an afternoon picnic at a nearby lake. The fact that it went no further seemed to hinge more on the infatuation's passing than it did on our marriage vows. But I was probably wrong about that. Those promises ran deep in her, and it would take more than a crush for her to break them.

I didn't know what it would take for me and hadn't given it much thought until the end of that October. It was a convergence of factors—the timing, an available person. Maybe there were other, more insidious reasons. A confidence that sleeping with someone else wouldn't really threaten our marriage, at least not more than other things had? A feeling that Julie had already cheated on me with her work? A suspicion that she wouldn't really mind? Julie had insisted the previous spring, when she'd floated ideas about casual and noncommittal sex, that it wasn't about me. "It's *me*," she said, "my own thoughts." I didn't believe that rationale at the time, and I didn't believe it any more when I was faced with saying it back to her.

ON HALLOWEEN night I went with eight friends to a haunted house, then ended up at Colleen's for beers and stories from Andy the psychic. We were all grad students. Andy brought us into the bedroom and read our shadows on the walls. He was an excellent bullshitter, but after half an hour and before my turn, I retired to the living room, to an overstuffed chair by the lamp. By midnight everyone was back out in the light, nursing beers and sitting cross-legged on the floor. But they soon started calling it a night, and by two o'clock, the only people left were me, Colleen, and one other guy. He was trying to outwait me—the default method of seduction: The last one left is better than no one. I stayed in my chair, as much to see how long he'd last as to save Colleen the trouble of getting rid of him on her own. It had to be close to three o'clock before he finally got the message.

Suddenly the apartment was very quiet. Earlier, in the darkness of the haunted house, Colleen and I had kept bumping up against each other, feigning fear and touching each other's arms. The contact felt fresh, and the tension from it was still high. Awkwardly tapping the leg of the sofa with the toe of her shoe, Colleen asked me to stay until sunrise, just to lie on the bed and hold her. Two hours. If I stayed, it wasn't out of the question that I'd fall asleep and Julie would give me an early morning call. That was my first thought. I knew my own alibi: I'd been out on a run. But Karl and Phil? Would they be too dull with sleep to give her a plausible answer when they checked my room and found I wasn't there, the bed hadn't been slept in?

And could two hours of hugging stop there? Offers like Colleen's meant more than their words. I considered what they could mean, not only in terms of actually getting under the covers and staying for a lot longer, but the bigger picture. I was living apart from Julie again, but the solitude wasn't accompanied by loneliness. Loneliness requires—or brings on—a feeling of weakness, and I felt energized, strong through and through. Nor was my solitude defined by sexual hunger. That was there, but I could see it as a circumscribed entity, like a thought that I could walk away from. Besides, I wasn't sure what her words did mean.

I followed Colleen to her room. I eased myself onto the bed and lay on my side, letting her spoon herself into me.

"You're thinking you shouldn't be here," she said.

"Something like that."

I stayed for an hour, and we didn't talk much. We simply existed for a while in, as Andy would have put it, the overlapping magnetic fields of each other's bodies. Nothing happened.

When I walked home the sky was denim blue. The red sign of the twenty-four-hour grocery was still lit, and so were the streetlights. I stopped and bought a Sunday paper, then went home and read every single section while I drank coffee and waited for Phil and Karl to get up.

At ten I was scrambling eggs and Karl was pouring a bowl of corn flakes. I told him I had a dilemma.

"You want to have an affair," he said immediately.

I said the possibility had presented itself.

"Colleen?"

"Hmm."

Karl was training to be a psychologist, and I hoped to have his input from that angle, as well as from the perspective of a friend. I knew, though, that his point of view was colored by an opinion he'd already shared with me any number of times: that my marriage was fundamentally flawed.

"It's not flawed, and you can't know," I'd argue with him. "You haven't met Julie, you've never seen us together."

"Exactly," he'd say.

"This has nothing to do with Julie," I argued over the scrambled eggs.

"Nothing?"

"Not much."

"Look," he said, "I don't personally believe Julie exists, if you want to know the truth. And if she doesn't, who are you cheating on?"

"Karl, c'mon."

He shrugged and spooned corn flakes into his mouth.

"All right, she exists," he said. "But I do believe that you're going to do this anyway."

"It's not decided."

He chuckled, reading the back of the cereal box.

"It's supposed to be more complicated than that," I said. "It's supposed to be a dilemma."

Phil came into the kitchen.

"Dan wants to sleep with Colleen," Karl said.

"Who wouldn't?" Phil poured himself a cup of coffee and fell into a chair. "Do it yet?" he asked.

"No, I didn't do it yet. Karl seems to think it's a sure thing, though."

Phil looked slowly around the room. "I don't see your wife around here."

"*Never* seen her around here," Karl added.

"And that's reason enough to have an affair?" I asked.

"It's *a* reason," Karl said. "Another is . . ." He pointed with his spoon to his crotch. Drops of milk fell onto his pants.

LATE AFTERNOONS, four or five times a week, sometimes after dinner. Always at her apartment. I wasn't counting, but it hardly seemed to take any time at all to surpass the number of times Julie and I had made love in the previous two years. And this affair wasn't work. Colleen made no demands on me. There was an odd predictability to our encounters, making them feel not risky but safe. It was Julie's thought-experiment in practice—mutual satisfaction with no commitment. It didn't occur to me to feel guilty.

And then early December arrived, Christmas was approaching, and I'd be spending three weeks straight with Julie. I eased out of the relationship. Not directly, but, I thought, clearly enough. After all, it wasn't really a relationship, was it? I began walking home by a different route, thinking it was best not to run into Colleen at all. But she saw things differently.

She called midmorning. I was standing in my socks in the chilly living room, wondering where I'd left my shoes. I had to struggle to bring the fact that I might have hurt her to a conscious level. But I began to understand more thoroughly as I stood dumbfounded, the phone to my ear, listening to her yell. I'd never been yelled at by a woman. What surprised me—stupidly, in retrospect—was how reluctant she was for us to retreat into our own worlds. Julie would have led the charge. I started to argue, but I knew I had little to say that she wanted to hear, and maybe with good reason. What I was doing wasn't the act of a generous person, the kind of person I'd tried to be through my marriage. And suddenly being called to account for letting that generosity lapse left me without excuses. Colleen didn't tell me I was a bastard right away, but she got to it before she hung up.

I SOUGHT OUT other experiences. Julie and I were graduating in June, and I was eager to see landmarks other than the 1958 Chevy perched atop a forty-foot pole south of Lancaster on Route 33, the road that stretched the seventy miles between Columbus and Athens. I decided to resurrect my plan from the previous summer to make a swing through Europe. I had five thousand dollars in student-loan money in the bank—enough for both of us, if Julie wanted to go. I asked. Teased her with visions of romance in Paris and Vienna. I unfolded maps and traced out possible routes. I offered weeks in Madrid, where she could practice her Spanish. I said that if she didn't come along, there would be nothing to stop me from having affairs with every olive-skinned Mediterranean woman I sat next to on the train.

"I'd love to, I really would," she said. "It's not the right time."

She had a job offer, to be a photojournalist for the *Gazette* in Charleston, West Virginia. The offer was too good to give up: a newspaper with a reputation for a solid, creative, and energetic photo staff.

"But *you* have to go," she insisted. "I know how much you want to, and it's the perfect time for you."

"What happened to that synergy they say that married couples are supposed to have, where they are in synch?" I asked.

"Who says?" she asked.

"They do," I said, waving my hand vaguely.

I WENT ANYWAY. I flew into London with a Eurailpass, two thousand dollars' worth of traveler's checks, and an itinerary that would take me to twelve countries in eight weeks. Sometimes I hooked up with others—two weeks with Conor and Rob from Ireland, three days with Edith from New Zealand. (We shared a B&B room in Cambridge, single beds, mutual convenience only.) I had a resurgence of the feeling I'd had after dropping Julie off at school the very first time: I was ready to inhabit the monkish, ascetic role of observer, controller of all my actions. So every alliance I had was temporary, each founded simply upon the accident of common destinations. Touring towns and countryside with strangers, I couldn't help thinking of the synergy Julie and I *might* have had. How we'd have sought out the same obscure places, rather than the overrun ones. How we'd have drifted in the same unconventional direction, away from being tourists.

Mostly, then, I traveled solo. I didn't always mind it, especially when body and spirit could merge in places where I didn't feel part of the great mob: the drizzly streets of Dublin; the rocky, windy beaches of an empty Greek island; the small museums of Arles. I didn't want to be part of the crowd, but I often wanted to be part of a couple. I sent Julie postcards, wrote her long letters from trains, called her from payphones in Barcelona and Vienna. But the five or eight minutes I could afford weren't long enough for abstractions, to explore how she felt about my being over there, or how she was going to feel about being part of a couple in Charleston. I recounted the briefest anecdotes—seeing a bullfight, riding across Yugoslavia with a hangover—but on the phone she seemed worlds away. I began to understand why people move to other countries to forget someone.

In Paris, I walked the streets in the evening, past cafés where couples kissed and laughed. I felt conspicuous, the only person not holding hands. The only person back in his room alone by nine-thirty. I roamed in search of French lingerie I could afford to bring to Julie, but my money was almost gone. I was down to only enough for meals and, minutes before I left the country and needed to unload my last twenty-five francs, a strawberry *tarte*, an apple *tarte*, a croissant, and a raisin bun.

I flew Paris to New York to Charleston. Julie picked me up and took me to the house she'd rented, a four-room, unglamorous but comfortable green shack on the side of a steep hill. You parked thirty feet above it and walked almost straight down to the front door. She'd prepared the interior for me, as if to make up for the previous summer. A space for writing. A double futon. A kitchen in which I could cook whatever I wanted. For days she drew out stories of my travels, studied my snapshots, wanting to know about the people and places in each. She brought me to the newsroom and introduced me to her coworkers. We walked the hills of the neighborhood, and went on Sunday afternoons to a theater downtown to hear bluegrass music. We drove up and down the Kanawha River through nearby towns with names like Confidence and Institute and Nitro. I got a feel for the place. It wasn't Paris, but I thought it could feel like home.

Then I went looking for a job of my own, and found one almost immediately, in Hamlin, the hometown of Chuck Yeager, first man to fly faster than the speed of sound. His statue was on the front lawn of the high school. I became a reporter for a small weekly newspaper. I drove twenty-five miles south to work each day in our orange Volkswagen through Sod and Yawkey and Sweetland. I spent the days chasing down stories that the editor (born and raised in Hamlin) thought someone might talk to me about. Usually they did, especially once I explained whom I was working for. Trying to trade on someone else's reputation was odd, but this was Lincoln County, West Virginia, and I didn't have a reputation of my own. I nevertheless managed to write all the news and features every week—the other reporter did the sports.

Suddenly Julie and I were a working couple again. We were living in the luxury of two mediocre wages, with a few hours in the evening and the occasional weekend to do nothing but spend time with each other. We started socializing with other husbands and wives, resuming a routine that felt familiar from years before: movies, books, food. Talks that didn't feel squeezed out by the pressure of having something else to do. Reading the newspaper and eating cinnamon rolls on Sunday morning. Buying presents for family birthdays and holidays, and signing the cards from both of us. Small routines that bespoke our settlement back into a marriage that fit the pattern, evidence for the skeptics that Julie and I knew something of what we were doing after all. I could sense relief in our parents' voices when we called them once a week. They didn't have to ask whether one of us had heard from the other. Sometimes they got brave enough to mention that since we were actually within touching distance of each other, this might be a good opportunity to have a kid. Julie's mom liked to hoe this row now and then, but she did so with humor and great patience. "We don't *want* a kid right now," Julie would tell her. "Maybe later."

I settled in as the fall went on. Julie went to work and came home, and I went to work and came home, and time seemed to pass comfortably. We hadn't yet reached the "later" that might involve kids, but we were already in some other kind of "later." The past few years, the slip toward and then away from divorce, took on the patina of another era. I actually began to harbor a certain pride that we'd lived through a rough patch, and to think of it as having happened to a person I used to be and not the twenty-eight-year-old I was now. And our past struggles colored our marriage in a way that I was glad to hold lightly onto. I didn't want to rehash them, but they were there as a history. Marriages became more real, stronger, more privately and culturally meaningful when they had histories. We had been married for five years, and when I imagined us living up to the longevity standards of my parents and grandparents, I knew we were just beginning to dig in for the long haul.

THE FOLLOWING summer, 1988, we rented a farmhouse fifteen miles south of Charleston for two hundred fifty a month. Very cheap, very roomy. It was white, two-story, and about a century old. Wood floors slanted toward the interior walls, and we had so little furniture that two or three pieces got swallowed up in each room. But we both loved the place. The house sat on the front end of two hundred acres of woods, and unless we went looking for it, the only other signs of life were the field mice that the cats brought to us and a German shepherd named Grits. He lived at a farm a half-mile down the road but slept on our front porch every night.

It seems in memory that we were operating in a deep-grained habit of love, by which I mean we could leave things unspoken, move within each other's lives with gentleness and subtlety and communion. We could understand what the other person wanted and move to give it without being asked. These were the ineffable qualities of our relationship, the payoffs for earlier struggles. I easily let them manifest themselves in the routines of our free time together and our plans: sitting on the wide front porch in the evenings, and imagining the vegetables we'd grow in a plot I'd dig over on the edge of the lawn. For me, the routine enclosed us like the thick woods behind the house, and it was comfortable.

But there were hints that Julie was experiencing everything differently. Even within the quiet of our surroundings, she wasn't escaping stress. She was working long hours, under short deadlines, sometimes four or five different assignments each day. Shooting, developing, printing. Then, at four o'clock in the afternoon, if there wasn't a photo for the front page of the morning paper, she had to go out and make one. Cruise the streets looking for a scene, a high-impact or touching moment. She worked hard and well, and it wasn't so much the pace that drained her as the fact that she didn't have weeks to delve deeper and deeper into a project, the way she had in school.

"My mind is being consumed," she'd tell me some evenings. "It wanders so much. I jump from thought to thought. I haven't had a full-length conversation in my *head* in forever."

I understood Julie's reliance on internal conversation, understood how such talks were a sign of her mental health, her centeredness and focus. She worked best, relaxed most enjoyably, was happiest when she had the time and energy to talk herself through the day. I had known this about her for years, and knew our relationship was better when she had those internal talks. I tried to think of topics we might delve into together, ones that might engage her passionately. At the same time, I knew that debating and exploring aloud, though important in its own way, couldn't be a substitute. She craved *internal* dialogue, and no number of years together, or intensity of intimacy, or habits of love can give anyone entrance into another person's consciousness. We could travel only so far along this road, and then—married, in love, and reliant upon each other or not—we, like every human being, were each on our own.

"I ought to be reading," she'd say. "I ought to be learning more about the world. There's *so* much I have no idea about. But I'm lazy—mentally lazy."

"There are plenty of books around this house," I'd say. "You've been reading."

"I haven't finished a book in months. Maybe since I left Athens. I pick them up, read a chapter, and then never go back to them. I *want* to read, but I can't concentrate."

I hadn't noticed, and suddenly I had to reconsider every feeling of tranquility I had thought we were sharing, every assumption that the road had smoothed out.

I was reading. Maybe too much, if I'd missed so many clues from Julie. But reading was what I did to relax, and what kept me connected to the writing that I wasn't doing because of my own job. *Well, just get a book and force yourself into it,* I thought. What could be easier than reading? It was a wonderful escape from stress and work, at least the stuff I was reading—novels, essays, biographies. When I asked Julie what she wanted to read, she didn't have any idea—like a hungry person with no appetite for any particular food, a whiny child who refuses to be satisfied by any toy or gooey treat.

Her distraction drove me crazy, and I thought that more than anything she needed to take naps. As often happened in our marriage, Julie thought the same of me when I began to throw up my arms in frustration. And then I decided that if she couldn't pull herself out of her funk, couldn't make up her mind what she wanted, couldn't *let loose,* I'd wait quietly until she could.

Julie interpreted my subsequent three days of quiet waiting as "callous" treatment. She was sitting in a kitchen chair and I was standing in the kitchen doorway when things finally erupted. She suddenly announced that she was sick of this shit, tired of my being a bastard. We had always been careful about insulting each other. We'd agreed early on that the teasing that so many couples do and the "good-natured" public put-downs that get laughs from everybody at the cocktail party were far from harmless. There was always some truth in them that hurt. We'd made a rule against teasing, against flippant insults, even if we swore we were only kidding. We'd never seen anyone who was really only kidding. So I was shocked to hear the word bastard, as I'd been shocked to hear it from Colleen. I had been getting ready to cook dinner—I'd gathered onions and garlic and carrots on the counter—but suddenly I felt my impulse to feed us fading.

"You made a face at me this morning when I tried to talk to you," she complained. "And you've been ignoring me. You don't listen. You're not being sensitive. I don't . . . *like* you right now."

What she wanted, she went on to say, was to be left alone—for me to go away. The mound of muscle below my lower lip tightened like a small stone. I don't know what she ate, but I drove into Charleston and got dinner for myself.

I had been a jerk. I thought I'd outgrown that kind of behavior since our days in Denver. To make up for it, I stopped at the mall after I finished eating and bought Julie a corny card. It struck the right tone of embarrassment and contrition, and didn't assign too much weight to my juvenility. She was asleep when I got home, so I left the card on the kitchen table and crawled quietly into bed beside her. She didn't wake, but she was up first the next morning and found the card.

She accepted the apology, and gave me her own when I walked into the kitchen a few minutes later.

"It was just one of those things that has to work itself out," she said.

"No hard feelings for calling me a bastard," I told her.

That night, cuddling in bed while a purple candle flickered on the small wooden table by the open window, we talked without anger. She admitted that her state of mind wasn't only a result of her job: Her old cravings for real solitude had resurfaced. No, she explained, *resurfaced* wasn't the right word. They'd been there all along. Pretty much ever since she'd moved to Charleston and I'd made my glorious return from Europe. She no longer needed to prove anything to herself—that she could get the car fixed, do the taxes, or be self-sufficient in any of the ways she'd worried about before she'd gone to grad school. Lack of self-confidence was no longer the issue.

"I simply enjoy solitude more than anyone can understand," she said softly. She wanted to be "more productive." She wanted to be independent. I knew where those words were likely to lead, but she didn't rush to get there. She ran her finger the length of my arm.

"I'd like to live apart. I want to live apart. Live alone. Think alone."

"I don't see how I'm getting in your way."

"You're not getting in the way. It doesn't sound good put that way. To tell the truth, it's not even just solitude that I want. That's *most* of it, but, also, I guess I want to feel free to see other people."

"Ah."

She asked me to be hypothetical, just for a moment. What, she wanted to know, did I think about affairs. "And not yours," she added. I had spontaneously told her about it months after it had ended. She had wanted to know, and she had reacted with more curiosity than anger or jealousy. I didn't have to argue, as I had with Karl, that it hadn't been about her.

"It's hard to think about them without thinking specifically about mine," I pointed out. "But you know I thought that was mostly a good thing."

"How so?"

"It put our marriage in perspective. I got sex." I laughed.

"That sounds like a ringing endorsement."

"Well."

"Is it an endorsement for me?"

"Why, are you having one?"

"Not at the moment."

"But we're living together," I pointed out. "It's a little bit different. The floors squeak in this house, so I'd probably hear anybody you snuck in." Then a whole series of images of other places to have an affair flowed through my head. "I don't know why I'm saying this. If anyone overheard me they would think I was spineless and self-destructive, and they might be right, though I don't think so. But, all things considered and given the right circumstances, whatever those might be, I'd probably be for it."

"Really?"

"I can be jealousy-free when I'm hypothetical," I said. "And a little kinky. Besides, tit for tat."

"I don't want you to like this idea for its kinkiness," she said, laughing.

"Doesn't there have to be some return? Don't I get something back?"

We were sticking to banter, and I didn't want to risk the tone by mentioning the other reasons I could imagine for wishing her well in her sexual endeavors. For instance, she might break through her funk in some dramatic way like this. And she'd then wake again to our marriage. Or I might have been hoping that she'd end up hurt by the experience, and I'd be the one to do the healing.

"I do have one reservation," I teased. "Any affair you have is automatically a part of your life that I'd be left out of." I couldn't decide if this sounded more sentimental or grim. Still, the truth of those words struck me hard as they hit the air, and I was sure that I was speaking from a position of real love.

"I can keep you filled in on all the details if you really want," she said.

"Pictures would be good," I told her. "Color."

THE CONVERSATION seemed so abstract as to be without real threat. And I had figured we would either pick it up again the next day without a lapse in tone, or that it would seem too distant and delicate to even mention once the sun rose, like talk during sex. But instead I found myself depressed and unhappy. I had to pound my way back into the subject.

"On an intellectual level," I told her haltingly that evening as we set the table for dinner, "I do think an affair can be an okay thing. It *can* be good. But on an emotional level . . ." I tried to choose words that would explain my new reservations without sounding small-minded. "I don't know that *I* have the self-confidence for it."

"Because you'd feel left out?"

"Living together," I said. "How is it possible to separate our day-to-day existences in only this one area?"

"I've already met someone interesting," she said.

"I figured."

"Do you want to know who?"

It suddenly hit me that she really did want to push this hypothetical scenario into the realm of concrete reality.

I shrugged.

"He works at the record store."

I knew immediately who she meant. I'd bought tapes from him. He was youngish, with thick brown hair like Bobby Kennedy's. He always wore loose white shirts and brown leather sandals.

"His name's Owen," she said.

I couldn't stop myself before I told her he looked like a twenty-year-old wimp.

WHAT WAS MY role in this evolving drama? For most men, there would have been only one answer. But for me, my part seemed to depend on what exactly was driving Julie. If it was stress from work, should I encourage her to quit her job? That was hardly practical. We couldn't live on my salary. Should I pick out books for her and encourage her to read? Try to force upon her the self-discipline that she claimed to be craving? I'd always trusted Julie's ability to work her way out of any dissatisfaction, to discover and act upon whatever was most vital to her. Now she was obviously making moves toward acting in some way. But it was still too early to tell how serious she was and how dangerous it would be for me to let her find her own way through the morass. I decided to wait and see, to play conservatively. I'd try to practice some self-discipline myself, become a model for Julie, a reminder of habits that she had lost touch with. It wasn't the easiest strategy—I was often working even longer hours than she was, and I didn't know if I could actually bear to let her do this. But in some ways it was easy. I knew how to be the rock, the steady presence she could count on. It was at the heart of who I believed I was. Quiet. Dependable.

I'd dig the garden and get some late vegetables in.

I'd stay cheerful and keep talking her through this phase.

I'd rub her back, feed the cats, take her on walks through the woods.

I'd play that role for weeks before I realized that a rock was really the last thing she wanted.

SHE HAD A CRUSH. And in truth, it was interesting to watch, seeing my wife experience the wooziness that I hoped she'd once experienced over me. I remembered a time a few weeks after I met her. She had shown up at the student center at two o'clock in the morning to see me participate in a dance marathon. I'd signed up with some other woman before I got my own crush on Julie. She had waited until a break to find me in the lobby, and had given me a little drawing she'd made of me striking a disco pose, along with a sweet note encouraging me to hang in there for the full eighteen hours. I knew what Julie was like when she had a crush, and I'd seen her move from a crush to something much more serious. The first time was fun, because I was the object of her growing affections. This time, fun wasn't the word to describe it.

She wasn't swept off her feet. I could tell she was starting cautiously, debating the risks of breaking the rules. How much I figured into the equation—my own feelings—was a mystery to me, but at least she'd been thoughtful enough to ask at the start.

When did she see him? I assumed she stopped into the music store. That maybe the two of them had lunch. That some of the evenings after work when she said she was running errands she was really at his place. After our initial ease and openness about the subject, we suddenly had difficulty talking about it. Was I supposed to rag her, quiz her about her day? His name came up now and then. "He's a friend," Julie always said. "There's nothing else going on."

Then, in mid-September, she invited him to go to Athens with her. She was going anyway, I had to work, and she had got up the courage to ask Owen. I had told her I didn't mind. It was a two-hour drive each way. Nothing could happen in the car or on the gentle streets of Athens that couldn't happen in Charleston. But then I found her at the kitchen table a couple of days beforehand, reading a map of Ohio.

"We're going to go camping," she said. "I want to stay up there for a couple days."

"Oh, great," I said. "Make sure you bring condoms."

"Dan." I could see she was on the verge of claiming again that nothing was going on. She knew I knew it was coming, and she mouthed the word. *Nothing.*

The dynamics of this triangle were taking on a bizarre form I couldn't have predicted. I continued to approach her with sarcasm, trying to get her to question how much she was in control, trying to get her to imagine consequences. Then I'd find myself reminding her of her responsibilities toward Owen, looking out for *his* emotional well-being.

"You haven't told him that you're married," I said. "Can you really imagine that he thinks you want to go camping and have nothing happen? Isn't that a little *intimate?* A little naive?"

She nodded vigorously. "I know, I know. You're right. I'll . . . I'll tell him. I'll stop by his apartment before work tomorrow and tell him."

For a moment I felt better that Owen was going to have some

cards laid on the table for him. Oddly enough, it gave *me* a feeling of control, which was more than I knew he had. He wasn't the force in this scenario. That was Julie's role—calling the shots, making the choices about how far to go. I felt a strange comfort in knowing that it wasn't she who was being used. I knew I might be oversimplifying things, but I couldn't help believing that Owen was more of a symbol to Julie than a threat to me. He was a momentary transport into freshness, into the succulence of a new beginning. Julie felt burdened by the routine of our marriage, and suddenly she was floored by a guy barely the age I was when Julie and I got married. I could understand her itch, even though the routine of our marriage was to me a source of assurance rather than despair. I felt threatened and not threatened simultaneously. In any competition between Owen and me, I still thought I had the advantage—even if it was no more than the inertia of a long relationship. What real comparison was there between our significance in Julie's life? So I backed off. Part rationalization and part liberation, I suddenly didn't care if she slept with him. I was sure I didn't. She'd had a brief flirtation with another man in Athens, but she hadn't slept with anyone since we'd met. I had, and I felt oddly unbalanced by the discrepancy.

So they went to Athens. They camped. And nothing happened. Nothing except the discovery, lying in the night air with cicadas chirping around them, that Owen was possibly Julie's soul mate. She used this term later that week, and it signaled an intensification that floored me.

What was a *soul* mate? I had no idea what Julie was talking about, not in the context that she was using the word. Was it simply, as she hinted, that they were linked by their common preference to live outside normal society (Owen had quit a shirt-and-tie job with an investment firm to work at the record store in his sandals and loose shirts)? Or was it that she and I weren't anything of the sort, that we weren't even close? I was scared to ask her to articulate it. Still, when I could stand to hear about him, which wasn't often, I could get her to admit that she was attracted to his innocence and his fresh eye. Apparently he had a habit of noticing the small details in everyday life, of living in the present and not thinking about future ambitions, and social connections, and climbing the ladder of success. As far as I could make out, this inspired Julie to be freshly observant herself, to re-inhabit a creative mindset that she'd had in college and grad school. She claimed she wasn't "infatuated" with him ("I don't feel out of control or impulsive, and my self-esteem doesn't depend upon his approval"), but that he "moved" her. Or reminded her how to be moved by the world around her.

But for the most part we didn't talk about the burgeoning affair. The atmosphere in the house became tense, grievous. What we talked about was separating, with Julie having more energy to be honest about all of its consequences than I did.

"I'm afraid that if I let you go, even for a little while, you'll be gone forever," she admitted. "What if it's a mistake to let you go in the first place? I know this is painful, but it's making me realize how close we are. How intertwined our lives are."

She paused. I didn't fill the silence.

"Yet at the same time," she continued, "I have a strong urge to live by myself. I feel more productive when I live alone. I feel like I've been humming along, noticing less and less, never feeling like I have any time. Then *boom*, I met Owen, hit a wall, and have to say to myself, Slow down. I'm so used to structure and goals—but at the same time I want to shake those things off and adjust my priorities a little. I don't know how, or what that involves."

I had no answers for her. And I don't think she was looking for any.

All I could say was that there were things I couldn't provide, forces against which even my greatest efforts at making our marriage work were powerless. And though as time went on I felt more and more that I would have gotten some satisfaction from pounding Owen into the ground, he wasn't my real target. What should be? I didn't know.

Another week passed, then another, and things with Owen seemed to be heading toward some resolution. Even from the distance I tried to keep, I could see an escalating passion that threatened to accelerate in one direction or another. Whatever was pushing them along down the road, I wanted to be well out of the way when they reached the fork.

I retreated to Columbus to spend a long weekend at my friend Andrea's house. I told her why I was there. She was shocked but not surprised. She'd met Julie and knew the history of our marriage. She cooked for me all weekend, and for hors d'oeuvres we went to the Big Bear grocery store right next to her apartment in late afternoon. Ladies in red smocks gave out samples in every aisle—cheese, wienies, chips and dip, apple cider. We could have eaten our whole dinner there, but Andrea could tell I needed the structure of sitting down to a meal and the focus of lending a hand with the cooking.

She asked me how I could abandon Julie to her tryst.

"I'm not giving it a stamp of approval," I explained. "I don't have anything to give it at all. I can let the relationship play itself out, or I can drive the four hours back down there and kick in the door and watch him scramble out the window." The latter course of action sounded absurd even as I described it, and I knew it would only embarrass me.

Each night we drank two bottles of red wine. I slept as uneasily on the futon in her spare room as the parent of a teenage girl out on her first date. Each morning I woke with the sun and a headache. I didn't call. And I drove back on Sunday evening not because I wanted to find out what had transpired but because I had to be at work the next day.

Julie was on the porch. It was still sunny. I parked and took my time getting out of the car, walked slowly across the gravel drive to the wooden steps of the porch. She was smiling, and calmer than I'd seen her in weeks.

It could have been right then or it could have been an hour later that she told me they'd made love. I had the words in my mind long before she said them. She spoke with relief about how she had needed to do this, clear everything up once and for all. She was amazed that she no longer felt any of the chaos from just two days before. The craziness was over. She swore that. He'd left that morning, and she wasn't going to see him again.

"Here?" I asked.

"I wanted to be on my ground—someplace I felt in control." She told me everything, not as a plea for forgiveness but as a distinct fact that had nothing to do with whether I believed her or not.

I walked through the house, sniffing like a dog. That night I slept on our futon, where twenty-four hours before, she and Owen had been discovering through the earthiness of sex that they weren't soul mates after all. I slept better than I would have guessed. I slept very well, in fact. Julie said that her last night with Owen had taught her mostly that she loved me more than ever, and the one thing that threatened to keep me awake was the annoyance of finding that I was thinking much the same thing about her. I knew I didn't love her less; nor could I muster the proper anger at having been cheated on. I wasn't at that moment interested in Julie's "growth," didn't want to be a cheerleader for something that stuck a knife in my gut. I realized that I didn't want to have the same nonjealous response Julie had had when I told her that I'd slept with Colleen. I had learned that a relationship without boundaries of any kind held little interest for me. That was commune stuff from the sixties—wide-eyed, doomed couples buying copies of *Open Marriage* in 1973—and it never worked.

Still, I fell asleep that night curled into Julie as she curled into me. Two days before, I'd left town knowing that another man would slip into my bed like a tomcat—and it didn't exactly feel like me who was now sleeping where that man had slept after he'd rolled off my wife. And it didn't exactly feel like me who was drifting off in a state of relief that the act had been more help than harm. As far as I could figure, I had finally learned how to relinquish myself in order to move on with the marriage. A long while passed before I thought that what I might really have been learning to relinquish was the marriage itself.

WHAT TO SAY about the rest of our time in West Virginia? Owen evaporated from the scene as quickly as he'd appeared, at least as far as I knew then. Years later, well past the time it mattered, Julie told me that she had continued to see him for several more months. Their relationship went through its own cycles of intimacy and distance, and Julie eventually began pulling away because of the very things that had attracted her to Owen in the first place: his youthfulness, his innocence, the fact that he seemed to have all the time in the world. Which was the last thing she had. Between me and work (she'd been switched to the swing shift) and Owen, she had even less time to be alone. She was more fractured in the midst of the affair than she had been before it.

Years later, when I found out how long Owen had remained in the picture, I felt a retroactive anger, a renewed indignation at having been duped. At the time, though, Julie and I simply got along better than we had in months. We talked, not about being soul mates but about our own differences and similarities, and about where life might take us. I felt a rejuvenated reliance on each other, a love that oddly felt at another peak, and from what I could tell she felt it, too. My friend Phil visited with his new girlfriend (they would marry the next summer), and Julie and I played the old married hosts. Word came through family gossip channels that two of my cousins were getting divorced, and Julie and I were suddenly leading our generation in longevity. People must have been befuddled by that reality, must have wondered how we had gotten ourselves into such a position.

AND THEN THE longest marriage in my family came to an end. Julie and I were at my parents' house, and my grandfather was on the phone, talking to each of us in turn. He joked about the new Chevy Impala he'd bought, telling us how it drove like a charm. Then he grumbled sadly about having had to put my grandmother in a nursing home. I heard a real sincerity in his complaining that convinced me he was suffering. I promised to come see him that winter, that we'd do some ice fishing. He agreed and said he'd teach me how to play the harmonica. But two hours later we got another call. On his way to the nursing home, with no other cars near him, he had swerved into a telephone pole—whether on purpose or not we never knew.

Maybe the heaviness of my grandfather's death contributed to an increasing focus in our house. Maybe we were both completely burned out by our jobs, and forced to choose between staying and going. Maybe it was time to really do something about the fragmentation in our lives and in our marriage. Julie had an idea. She wanted to take a walk. A slow and gentle walk, like the one we took in Jamaica to escape the noise. But she wanted to walk miles, so many of them that she'd be immersed in their power and profusion. By late fall 1988, she had decided she would.

WALKING

STATS: JULIE SPENT SIX MONTHS PREPARING FOR HER HIKE—AND
another six walking the 2,138 miles from Springer Mountain in
northern Georgia to Mount Katahdin in north-central Maine. It was
the Appalachian Trail, that thin spine that winds through woods and
across mountain balds, marked only by packed dirt and white blazes
splashed here and there on trees and rocks.

In her six months of getting ready, she asked me every few weeks,
"Are you *sure* you don't want to go?" She posed the question with the
enthusiasm of a parachuter who can't imagine passing up the joy of
free-falling, but also with the pride of one who never really expects
that anybody else shares his kind of lunacy.

We had talked about such a walk, in the Peace Corps, imagining ourselves going together from coast to coast. Now I was ambivalent, and taken up short by the *concreteness* of the proposal.

"I *like* to walk," I'd assure her, "but less diligently." In high school I'd read Peter Jenkins's *A Walk Across America,* and the book had inspired me to take long, solitary treks across my hometown of Dayton. I wound in and out of subdivisions and trailer parks I hadn't known existed. I was always satisfied to arrive home, exhausted and hungry, by sunset. Hiking the entire AT (as hikers call the Appalachian Trail) had been a childhood dream of Julie's but not of mine. She grew up in Massachusetts, taking vacations in the White Mountains of New Hampshire to walk small sections of the Trail. She used to describe for me how the Trail hooked her early: the beauty and isolation of a simple footpath through the mountains. Maybe her desire to walk such astounding distances had even more basic origins. Thoreau, in his essay "Walking," claims that being a true Walker "comes only by the grace of God. . . . You must be born into a family of Walkers." I assume he means a family beyond relatives, a group bonded by passion rather than blood. Certainly no one else in Julie's family was the kind of walker she wanted to be. They were no more likely than most people to think that walking for six months was something to do, no more likely to have the concept enter their heads and replace archetypal visions of vacations in the Caribbean or Paris. When Julie nervously broke the news to her father that she was going to walk the Appalachian Trail, he actually thought she meant the Freedom Trail—the three-mile-long path through downtown Boston on which tourists can see the Old North Church and Faneuil Hall. "So?" he asked.

It became increasingly clear that I also was not the kind of walker that Julie was. Perhaps she and I weren't in the same family, the kind inhabited by true Walkers, despite our thinking for the previous six years. We were family surely, but on a level that was being overpowered by an emerging exchange family of sorts—a group she'd live within temporarily for the convenience and instructiveness and companionship of all (except me). She simply had no idea who'd be in that family until she met them in the woods.

She did begin to look, though. In the *Appalachian Trailway News*, she scanned the classifieds for hiking partners. "Going all the way? Need partner for north-bound thru-hike, leaving Springer early April. Frank." "Plan on 20 miles/day and want partner for motivation and ambulation. Can leave late March. David." "Katahdin bound! Trek with me! Good conversation and a sane pace. Pumped! Gordie."

"They're all men," I pointed out.

"What a drag," she said sarcastically. "Guess I'll have to share a shelter with a bunch of muscular, outdoorsy guys for half a year."

What she was looking and hoping for was plenty of solitude, quiet, time to think and evaluate, as she put it, "where I am in life." Career mostly. Did she really want to be a photojournalist, a job that left her limp with exhaustion every evening? Did she want the stress? If anything, she was nervous about meeting *too* many people out in the woods, having the trip be too social. So when she asked, when she insisted—"You *can* go if you want"—I picked silently at the undercurrent of reluctance in her offer, hearing most distinctly the politely forced generosity in her words. I let her forge ahead buying supplies: a one-person tent, boots only for herself, cooking supplies for one. I joked about how I'd be a drag on her out in the woods, telling her when to stop for a break, where to pitch the tent, how much faster to walk.

"Yeah, probably," she said.

It wasn't just that I didn't want to impose. A marriage may not give one the right to impose, but it ought to give one the invitation. It was also—more—that the hike, even before it started, was surprisingly pushing me further into my own individual identity, as it was pushing Julie into hers. I'd learned at least one thing in six years: that being patient with a strong and independent woman could garner more admiration and wonder than any action I might take on my own. Our reversal of traditional roles seemed mysterious and rare to some people, like a marriage in a movie. Rather than hike, I saw other territory I could stake out—in the forest of contemporary marriage, in my place as a husband. What other man would let his wife go off alone like this? My talent, I knew, was not in walking the AT myself (I *could* walk it, I reassured myself), but in letting Julie walk it. It was the art of sacrifice. I chose to think of this separation positively, as the ability to make a statement about *how* one can be married. Besides, if *I* went on this hike, there was one huge claim I'd have to give up: that I was married to a woman who walked two thousand miles by herself.

Faced, then, with her determination, my own contradictory desires, our unspoken brands of (what else to call it?) selfishness, and the fates that were on Julie's side, I gave her my blessing: "Go! Have a good time!" But I was speaking only to hear my own voice. She was going regardless.

THE TERRAIN behind our house was rough, with ravines so steep and rocky that you either had to run down them, if they weren't too muddy, or descend slowly by digging your heels into whatever soft dirt you could find with each step. Going up was always slow. It was prime training ground for an aspiring hiker. In early October Julie began frequent walks through the dense stands of black oak, dogwood, and (along the bank of the Little Coal River, a half-mile behind the house) red birch. She would get her legs in shape. Often we went together. Or if the neighbor's dog, Grits, was around, we made it a threesome. We went along the main dirt road until we decided which trail we wanted—the one that went almost straight up initially and passed through a dilapidated family graveyard; the one that made the biggest loop and kept us out in the woods for a good two hours; or the one that bordered the railroad track for several hundred yards, then switched back and up so dramatically that within minutes you were three hundred feet above the river and could see well into the scrubby hills of Lincoln County on the other side.

We went out in the early mornings. I tried to get Julie to wear her new backpack, fill it with rocks and train like a marine.

"I don't want to wear the pack out here," she said. "We're only walking a mile."

"But it's practice. Now's the time to push yourself."

But she didn't want to be pushed. She walked slower than I did, and when I got ahead of her I'd jump up and down on fallen logs until she caught up.

"I'm doing it at my pace," she'd insist gently when we got back to the house. I'd close the door to the bathroom, and let a hot shower soak away my coaching frustrations.

"I want it to be *fun,*" I could hear her explain through the door.

Then when the November and December cold set in, it was not only easier *not* to walk in the woods, but safer. Squirrel season had begun, and every day hunters drove their pickups down the dirt roads that swung around the back of our property. They got out by the river and traipsed through the woods, more and more of them as the season wore on. Ours was private land, but shotgun blasts echoed through the trees so loudly that we couldn't tell if the hunters were honoring property lines or not.

In our warm house Julie began poring over catalogs, ordering the big items—Gore-Tex rain gear, Polarguard sleeping bag (good to five degrees), camp stove, aluminum fuel bottles. She made trips to Mountain State Outfitters for equipment that needed a good fit or that she couldn't get any cheaper through the mail—boots, backpack, waterproof matches, seam sealer for her tent, a wool shirt. She bought foot powder, Dr. Bromer's Peppermint Soap, a snakebite kit. She wrote down, on a neat chart, every meal she would eat from April 13 to October 6. Then she bought the food: rice, pasta, dried vegetables, some fawn-colored spongy substance called textured vegetable protein, spices, carob snack bars packed with protein. She measured out helpings and put them in small Ziploc bags.

In "Walking" Thoreau says: "If you are ready to leave father and mother, and brother and sister, and wife and child and friends, and never see them again—if you have paid your debts, and made your will, and settled all your affairs, and are a free man—then you are ready for a walk."

Julie worked to make herself as free as she could be. She made six advance payments on her student loan. She quit her job. She bought a one-way bus ticket.

But none of this could give her a freedom as complete as Thoreau's ideal. Like Thoreau himself, who borrowed land from Emerson for his cabin and brought his laundry to his mother in Concord, Julie conceded that freedom does not mean isolation or fissure—that it involves, paradoxically, dependence. She would rely on me, then, not only for holding down the fort and keeping the cats fed, but also for her very sustenance. Every two weeks I would mail her a box of food, care of general delivery at post offices she had picked out on the map. A dozen boxes sat stacked in the drafty hallway, already addressed and packed full of Ziplocs.

But what, besides redefining the role of husbandhood, was I going to do with myself?

I didn't have any great loyalty to the newspaper, and I was ready for my own journey, my own sort of escape. I'd applied to grad school, and Iowa had accepted me. School would start in August. When Julie left West Virginia in April, I wouldn't be far behind. I still had some friends in Columbus, and I could get temp jobs there to carry me through the summer. I'd go there, hole up in an apartment, and read.

While Julie was still around, though, I read what she read, boning up on Trail history and geography. She brought home AT and backpacking books from the library, got letters from former hikers she'd written for advice. She ordered topographical maps from the Appalachian Trail Conference. The maps unfolded into pale green sheets full of hairlike lines, the detail surprising me. Marks for tiny wooden shelters along the trail (one every fifteen or twenty miles), creeks where drinking water might be available. Faint numbers for elevations. I felt the sensuality and otherworldliness of these maps as I slipped them from their waterproof plastic sleeves and unfolded them across the table. I was used to road atlases, the best of which showed the AT as only a fine-spun dotted line almost invisible unless you were searching for it—a capillary amid all the arteries.

I pored over the maps. Each covered a small section of the trail—one state, maybe two. I imagined Julie on the paths that those lines represented, and kept running up against a tiny stick figure with a hiking stick at the end of its slash of an arm, walking along the map itself like a cartoon. Any further leap of the imagination felt impossible, though it wasn't a limitation that made me uncomfortable. I was willing to wait for the midst of Julie's hike, when I'd find out from her reports what it was really like.

So I was reading, following along with Julie's preparations, helping her fill Baggies, keeping my eye open for tall, straight walking sticks when we wandered out into the woods after squirrel season. But I was elbowing my way into a lot of these activities. I knew it was a way for me to have some control, which, like a parent, I disguised as concern. I'd already given Julie my go-ahead. What could *my* second thoughts matter now? And what could I do with them except keep them to myself?

Still, one night with little consciousness of my own motivations, I impulsively told Julie that I didn't want her to go after all. We were lying in bed. "This is a joint decision, and I'm changing my vote," I said out of the blue. She was drifting off to sleep, but I spoke loud enough to make her look at me groggily, struggle to guess whether I was joking. I didn't smile.

"Six months *is* a bit much, even for us, don't you think? Do you really think we can survive that long apart again?"

"You want to go?" she asked slowly.

"I don't want to step aside and let you go as if I have nothing at stake here."

She sighed, reluctantly pulled herself further away from sleep. She was trying to open her eyes wider, while I breathed in deeply. "You're doing what you want, too, remember. I'd *love* the chance to sit and read all summer."

It was patronizing. I resisted the temptation of asking why, then, she *wasn't*. But it was, in truth, patronizing only by my interpretation. Because she *would* have loved to sit and read all summer. This other thing had simply come along.

"Besides, you can't change your mind at this stage," she said. She wasn't trying to convince me, only stating what she took to be the obvious. "I've already got everything planned."

"I know about the plans," I said. "I helped with them."

Maybe it was more tiredness than politeness that kept her from correcting my exaggeration. My input might not have been actually a help, but at least it had given me an excuse to be there and witness the structure of her evolving plans. It was a way for me to feel included, because I'd felt those plans take up more and more space in our house, like the hiking equipment that was being stacked in an unused room upstairs. I'd moved aside to make room for them. And now their very idea—those defiant, balky plans—hovered behind Julie like a thug in the shadows.

Of course I had no intention of stopping her. And she knew it. And that was part of how we worked together, part of the give and take we'd established over the years. What *was* unclear was whether she also knew that the only reason I asked was to find out whether she loved me, whether she *would* give up going for me.

And is that what I really wanted? Or was my sudden revolt only by way of stringing her along? God ordering Abraham to make his ultimate sacrifice—me only to insist once Julie agreed to stay home that she *had* to go. It seemed mean and nonsensical, except in the dark recesses of my mind, where I thought about the evolving history of our marriage. I'd be able to store the moment of her insistence in the category of other moments I could later point to and say, "I tried. The divorce is not my fault."

There was silence. Julie's eyes closed then reopened. I could tell she was afraid she'd dropped off, could see her trying to figure out how long I'd been sitting there, breathing.

"I've got to go to sleep," she mumbled.

"Go," I said.

MEANWHILE I ARGUED the merits of Julie's trip with other people. "You two are *married*," friends kept reminding me when I told them what I'd recently learned about the geography of the Trail or repeated the stories Julie was hearing from those previous hikers. Their enthusiastic letters filled with tips were pulling her deeper into a new society. But to our friends, it seemed, the word *married* was as heavy as a medicine ball. It was stuffed full of expectations that Julie and I would share every passion, that we'd always live together, that we had the authority to direct each other's lives.

"So?" I'd ask, playing the devil's advocate, ignoring the obvious absurdity of this situation.

"Married people don't take six-month-long vacations from each other," they'd say. I saw actual fear in their faces, and I chose to interpret it as fear not for my well-being but for their own conservative safety. I read in their questions every inhibitive assumption about marriage, all of which I boiled down to this: With love comes authority. My mistake, I could sense them thinking, was that I was giving out love and getting no authority in return.

"Says who?" I always answered.

OUR SEPARATE preparations fell into greater and greater relief against each other. Though I was acting, not merely being acted upon (wasn't I *giving* permission? wasn't I *making* decisions?), Julie's actions seemed so much more concrete. For the last month or two before she left, I watched Julie winnowing out any extraneous supplies so she could keep her backpack to fifty pounds, running her new flannel shirt through the washer and dryer a half-dozen times to soften the fabric. I envied the exactness of her starting point: Springer Mountain, in northern Georgia. The bus ticket. The timetable. The maps. I envied the precision of it all—as if she were planning an invasion! It could have been a jumbled mess—I didn't like to think about how unorganized I would have been. But Julie was leaving as little as possible to chance—except, I thought in moments of doubt, our marriage. I looked at my own piles of books—novels, histories of American literature, collections of essays—that sat around the house like footstools, and had no clue where to begin.

"We'll write," I told her before she left, on April 2.

"And I've got the calling card."

"We'll think about each other," I said.

"Yes."

JULIE LOADED her backpack on a Greyhound and headed south to Georgia. While in West Virginia we'd acquired two new cats—for a total of three—and I loaded them into the car and drove four hours north to Columbus.

Even if we had attempted a rendezvous on the Trail, I would have needed better Boy Scout skills than I have (none) to find her in the woods. Though she often passed through little towns, her schedule once she was on the Trail became as indeterminable as it should be for a person following the spring northward, and she rarely knew exactly when she'd reach any outpost. Still, she did usually call or send a postcard at least once a week. On my refrigerator in Columbus, I taped a small Xeroxed map. It showed the eastern states tilted en masse about forty degrees so that a crooked, bold black line that signified the AT was approximately vertical. With each weekly update, I colored more of the black line with a red marker. The going was slow, and the red crept upward—across the long border of Tennessee and North Carolina, northeast across the long stretch of Virginia—as sluggishly as the long summer days passed.

In some ways, the map on my refrigerator made Julie's trip more abstract to me—neat and uncomplicated, the safest and simplest of excursions. But I wasn't without worry and fear. We'd read about two women thru-hikers who'd been shot—one of them killed—as they camped along the Trail in the early 1980s. The attack wasn't random; they'd been stalked by a man they'd met earlier, but that hardly reassured me. Nor did I find a lot of comfort in the fact that a woman out in the woods was statistically safer than a woman in most cities. And what scared me more still were things like bears and moose (known to attack if provoked or surprised) and random accidents— one woman had drowned in Maine as she was fording a river a mere hundred miles from the end of the Trail. So perhaps it was better that I got only weekly updates from Julie, that I didn't know right at the moment how she might be suffering.

Through one of the ads in the *Appalachian Trailway News*, Julie'd teamed up with a hiking partner, a former Marine in his forties named John. They left Springer together, but he'd quickly become obsessive, walking too fast for Julie to keep up. After five days he forged ahead, leaving her tent (which he had agreed to carry) in a shelter with a note signed "Godspeed, John." Julie convinced herself to stay at her own pace. "He'll probably blow out his knees by the halfway point," she wrote. And though she was in good physical condition herself, her own body was in danger of failing her. For the first two weeks she had blisters on her hips, from an external-frame backpack that didn't fit her body tightly. (When she got to Virginia, she mailed that pack home and bought an internal-frame one, which molded itself to her shape.) Her feet, too, were tender and painful, the soft skin pulled back and forth no matter how lightly she tried to walk in her new boots. She was ravenous, her servings of seasoned rice and textured vegetable protein not enough to replace the energy she was burning up. And on one surprisingly hot afternoon, walking across a stretch of rocky mountaintop in North Carolina, she ran out of water. "I was stuck for hours with an empty water bottle," she told me the next time she called, angry at not having filled up completely before setting out that morning. "I just kept walking, with my bandana tied around my head to catch the sweat. Then I started hallucinating. I could actually see the Kool-Aid pitcher with the smiley face sitting in front of me, the one with all the flavors combined." She told me how she began listening closely—Indian-like—as she walked, and finally heard what could have been a stream. She crawled on her hands and knees across the wide rocks, searching, holding still to hear the sound now and again. After fifteen minutes, she discovered a dripping of water in the seam underneath two boulders. The space was too small for her water bottle, but she could squeeze the cap in. The drops filled it slowly, each capful only enough to wet the inside of her mouth. "I sat there and drank," she said, "about a hundred capfuls."

IN COLUMBUS, I had found only one apartment I could rent on a month-to-month basis, and it was filthier than anything I could imagine Julie encountering out in the woods. This was grime, not dirt, and it wasn't until I'd spent two days scrubbing linoleum floors, the bathtub, Formica countertops—wearing out sponge after sponge— that pale yellows and greens began appearing. I figured then that I could stand to live there for three months. But it was hard to civilize the place completely. When I'd been there a week, I told Julie she had it much easier in the woods than I did in the city.

"I'm the one being attacked by wild animals," I said. I'd woken up at four A.M. to a high-pitched squeal, and after snapping on the light I squinted at something as flat and large as an open magazine flopping on the floor—flopping, that is, as best it could with one cat on each wing and a third straddling its belly.

The cats had jumped when my feet thudded onto the thin carpet, and the bat scrambled free. It rocketed clumsily to the ceiling and began pitching and yawing in erratic circles around the wicker swag lamp. When the bat found brief refuge in a high, cobwebbed corner of the room, I grabbed my robe from the closet and scudded bleary-eyed into the hallway, out of the flight path. The bat launched itself again, and the cats, clucking dramatically in their throats, chased it like silent-movie firefighters trying to hold a net under a crazy man dashing back and forth on a tenth-floor window ledge.

"I don't know anything about bats," I told Julie. "How was I sup-posed to know whether it had rabies? The cats had probably already sunk their teeth into it."

"Did you hurt it?" she said from the safety of the woods.

"Of course I hurt it," I said. "I waited in a little alcove off the hall-way with my tennis racket. The bat finally swooped out of the bed-room doorway and barreled down the hallway at waist height, with the cats jogging several feet behind. I hit it with a solid forehand, and sent it tumbling in a small clump all the way back to the bedroom door. I got it covered with a bag before the cats had a chance at it though."

"Oh god," Julie said.

"Hey," I told her, "take care of yourself out there. I'm doing what I have to here."

I'D GOTTEN A temp job as a technical writer. The large office wasn't busy, and I discovered early that I could sneak out at two each after-noon and no one would miss me. At least no one ever said anything. We were on flex-time, and each person had a different schedule. I usually went home and took a nap, then came back the next morn-ing around nine.

Two cubicles down was a man who was that summer in the midst of a classic divorce: bitter and devoid of any realization of what might have been good in the marriage. His wife had thrown him out. He looked to me, I think, because I was the only other man in the office whose wife was gone. But he was shell-shocked by his separation, and I found it impossible to encourage him to stick it out (he seemed to have no strength left for it) and too presumptuous to tell him to call it quits. A couple coworkers took longer turns counseling him and liked to joke that we'd be reading in the paper one morning of how he'd gone berserk and murdered his family. It was a cruel running gag, and tossing it around felt like tossing around a lump of plastique, which could blow up one day as absolute truth.

But there was an advantage, to put it crassly, to his presence in the office: The disaster of his own marriage drew the idle attention that otherwise would have been directed at the oddity of my marriage, and the fact that I, too, was alone that summer. Still, I suspected that people who didn't look too closely saw similarities between us, and any suggestion that he was crazy troubled me because I didn't feel immune from that characterization myself. Nor did I feel that Julie was immune. But the word had a different ring when applied to her. Julie's was the good kind of crazy, admirable and to be envied. Pure energy and naked spirit. (It was a difficult concept even for those close to Julie to explain, as I'd be reminded later in the summer when her mom reported that she'd quit telling her friends about Julie's hike. "They look at me and say, 'Is your daughter nuts?' ") But if people were calling me crazy, it wasn't indicative of approval or flattery. They would be talking about a craziness that came from my being married but alone.

I found it difficult to spend my days with people who went home in the evenings to families, who called to check in with spouses and kids throughout the day. Worse, my solitude was not the result of leaving but of having been left. Julie and I compared the questions we got from initiates to our story. When she told people out in the woods that she was alone, their first question came with more respect than alarm: *How can you travel so long without your husband?* On the other hand, people asked me: *How could you let her go?* And their tone made it clear what each of them would do if his or her spouse ever got the notion to take off alone on an adventure any longer than a three-day weekend.

ON MY DESK at work I had a framed snapshot of Julie standing, gloriously healthy and muscular, on a mountaintop in Virginia. She was wearing shorts and a black tank top, her right hand grasping a walking stick. Her legs showed the effects of the hundreds of miles they'd hiked, as hard and coppery as a chain-saw sculpture. One was ramrod straight below her, the other propped casually forward. Her red backpack lay in front of her—sandals, a sweatband, and an aluminum drinking cup dangling from it. A half-dozen tree-covered mountains faded into blue behind her. Her dark hair stood up in a breeze, and the sun glowed off her chest, where her tank top scooped down. She was smiling, almost laughing. I noticed that she was slightly out of focus, but no one else seemed to.

Bringing in the picture had the effect I'd imagined: impressing people who could finally see whom they'd begun to call "the mysterious hiking wife." Suddenly, something about my marriage became more "real." The picture was small proof that I was living a life vaguely similar to theirs, that I wasn't a complete oddball. A couple of the women liked the way that Julie looked tough.

But there was Marty, who sat most of the day at his cubicle with his headphones on, the yellow wire running to a Walkman hidden in his desk drawer. He was a weightlifter, a triangular torso rising out of his chair. He lumbered to the bathroom every few hours, or to the break room for a diet Coke, but stayed out of the gossip. When Marty walked by my desk and saw Julie's picture, he said, "I'd be rooting for her, but I'd want to kill her." He shrugged his titan shoulders. "Then again, I'm a very jealous person."

I took his remark as unvarnished truth—tactless, and thus a rarity among the comments on my situation. I didn't welcome it, not because I hadn't ever imagined his words myself but because I knew that spoken aloud they would hang heavy with the danger of disloyalty. I tensed up, not wanting to have to defend my own attempts at being accommodating and supportive, at being the liberated husband. I felt something at stake, and thought with a recognition of the absurd that it was his respect for me as a man. That's what annoyed me most about the moment, that Marty had caused me to feel something so cliché and worthless. Still, what was he seeing? Dainty me, staying at home and taking care of the cats, showing off pictures of my wife in her travels? Me, being domestic?

He'd picked up the picture and was studying it. It looked small in his hand. I wanted to snatch it back and reset it in the corner of my desk.

"No one said I wasn't jealous," I told him. "Healthy jealous."

"Which is?"

I shrugged. "I don't want to *kill* her. At the same time, I don't want her screwing her way up and down the Trail. Somewhere in between."

He waited. Then he said, "Well, you're unusually enlightened." It wasn't a compliment. He handed me the picture.

I could have explained it to him. I could have squeezed him into a chair and spelled out every oddity of my marriage, every philosophical underpinning of my role as a husband. Julie was not walking away from the marriage, but walking within it. And if in fact I was giving her the opportunity to exploit my patience, well, we trade off some certainties for the sake of trust. The ledge was narrow—patriarchy on one side, rationalized martyrdom on the other. And it certainly wasn't all intellectualized. I could have claimed outright that much of the time I went with gut feelings—a trust within myself of what was right. I could have defended both Julie's hike and our marriage, not caring what I was defending more—Julie's free-spiritedness, romanticism, and self-indulgence, or my pragmatism, responsibility, and self-sacrifice.

But he wouldn't have believed me. And I might not have believed myself. Besides, what was I supposed to do? Stop sending her food?

TWO MONTHS into the summer, I condensed my updates of Julie's progress and reduced my audience. To certain people I dropped small highlights like bread crumbs: She was crossing the forty miles of Maryland, or she was in the rocky portion of southern Pennsylvania, where her boots and her ankles were getting their hardest workout. But more and more I considered the hike a private matter. And I'd begun to worry that I was bragging. To speak of events so distant from my own day-to-day existence seemed to embarrass most people, somehow, and I began to think I should spare everyone. But at the same time, I wondered how different I'd feel if *I* were the woman and my husband was out hiking.

In a secondhand bookstore, I had found a copy of a National Geographic book on the AT. It lay on the table next to my bed, and I occasionally flipped through it when I was dropping off at night, with the cats packed around my legs like hot-water bottles. I tried to imagine Julie within the photographs of a narrow dirt path winding through thick stands of trees, or in pictures taken from atop some bald in Tennessee, the Appalachians undulating for ten or twenty miles in the distance. Julie had also left me with a video documentary on the AT called *Five Million Steps*, which allowed me to see and hear the scraping of boots across fallen leaves, the tapping of hiking sticks against hardened dirt, and the splashing of feet through shallow streams. And there were always the images that Julie described over the phone or in her postcards—like the afternoon she and her friend Judy hiked topless for fifteen minutes, before their modesty and a group of people they heard coming toward them ended their brief liberation.

WHEN SHE REACHED the halfway point at Pine Grove Furnace State Park, just southeast of Harrisburg, Pennsylvania, Julie ate a half-gallon of ice cream in one sitting. It was the traditional rite of passage for thru-hikers, and the local ice-cream store was the home of the "Half-Gallon Club."

"Fifty minutes," she told me proudly over the phone that night. "It was Neapolitan, so I didn't get bored."

She was ecstatic and proud, and I felt good for her. The next day I would even break my self-imposed ban on bragging, though I regretted it a little when my office mates began joking unceremoniously about the ice cream. But even that didn't mar the relief I felt at Julie's having gotten halfway—especially without having blown out her knees or been attacked by a bear, despite how slim she kept telling me the chances of the latter really were. I was also glad that she had moved beyond the worst pain of hiking, and that now her movement was more like Thoreau's sauntering—more meditative and less all-consumingly physical.

BY SEPTEMBER she had walked more than fourteen hundred miles and was in Connecticut. I had moved five hundred miles west, to Iowa City. Everything familiar began to feel further away.

Julie was still checking in weekly—now each time from a different state: Connecticut, Massachusetts, Vermont, New Hampshire—but I felt as if she were on the other side of the world. I had been coloring my map in red for so long that it seemed like only a piece of paper taped to the refrigerator, rather than the heartfelt symbol it had been of Julie's location—a badge not only of how far she had walked but also of what we, our marriage, had undergone that summer. I began to feel adrift, to feel the helplessness that comes when you know that someone you love is beyond your reach. The feeling was heightened by the more frequent thought that she was in danger—a fear that I'd been able to suppress for several months but which was reappearing now that the summer was waning. I was beginning to imagine the bitter cold that could hit the northern mountains without warning. So I struggled to gain influence.

I thought of the year I was thirteen, when my dad had been sent to Thailand. My mom had snitched to him in a letter that my hair had begun to creep over my ears. He fired a letter back, from the other side of the world, with orders for me to march to the barber shop. The order could've come from the kitchen table. I went.

With Julie, I didn't want a father's authority. But sometimes, like the night she called from Maine to describe how, earlier that day, she and her friends had forded the Kennebec River, I thought I would have taken even that. The water had reached their upper thighs and had been running rapidly. To avoid losing their footing, they had used one or two walking sticks apiece.

"Julie," I told her, able to muster no more force than that with which I had told her months earlier that she couldn't go on the hike, *"don't do that."* This entreaty also was too little too late. But I nevertheless reminded her of the woman who had drowned in 1985 in that same river, trying to do the same thing. We had agreed, before Julie left, that she would take a boat across any river she could.

"The boat was only a canoe, and it only ran two hours a day," she said, "from ten to twelve. We didn't want to wait, so we camped by the river's edge last night so we could get across before the dam upstream opened, at eight o'clock. *That's* when it gets dangerous. But we saw some gravel bars and decided it was okay to go."

I breathed deeply, searching for a reason to yell at her. But she was already across the river, her boots had dried out, and she was safe and thrilled.

"Be *careful*."

She agreed, as a teenager will agree to drive carefully.

FINALLY, on an early Saturday morning, one week into October, Julie called to say she'd finished. I hadn't heard from her for a week. She'd been in the last stretch, the hundred-mile wilderness, no towns, no phones. I'd been telling our three cats every day: "Guess who's coming home in a few days! Your mama, your mama is coming home to see you!" They sauntered to their bowls and ate.

She called from a friend's house. She had climbed Katahdin on Friday, October 6. Her final ascent was made in snow and freezing winds, the temperature was twenty-five degrees, and the wind chill far below that—a Class-III day, the next-to-worst classification. Hiking was not recommended.

"We went anyway," she said.

"Surprise," I said.

I asked her whether the last moment was emotional.

"Too damn cold for that," she said. But she had been preparing for the end for three weeks, often crying while she walked. Once at

Katahdin, it was up, snap a few pictures, then down. No time for standing and wondering at the magic of it all, as she had in April, in Georgia.

She spent a week in Boston, reacclimating with her parents, letting her mom buy her new clothes—a signal of her transition back into mainstream society. A stronger signal, though, was the difficulty she had in letting go of the thrill of climbing mountains once she was very far away from them. When she flew into Iowa on October 15, all she could say was, "This place is flat. Flat cornfields. Flat roads."

"That's actually a myth." I corrected her. *"Western* Iowa is flat, but eastern Iowa got scrunched up by the glaciers and is actually quite hilly."

"Uh-huh." She was unconvinced, staring out the car window as I drove us home from the airport, no doubt comparing what she saw not to the Great Plains but to the Appalachians. But she looked determined to give Iowa a chance, to make a new home in this place she'd never been, where I had made my commitments. At the house, the cats welcomed her, holding their tails high and wanting to be petted ("They remember me!" she said), and she showed me her "hiking tan"—dark legs down to just above the ankles, then milky-white ankles and feet, which had been enclosed in her hiking boots for six months.

"I can take you to the Tan 'n' Wash," I told her.

We could joke for a while about how skin browned by the sun would differ from skin browned in a booth, about how Julie could set up her tent out in the yard if she needed a burst of nature, and about how the local senior citizens' group sponsored a mall walk every Saturday morning and she could do eight hundred laps past the storefronts. But clearly Julie was missing the Trail, the body she had created out there, the quiet, and the substitutions I was offering were artificial. She didn't say so, but I suspected she wouldn't mind letting her feet stay milky white.

It didn't take long, either, to see that the whole transition—Julie settling into small-town Iowa, both of us settling back into "conventional" marriage—wasn't going to be easy. Rarely a day went by that she didn't wish aloud—sometimes wistfully, often sullenly, occasionally angrily—that she was back in the woods, hiking, being with her Trail friends, existing as freely and austerely as she could. She made small attempts at creating a Trail feeling in her home life. Most nights at dinner, instead of drinking from the nice glasses in the cabinet, she drank from either an awkward aluminum camping cup or a red plastic thermos top. One evening as she was mixing an oil and vinegar dressing in the thermos cup, she announced, her eyes glistening with nostalgia, that that cup had once allowed her to stay in her tent rather than take a midnight nature-trip into the trees. My nostalgia for her trip wasn't so strong, and neither was my appetite. I told her she could eat my salad.

I began to consider what my father had told me about his return from Vietnam: "It wasn't too difficult to readjust to each other," he'd said, "even after a year. We did it right. Your mother met me in San Francisco, and we spent five days on a second honeymoon."

My mom had joked: "You remember that earthquake in San Francisco, don't you?"

SYMPATHY

HOW COULD MY PARENTS HAVE MADE SUCH A RUCKUS IN SAN
Francisco when they must have been virtual strangers to each other
that first week? Despite the years that Julie and I had already spent
more or less together, despite our writing and calling as much as we
could in the previous six months, despite the fact that our friends expected us to spend our entire first week in bed, we were taken aback
by the awkwardness of this reunion. Julie's longing for the Trail was
sharp, and my own protectiveness of a house I'd already set up to my
tastes was strong. Though the gap that had inevitably opened between
us since April was nowhere near as wide or deep as the one we'd had
to fill during that muggy summer in the trailer, our reconnection
flickered like an old lamp. It was Julie's turn to feel like a transgres-
sor in my space. And that didn't mean simply getting used to me. It

was obvious from the moment she walked into the house—the way she glanced up and shifted her eyes quickly from corner to corner, as if calculating dimensions—that she would have to readjust to the very walls and ceilings.

"It's my mission to recivilize you," I told her. "But if it makes you feel more comfortable while I'm doing it, you can walk around the house topless."

I let her drink out of the camping cup, but I worked on other points.

"This is a plate," I said slowly. "Eat off plate. No hands. Fork."

"Shut up." She laughed.

"Stove," I said, pointing. "Not portable. Do not put in backpack when done cooking."

I had some pressing questions about our roles now that we were together again. Some concern about "evening things out." I didn't say them aloud just yet. I wanted to be more subtle and gentle about my desire for Julie to redirect her Trail energy toward our marriage. I had the idea we needed to reconnect slowly, like liquids seeping together. We could slip back into some of the routines of marriage we'd created in West Virginia—taking walks together, reading in the same room, making love—but almost everything else was uncertain. Could we have said, for instance, what the state of our love was, exactly? That love felt strong, even in the midst of the awkwardness of reconnecting. Comfortable in deep ways. But was that our history talking, the fact that we'd been married for so long and knew each other so well? Or the fact that we'd begun counting on things being in flux? With the hike over, I was surprised to be asking myself the questions other people had been asking of me: *What kind of marriage is this? If we are in love, why would we want to spend so much time apart?* And I wanted to ask Julie these questions, to hash out answers. I decided that what we needed was a second honeymoon—not in the Appalachians and not in the farmland of Iowa. Maybe back to the Rockies, or L.A., or even San Francisco. A place where what dominated our vision was not the lay of the land but the lay of our marriage. Unfortunately, Julie had spent almost every penny of her savings on the hike, and my own bank account hung precariously in the double digits for most of each month. It was midsemester. I had three papers to write, a half-dozen books to read. Julie had to find a job. And she had to settle in. First things first. And so she finished emptying her backpack and hanging up her clothes. Then we began with one small ceremony: a dinner—of anything, Julie had insisted, except rice or textured vegetable protein—to celebrate our seventh anniversary, which arrived one day after Julie did.

IN THE WEEKS before Julie's homecoming, my eye had been bothering me. At first I thought it was strain from all the reading. But it was just my "bad eye": I'd been blind from birth in my right eye because of a congenital cataract. My left eye was fine, but my right one was so dry I was blinking constantly. Then it began to feel swollen. I looked in the mirror but couldn't see any difference. I ignored the discomfort for a while, until I had to go in for a new glasses prescription anyway. The doctor asked me if I'd had an injury lately.

"I got poked a few months ago, playing basketball," I said.

"Your retina's flopping around back there like a torn curtain." He turned on his office lights and sat down. "We could let it go, since you can't see out of that eye anyway. Reattaching the retina isn't going to give you any more vision. But even if this eye can't carry its share of the visual load, I don't like the idea of losing an otherwise healthy organ."

"What happens if we don't do anything?" I asked.

"Probably that eye will begin to shrink, become painful, and have to be enunculated. Taken out."

"Enunculated." I let the mellifluous but frightening word roll off my tongue.

"Worst-case scenario," he said. "With one injured eye, there's always the chance, however slight, of sympathetic ophthalmia—the good eye tagging along into blindness for no reason other than loyalty to its injured partner."

I proposed the idea of the surgery to Julie. "You're having it," she said immediately.

"But this is the worst time to be laid up. And I can't see out of that eye anyway."

"You can't not have this surgery. That would be stupid."

"You're going to have to play nurse. Wait on me, cook all the meals, read to me. And I'm not a good patient."

"Call the doctor and tell him yes," she said.

I WAS A lousy patient. I always had been. Julie, though, had her own shortcomings as a nurse, such as her tendency to laugh when I was in pain. She swore it was a defense mechanism and that she was helpless to stop.

"*Try*," I pleaded.

"I'm sorry, I'll try," she said, laughing.

Sometimes I had no choice but to let her giggling elbow in briefly upon my misery.

Instead of looking for any early sympathy, therefore, I spent the week before the surgery reading about St. Lucy, the patron saint of eyesight. Her eyes, according to one legend, were miraculously restored after a judge ripped them out because she had been denounced as a Christian by her rejected suitor. Another legend said that the suitor had admired her eyes, and that she tore them out herself and gave them to him. Either way, she got them back, good as new. The only part of the story I didn't like was that she was martyred soon afterward by a sword thrust into her throat.

I was going under the knife at seven A.M. At four-thirty I shook Julie awake. It was dark and cold, and we rode to the hospital in yawning silence. By five-thirty I was seated in front of a nurse with tiny scissors. "Such gorgeous eyelashes," she whispered as she cut them off. "I know women who would kill for these."

Julie walked alongside as I was wheeled down a series of hallways on a gurney. At the elevators, where we'd have to leave her behind, the attendant paused long enough for her to bend down and kiss me.

"Any advice?" I asked.

"Don't blink," she said.

She forced a smile, through what seemed not so much sleepiness anymore as worry.

In the OR I slid, with help, onto the operating table, and looked into a huge bank of lights, then up my doctor's nose. "Feeling all right?" he asked.

The moment was lonely. I thought of Julie downstairs—reading a book, watching TV, leaning her head back against the wall to catch a short nap. Years later I met a couple who on their honeymoon both had intense toothaches. When they found a dentist it turned out only one of them had a tooth problem. The other had sympathetic pain, which disappeared as soon as the dentist had finished working on the first one. "We see this a lot," the dentist told them.

How common is it? Did such psychosomatic sharing indicate a level of resonance that Julie and I had never reached? Or was she downstairs at that moment rubbing her eyes, feeling the strain and the dryness? I didn't wish my pain on her, but I craved the intimacy of such involuntary sympathy—and that craving made my loneliness stronger. Because I worried that really she felt nothing of my experience, as I had felt less and less of hers as she'd journeyed deeper into the mountains and herself.

Suddenly it was late afternoon in a darkened room, and my eye hurt like hell. I was bawling and moaning, and I could feel Julie's hands on my arm.

"I'll get the nurse," she said, with some panic in her voice. The nurse came and stabbed me in the hip with a shot of Darvon. Within a minute I was out again. And hours later when I came to, I couldn't open my eyes but sensed Julie next to the bed.

"The Berlin Wall came down," she said.

"Wha?" I mumbled. I couldn't tell where I was between consciousness and unconsciousness.

"I'm reading the little sheet of news summaries the hospital gives all the patients. The Berlin Wall came down today. Are you awake?"

I HAD TO lie on my left side all day. There was a gas bubble in my eye, and I had to let it float up to my right side, to hold the reattached retina in place while it healed. I was better off than the man in the next bed, who had to lie on his face so his gas bubble would press against the back of his eye, but the position became uncomfortable nonetheless. I wasn't supposed to open my eyes for a day, and when I sat up to eat I did it by feel. Julie watched with amusement for a minute, then took my fork and fed me.

"Fork," she said. "Use to eat."

When I felt up to speaking I told her I'd decided I would learn Braille, get a head start so that I wouldn't flounder in depression when the time came.

"You're not going blind," she said.

"I should also take a typing class and learn the touch method. When I'm blind I won't be able to pick my way around the keyboard anymore."

"Quit making it worse than it is."

"Did you know," I asked her, "that Roman gladiators used to become eye doctors and gouge out the eyes of their patients just as they had those of their gladiator opponents?"

"Well, next time your doctor comes to check on you, I'll ask him what he did before he went to med school."

My eye really did hurt. During the surgery it had begun to cloud up, and my doctor had relieved the clouding by scratching my cornea with his scalpel, like popping a blister. A common procedure, he assured me, and added that these scratches heal within days. He sent me home and instructed Julie to keep me from blinking if she could.

She took her work surprisingly seriously, four times a day tugging gently on my lower eyelid and squeezing ointment across the bottom of my eyeball.

"Goop me up," I said.

"Hold still. God, your eye looks like somebody stomped on it. Ugh."

The coolness of the ointment was the only thing that made my eye feel comfortable. I sat stone still while Julie folded gauze eye patches in half, stacked them atop each other over my eye, then covered them with long strips of white tape. I could do nothing but keep both eyes closed. Taped up like a battlefield casualty, I tried not to move around, not wanting to disturb the delicate patch. At night, Julie had to lead me upstairs. She'd sit me on the edge of the bed and dutifully fluff my pillows before she'd let me lie down.

When she got bored with playing nurse, she asked me if I was ready for sex.

"Oh, Dan, loo-ook." She began to do a slow striptease at the foot of the bed.

I could barely crack open my eye, so she was blurry and distorted. "Put it back on," I cheered glumly. "Too bad you didn't become a nurse's aide out in Denver. The geriatrics would have loved this."

"Oh god. I had no idea what I was doing with my life then. What the hell was I thinking?" She laughed. "Wait, I have to get my journal."

She went to the next room and came back.

"I know right where it is," she said, flipping pages.

She read passages about our aimlessness in those months, about our days spent locked in that apartment, about the time we'd argued over how much salt I was cooking with and then didn't talk to each other for a full day. The embarrassing memories made my eye hurt more, but she could barely get through a paragraph without splitting her sides over our immaturity or what seemed in retrospect our unending optimism. This despite a grim paragraph about me pouting for hours on the couch.

"The more things change," I said.

"You're not pouting now," she said. "You're sick. I, on the other hand, still don't know what the hell I'm doing in life."

I didn't like thinking back on Denver. There always seemed to be the possibility that the same kind of inertia could set in. None of it seemed like such a distant past to me. Even the scratchy feel of that apartment's carpet on my spine as I did sit-ups was immediately available to me with the merest flip of my memory. Of course, we had been overly optimistic. But our optimism had gotten us through some days that otherwise would have been unbearably oppressive. What I wondered instead was whether we'd been right in assuming that the stagnation was either imposed from outside (a slump in the economy) or the result of lousy choices (leaving the Peace Corps early, moving to Denver instead of any other city). What if the forces weren't external and came instead from the center of our marriage's gravity? Would that mean they had determined every other direction our marriage had taken—the contractions and expansions of our relationship—and were still with us?

I didn't know whether this was as fresh and dangerous a thought for Julie. Traipsing through the woods, she could not have imagined the immobility that would greet her in Iowa, not only from my slow recovery but also from the patterns we might have set long before and simply fallen back into. And there was the weather. Winter had come early and fiercely. There were heavier December snows than normal and, in the weeks around Christmas, wind chills of sixty to eighty below zero. The windows rattled. Maybe at least Julie could think back on her quick and snowy ascent of Mount Katahdin as a transition to an Iowa winter. To go outside we had to spend twenty minutes wrapping layers and layers around us, and then could only spend half that time in the open air. On days when the wind was calmer, we walked the dozen blocks to downtown. But each time, by block eight we were cursing through our scarves that we'd been out of our minds. Sometimes I forced myself out into the cold to freeze away the pain in my eye. Having the rest of me go numb was a worthwhile trade-off, for as long as I could stand it.

JULIE READ to me endlessly. Mostly articles on sex and fashion from women's magazines. Frivolous stuff. A novel seemed too heavy, and I wanted to be able to drop off to her voice. She did find a story in the paper one day, though, about a guy who went blind. He was thirty-seven and had had diabetic retinosis since he was eleven. The disease caused the blood vessels in his eyes to become weak and rupture. Then one morning he sneezed and detached the retinas in both eyes. There didn't seem to be any point to the story, other than to tell of the suddenness with which the lights had gone out on this poor fellow. It was a story of fragility, which I didn't need at the time. (Julie had read it innocently, not thinking that it might scare me.) But nevertheless I stored it along with other evidence (tree branches that dangle at about the six-foot level, I'd become suddenly aware of) that some things seem to come out of nowhere, but don't really.

It was clear though that I'd recover. I didn't need a full-time nurse, and Julie was becoming bored with being one. We also needed cash, and though she had a couple of interviews, they weren't for the right jobs, and they didn't come through anyway.

But what sort of job would make her happy after six months on the Trail? National Park ranger? I didn't know if there was even a *state* park in Iowa. If you hike anywhere outside town, you're likely to trespass on somebody's corn or soybean field. Any job Julie got would almost certainly be indoors, with not only walls but schedules—taking her recivilization one step further. Not that she wasn't up to work. She was craving it, in fact, by the time her money was low enough that she didn't have any choice. Still, I didn't dismiss her from whatever she chose to see as her nursing duties. I remembered the game we'd played in our early years, how long we'd each stay around if the other became a vegetable. And I remembered the bluntness with which Julie had relegated me to a nursing home and got married again. I lapped up all the sympathy and attention she gave me.

She signed on with a temp agency, to tide her over until something better showed up. For three days they sent her to clean sorority houses. For another four, she organized the scrambled records of the catering department in a local hotel. And for another four after that she was a substitute secretary at the town water treatment plant. The full-time secretary had gotten ahead in her work before she took a vacation, and Julie sat for most of her eight hours in a concrete office only answering the occasional phone call. "Don't you have anything to do?" one of her coworkers said when he caught her looking out the window. "You could be cutting up paper or something." She swore to me that he was serious.

Why was she in Iowa? Julie had begun to ask, insisting that the question wasn't meant to insult or hurt me, but that it rose in her throat almost involuntarily. Iowa! Where was the sense in it, when for so long she'd been trying to find the place she'd be most happy and had rediscovered every day for six months that it was in the gentle Appalachians? "The happiest time of my life!" she was free to admit. She couldn't live on the Trail forever, of course, couldn't hike endlessly. But what about living closer to it? Having it cut through her backyard like a creek? What in Iowa could compare?

I cleared my throat, gave her a small wave.

"Of course you!" she said. "I wouldn't be here at all if not for you."

"That sounds like an accusation."

"No, no, it's not. I *love* you. That's why I'm here."

SHE'D SPENT a few months in Iowa. Not the most entertaining months, but good, intimate ones in many ways. Was I supposed to take that as a good faith effort and let her off the hook? Give her the nod to move away from me again for the sake of her own . . . goals? dreams? professional needs? And if she did stay, did I have the energy to motivate her, to keep her from being so depressed that she was bound to be unsatisfied—as in the Peace Corps, as in Denver? Did I want that responsibility? Was it my responsibility? I had looked out for myself in West Virginia and didn't suspect it was unfair for her to do the same in Iowa. I'd sacrificed. On the other hand, my willingness to compromise my own goals for the sake of Julie's struck me as a rare trait, which sometimes I didn't admire much and saw rather as weakness. Which was, I knew, the reason I couldn't leave Iowa.

"There was nothing in West Virginia for me," I said. "I *found* something once I got there."

"I know, I know. You were good at that."

If I were my dad would I have been able to tell her to stay? If I were my grandfather? Would I have been able to do it with more fairness? More equanimity? More emotion? My grandfather's habit was simply to "put his foot down." Not a tactful or caring way to express his desires, and not one that took my grandmother's wishes into account. What, though, if he had begged and wooed her instead of making demands of her? What if he had spoken from his heart and not his pride? How would their marriage have been different? Would the ability to talk about matters of the heart have inclined her to make sacrifices for him willingly? And what if she had spoken to him in the same way, and he had listened? Would he have understood her better then? Would *he* have sacrificed?

How could I be a man and yet respect my wife and our relationship—while at the same time protecting it—if I retreated into my mother's position and sacrificed myself and my needs (again) for the sake of "us"?

If I finished school at Iowa, it would be another four years, minimum. Iowa City was a small town, clearly not on the map of Julie's career path. The photography departments at the local newspapers were amateurish compared to those where she'd already been and the level of work she aspired to. I could see what was going to happen. So we left our plans uncertain. School started again. Julie drove me there and picked me up. I sat in class with the patch over my eye, worn out at the end of each fifty minutes.

At home I'd assured her, "Something will come along," but neither of us had any idea what. And when the money she'd saved before her hike was nearly gone, we agreed to find out what kinds of jobs were available elsewhere. No risk. She had some contacts, made some calls. There was a photojournalist opening at a good newspaper in Knoxville, Tennessee. Julie shook her head at the ominousness of fate when the editor offered her the job almost immediately.

Eight hundred miles. A twelve-hour drive. We took out the atlas and traced the interstates, down the empty length of Illinois, across the toe of Kentucky, east to the far end of Tennessee.

"That's no weekend trip," I said.

"Should I go?"

"Well, what happens once you get there?"

"I work. I can send you money. You can come out for the summer."

"My mom would be annoyed about having to add another address to her book." She had pages of addresses for the two of us, many with a circled "Dan" or "Julie" in the margin to indicate who was where.

"I'd have a paycheck. I could buy her a new book."

"Do you want to go?" I asked.

She hesitated. "I don't know. It's nothing to rush into. And I *know* it's my turn to come to where you are. You came to West Virginia. It's only fair to trade off."

"But?"

She shrugged. "It *is* a job. It's sort of hard to imagine being ordered to cut up paper for five years."

"I haven't even finished civilizing you yet."

After more than seven years of marriage, a separation that had no immediately foreseeable end (a graduation, a mountain ascent) seemed immensely more threatening than any we'd survived before. We were older, less able to treat the idea of having to get used to each other again casually.

I would finish out the school year; we'd see what came of it.

NO ONE SAID we were crazy when Julie left this time. There were expressions of sadness. But she had a job to go to, and what could be more sensible? It seemed an odd time to impose practicality on a marriage.

Her backpack was gone from the living room. The cats' dishes. The cats. The driveway was empty.

A week after Julie left I rode the bus to the hospital for my three-month post-op check-up. The doctor shined a pinpoint flashlight in my eye, making me look up, down, left, right. He pulled up a stool hesitantly after he'd flipped the lights back on. My retina had flopped loose again. The only thing he could guess was that there had been too much scar tissue for the retina to get a good grip. We could do another operation, though it would be much less likely to succeed than the first one. Or he could do a less radical, outpatient procedure—inject another gas bubble to get the retina back in place, rivet it down with a laser, and cross our fingers again that the connection would hold. But I sensed he was offering both options not for their chances of success but for an appearance of effort. He told me to take a month to think about it, let him know. I barely even talked it over with Julie.

WE RAN UP phone bills. Then in May, I flew to Knoxville for the summer. She met me at the airport and brought me to her apartment, a one-bedroom place in a complex with a pond that was home to two irritable swans. The week before, one of them had chased a tenant up to his patio and bit him.

In her bedroom was the futon. A small table with a bedside lamp. In the living room, a wide expanse of gray carpet with a few cushions tossed here and there.

"It's . . . simple," I said.

There was no decoration except, on the wall of the tiny dining room, a three-by-five-foot glossy map of the Appalachian Trail.

LAST MEALS

I'D BEEN THINKING ABOUT FOOD BEFORE I ARRIVED IN KNOXVILLE, and I found when I got there that Julie had been, too. I'd been thinking about it in terms of the mundane tasks we could share, the activities over which we could linger: cooking in her galley kitchen, eating at the small table in her dining room. I'd hoped to cook a lot that summer, and wanted the food to be a communion, in the broadest sense of it bringing us together, of giving us physical and emotional sustenance.

Julie however was trying to reduce her hunger. The previous summer and fall, when she'd been walking the AT, she'd eaten anything and everything she wanted. Hiking twenty miles a day, such habits made sense. Then, in the cold of the Iowa winter, we'd eaten heartily together. But in the universe of Knoxville in the summer of 1990, she had a different idea. Not long after I arrived, she told me about a class in macrobiotic cooking she'd seen advertised and suggested we take it. My first thought was that I was in Knoxville to spend all the time I could with her, to fall into the sort of full rhythm that other couples enjoyed, to pursue small ways of being "normal." Taking a class together would be perfect. But after we'd bought a macrobiotic cookbook, I began to understand what was actually meant by "simplicity." I read about the plainness of macrobiotic staples (brown rice, beans, miso, seaweed, kale, tofu, millet), the exhortations to pare down and distill. And I began to think that this class was trouble.

Julie seemed as willing to give herself over to eating only rice and beans as she'd been to wolf down that half-gallon of ice cream at the halfway point on the AT. Even seven months after she'd quit hiking, she was "getting used to sitting still again." I, on the other hand, had been sitting, recuperating, most of the spring. I didn't want a plain and austere summer; I wanted a messy carnival, a beans-and-franks season. I wanted to go to theme parks, join a softball team, rebuild a car engine. This idea of macrobiotics made me worry about what might come with it—meditation, solitude, silence. I wanted *talk*—not the sultry, sweating hush we'd had in that skinny trailer outside Athens four years earlier.

We of course had a lot to talk about. I came to town with that in mind, and I knew Julie understood what we'd have to do, but I still spent most of the plane ride down trying to refine a good way of beginning a dialogue. I wanted words that would convey a sense of urgency and push Julie up against a wall. We had three months; Julie wasn't coming back to Iowa at the end of summer, and I didn't plan on leaving Iowa. Maybe the logistics of our individual situations meant that we began the summer with an insurmountable obstacle, a decision already made for us, and that we really didn't have to talk about our future at all. Maybe we had an unspoken agreement to pretend that the obstacle was not insurmountable. The latter seems more likely from a distance. But in reality I think we truly hadn't decided. Things had turned around before, had worked out in ways that surprised us. We were open to that happening again. But we also were open, I think, to it not happening. I didn't make any early predictions, and went into the summer with a confidence forged from having survived all our other separations. Julie had the same confidence, and for both of us it might have been greater than ever because we'd been in worse situations. I don't mean that we were sure we'd save our marriage, but that we thought we'd figure out something one way or the other. Perhaps rearrange expectations and duties and reliances in a way that would take us to the next place along the path.

That's why I told Julie we had to "settle things once and for all between us." The phrase came out sounding much harsher than I'd meant it to. But she didn't argue. She said, "We do."

THE MACROBIOTICS class was on the other side of town, in a solar-heated, six-room cabin at the end of a dirt road. In a field fifty yards up the dirt road were a dozen abandoned beauty-parlor chairs side by side, with a hair dryer hovering over each like an eggshell. They were strangely disconcerting. When we walked up onto the porch, a dozen pairs of shoes were already lined up outside the door—other students, padding around inside in their socks.

The teachers were Amy and David, a married couple in their late thirties who were equally devoted to macrobiotics and equally skinny. One of the first things Amy told us was that her body had been purified by her menu. Her system was so cleansed she could hear the food she ingested talking to her. In a restaurant once, she had begun to feel woozy after only a couple of bites. Suspicious, she called the waiter over and asked him if the food had been microwaved.

"Yes, ma'am."

She had held her fingers to her temples. "I knew that," she said, "because I'm having deep brain pains."

David was red-haired and stringy, with muscles like a young boy's just taking shape. He claimed to have attained his physique naturally through macrobiotics. His perfect weight.

Like parents, these two cooked us a meal every week, letting us watch the careful preparations, letting us chop vegetables or stir simmering sauces. During the cooking, they fed us a steady stream of hints and advice, meant to make eating a healing experience.

"Never go into the kitchen to cook when you're in a bad mood," Amy said. "The negative energy will transfer right into your food, and you'll end up with a stomachache or diarrhea."

"If you come home in the evening angry, go for a walk first, or meditate, or take a warm bath. Then cook."

"Never use any electric appliances in your cooking. Bad energy. Use gas or a woodstove."

They threw in suggestions for daily living: Never wear synthetic clothing; keep every corner of your home in good order; avoid taking long hot baths and showers; don't watch TV, especially color TV, which shoots out unnatural electromagnetic radiation; live each day happily.

I entertained myself by extrapolating their common sense into more personal bits of advice: *Never go into the last summer of your marriage when you're in a bad mood. Never drop an electrical appliance into the warm bath of your soon-to-be ex-spouse. Never watch TV—especially a color TV—with your soon-to-be ex-spouse, since the three-way combination of bad energy will be toxic to your system.*

In rebellion, perhaps, I got myself hired as a grill cook. I had to get a job, and at a place I could walk to (Julie took the car to work), which meant convenience stores, muffler shops, or restaurants. I went with the most romantic option.

The breakfast shift: six to one, every day. The restaurant was busy, three or four grill cooks working at once, and since I had no experience whatsoever, I started off with the easy stuff—frying walk-in refrigerators full of bacon and sausage. I stood over the grill, tongs in hand, while so much grease spattered onto my chest and face that I constantly had to go to the bathroom and run hot water over my glasses simply to be able to see.

I felt oddly comforted by comparing Julie and me to the married people who worked at the restaurant. We seemed no more or less normal than anyone else, to me. Sheila, whom I admired, had gotten pregnant and married at seventeen and worked a variety of minimum-wage jobs during the course of her twenty-year marriage. Barb and her new husband had recently bought a house, and she was looking to be in management by the time she was twenty-five. Bill, who'd owned restaurants himself, was bringing in some extra cash in his retirement so that he and his wife of forty years could afford a few trips every year. I heard all the gossip about their marriages and affairs and children and dreams, but I didn't know what they were really like. I simply grilled; then I walked home in the middle of incredibly hot afternoons and rested until Julie got home, when I could live out the course of my own marriage.

IN OUR macrobiotics class, there was a forty-five-year-old man named Frank who wrote down each piece of David and Amy's advice in tiny handwriting on a yellow legal pad. When they advised us to chew our food at least fifty times, Frank began staying at the table longer than anyone else, scooping a small bit of brown rice into his mouth and chewing like a bored horse, his eyes focused on a point about eight feet in front of him, his cheeks stretching and contracting. During any lull in the after-dinner conversation, we could hear his tongue moving around the mush like a paddle. If anybody spoke to him, he'd raise one hand off the table, where it had been lying palm-down, and signal that he'd be able to respond soon. After everyone else had finished, Frank still sat at the head of the table, shoulders square, his jaw doing the work that his stomach would otherwise have to do.

As the weeks went on, his chewing took on metaphoric dimensions, and I saw him forcing every ounce of pleasure out of his food. It was the danger in Julie and my living that summer together, that we'd grind every moment of pleasure out of our marriage, till we were left with nothing but a tasteless pulp.

WE FILLED our free days and evenings with activities. We went miniature golfing on absurd, fluorescent courses in Pigeon Forge; we rented a rowboat at Big Ridge State Park on a cloudy day and had to race to the dock before lightning started stinging the water; we took in a folk music concert at a small club; watched videos, sat together and read books; refinished an old maple table.

One day in late June we drove thirty miles to the Smoky Mountains and hiked for most of an afternoon on a stretch of the Appalachian Trail. I had been excited and wary about entering a space that was so much Julie's, a space I knew only through the filter of her experience. Such entrances had been difficult in her old dorm room, in her trailer, even a little in West Virginia. But the day was hot and sunny, the Trail was crowded, and it quickly became clear that the AT had been Julie's space only when she'd been moving through it—and then only partly. The Trail was inherently shared space, and while we were on it together she made no proprietary claims.

"Day-hikers," Julie said. "You could always tell them, just like you could tell a thru-hiker."

Julie was dressed like a day-hiker, wearing jeans and a pair of sneakers (she'd worn out her boots on the trail). She was also missing the tan, the rugged look, the fifty-pound backpack. We walked slowly, stopping to look at plants, rock formations, the slashes of white paint that blazed the AT. And it was pleasant to be out there with her, to imagine that by the time she'd walked these few miles the previous May, she'd already done several hundred beforehand.

"What did you look like by this point last year?" I asked.

"I was in *shape*," she said. She raised her leg and knocked the side of her fist against her calf.

We did three or four miles northward and then retraced our steps. Julie kept a lookout for thru-hikers, but most of them would have passed this point a month earlier if they were going to have any chance of making Maine before the cold weather. Some people went the opposite way, north to south, but we didn't see any of them, either. Still, Julie knew people who were out there again, friends she'd hiked with who had decided to walk two summers in a row. She'd been in touch with her closest Trail friends, and the antsiness seemed to be active in all of them. Some who weren't on the AT right away were on other, similar ventures: hiking the Pacific Crest Trail from southern California to Washington, or canoeing the length of the Mississippi.

THESE ACTIVITIES gave shape to our days. We did them together, the two of us as much a couple—trusting, knowing the other's tastes and wishes, touching easily and often—as we'd ever been. And in the significance and safety of that, we could almost forget the need to settle anything once and for all. We didn't count days, though we knew there was a countdown. We didn't rush into discussions, though we knew we had only a small stretch in which to talk face to face. We lived within the knots of our mutual and shared intricacies, with as much unspoken between us as there was between two people in any long-spun marriage.

WE TALKED around the hot topic of the summer. "If we get divorced," Julie said, "I predict you get remarried before I do."

"Why do you say that?" I asked.

"I mean that you like being married more than I do. I mean . . . I don't mean that *I* don't like being married to *you*. Only that you're better at being married. You're more . . . generous."

"You trying to make this a compliment, right?"

"*Yes.*"

"Because I *could* hear you saying that I'm the one who *needs* to be married. I could hear it as a comparison of who would survive better alone."

"*That's* not what I'm talking about," she said.

"What you want to say," I said, winking, "is that I'd be as good at being single as I would at being married."

"You would."

"Thank you very much."

"But you'd be *happier* married."

"But I wouldn't *have* to be married."

"But you *should* get married again."

"I'm not even divorced yet."

"I'm just speaking hypo*thet*ically . . ." she said.

RARELY DID we land any more directly on target, and then only for brief moments. But I found other ways to give the issue weight. Small ways. Ways to make things ugly, to get Julie angry and me angry, so that the decision would make itself. I'd criticize the boring food we were eating, bitch about the crummy job I'd come all the way to Knoxville to work, complain about the heat and then about letting the air-conditioning run all night. I was grasping at anything, and after a day of tension that felt not only painful but insincere, I'd relent.

Seven years before, when we were unemployed in Denver, Julie would have said that I was being "a real baby." This time, she said, calmly, sensibly, even with what sounded like a hint of nervousness, "Let's make it nice. We may not get another chance."

SO WE COOKED, we ate, we worked. We lived a rhythm of simplicity, but not oversimplicity. Which is to say that nothing would have been simpler than to walk away from our relationship, not to drag things out any longer. And then suddenly August had arrived, and we were standing on a hot morning in the parking lot next to my rented car. What had we agreed on? What had we accomplished?

We had gotten this far: We agreed to "separate informally." We'd be free to date, with the understanding that we would see what happened and not make any official moves. The decision was so ambiguous as to be almost no decision. But there was a rightness beneath the surface, a safety and a protectiveness of all the shared years that we didn't want to give up too easily. We had to trust that, because there actually had been something deeply satisfying about the summer, all the way up to its irresolute end. We'd seen each other as lucidly as we ever had. We felt that we had come to know each other again, and to know ourselves. If it was too early to articulate that knowing—and the consequences that would unravel from it—then at least we had it, right under our skins.

Years later, my psychologist friend Karl and I were talking about whether it's possible to really know someone. He proposed the tragic Freudian theory that we never really know others in our world, but instead project our expectations on them. "Your relationship with Julie may have lasted as long as it did," Karl said, "in part because you imagined her to be who you wanted her to be. And the person she wanted to be may have been, in part, a reflection of the person you wanted her to be. She may not have been ready for years to give up your idea of who she was, which she would've had to do if she gave up you. But in the end that wasn't the dominant part of her. You two ultimately had to choose between what you wanted in reality and what your fantasies about each other were providing." Karl probably had a point.

There were certain impracticalities to our informal separation. What would I *tell* someone I wanted to go out with? That I was married but free for the time being? It sounded fishy to me, and I couldn't imagine wanting to date anyone who wouldn't think so, too. But there seemed no need to refine it all further at that point. I couldn't imagine whom I'd go out with anyway. Other things were left unsaid, too, things that hinted at how long this informal separation would last. We didn't, for instance, discuss who would visit whom at Christmas, or when we might try to see each other before that. Only: "Let's see what happens."

The whole thing was anticlimactic, a fizzling away of connection. But maybe this is the way it happens for a lot of people. Despite the flatness of a fading away, I think we both at least liked an end free of the traditional swirl of recriminations. We thought we could count that a success.

So we relied on sparse and affable words—thanks for the summer, jokes about bacon grease and the effects of too many macrobiotic beans—to take us through those last moments before Julie had to go to work and I had to start driving so I could make it to my parents' house by dinner. Maybe for that parting we had no other words left—just as, I think we were both slightly embarrassed to discover, there were no tears.

"This is so much like when I was on Mount Katahdin," Julie said after a moment, when I finally opened the car door. "I feel like I've already cried myself out about this, and now it's almost easy."

I SPENT THAT night in Dayton and let my mom buy me lunch the next day at a department store downtown. Waiting for the sandwiches, I told her Julie and I had separated—my first time using that word aloud to anyone but Julie. It didn't get caught on my tongue.

My mom's response came easily. "For years people have been asking me, 'How come they stay married?' " she said. "I told them, 'They're happy. They're too involved with their work to be concerned about not sleeping together.' "

"That's not quite true," I answered.

"No one thought so," she said.

EARLY TERMINATION

MAYBE THERE SHOULD BE PROPOSALS ON BOTH ENDS OF A MAR-
riage, if only for the sake of marking the moment when one person
asks the other to take him on or put her aside. There's an attraction
to such definitiveness, and I've sometimes envied couples who've experienced it in various forms: the suitcase heaved out onto the lawn,
the locks changed on the doors, the slap across the face. But I believe
that such action requires intense bad feeling: despair, rage, hate. Or
a taste for high drama. And I believe that one ought at least to be true
to the rhythm of one's own waning marriage, and play it out the way
it asks to be played out.

Julie and I slipped, within four weeks of my return to Iowa, into
the specifics of divorce—dates, procedures, fees, parents' likely re-

actions—as easily as if the participants were two people other than ourselves. Just as smoothly, we began divvying up our few possessions, restoring items to their proper places: "I found one of your sweaters up here. I'll put it in the mail." Then Julie found a lawyer, a boyfriend of a coworker, who agreed to do everything for half price. I began getting certified letters. The first document jolted me. It suggested a confrontation, an enmity, a hostility that I didn't feel. I was the defendant, Julie the plaintiff. The Division of Services' (what was that?) summary was blunt: "irreconcilable differences for which these parties should be divorced and forever live separate and apart." I called Julie to ask whether they had another form for nice divorces.

"It's the language they have to use," she said. "The lawyer said it doesn't mean anything."

THE LAWYER told me I had to make a couple public announcements concerning my familial status. One was pure formality—a small-print legal notice in the newspaper. He'd take care of it. For the second, he'd await my directions. What was I doing about my name?

Julie was dropping her hyphen and my name. It felt, to me, like someone dropping a book to the floor.

"That didn't take long," I told her, feeling a little hurt.

"It's not like I have unlimited options," she said.

Options seemed like all I had. Her name wasn't tagged on to the end of mine where I could shed it like an outer layer. It was lodged in the middle and would have to be dug out with some effort. I'd moved way up in the alphabet, and now felt as if I'd been taking cuts in line from Julie. I understood the expectation that I was now to move gracefully back to the R's. But I didn't feel ready. Something unexpected might unravel when I pulled on that hyphen.

THE PREVIOUS SPRING, before I'd known whether or not Julie might be coming back to Iowa with me, I'd signed a lease on a minuscule apartment, the smallest I'd been able to find. I was living in it that fall, and would live there for the next year, its close walls wrapped around me like a shell. And it was truly tiny—"like a cave," my mom said the first time she walked in. The building, constructed in the 1820s, was stone and more like a shed than a living space. It had one room on the main floor, which I nearly filled with my double bed and sofa. As I lay in bed, my body almost spanned the width of the room. At the bottom of some concrete steps, which I had to duck to get down, was an even smaller basement. It held a gas stove about the size of a hamper, a sink in one dark corner, and a half-inch water pipe along the top of the back wall from which I hung my shirts. The bathroom was tucked at the top of the steps, near the door. My house was actually part of a larger complex, with a big Victorian house that had sprouted up in front a decade or two later, and two or three other rambling buildings. All of them had eventually been broken up into apartments. There must've been a hundred people living more or less on top of each other—many of them artists or frowzy grad students, but it was somehow private in the midst of the sprawl. I didn't see many people, only occasional signs of them. For several months, one art student kept a few dozen cow bones spread over the small patch of dirt between our doors, drying and bleaching them for some project.

When I'd first moved to Iowa City and known that Julie was coming, I got a house and created a space in it for her. When I'd locked into this apartment, though, I was locking her out. It was a subconscious thing, because I'd operated under the assumption that it could very well be the two of us there, plus the three cats. I mentioned that unrealistic scenario to that landlord before I signed. He stared at me, and I assured him we'd lived in smaller places, though even the trailer in Ohio could've held four of these cottages. It didn't matter to *him*, he said, because he and his wife had lived in places just as tight ("but in *Paris!*"). "If you want to risk it," he told me, "be my guest."

THE APARTMENT gave me a monkish feeling, invited me to think about who I was as the sole occupant of this bare space. When I'd lived on my own before—in my dorm room, in the house with Phil and Karl—the space had never been mine alone. Whether Julie showed up or not, she had a space reserved for her. Not so now. That feeling of ownership was a feeling of control, and as such it was mentally liberating. I could live as I wanted, I could imagine any connections that would replace the dissipating one with Julie.

I couldn't stay Elman-Roche. One night, I sat on the sofa and filled the pages of a yellow legal pad with my mother's maiden name—*Matthews*. I'd been thinking about it as a route back into the fold of my own family that at the same time allowed a jog outside the path worn so deep by my father and brothers, my uncles and their sons. *Daniel Michael Matthews. Daniel Michael Matthews. Dan Matthews.* I autographed with a flourish and scribbled tiny, compacted signatures. I played with the initials. I printed in a blocky architectural hand. But even after fifty or a hundred signatures, after speaking the name aloud in the gray silence of that room, the sound rang strange in my ear. It didn't have the mellifluousness of Elman-Roche, or the barkiness of Roche itself. Its one aesthetic advantage—that it didn't call to mind long-antennaed insects—wasn't insignificant, though it would have meant more to me twenty years earlier. So what would Matthews really allow me to detour? Some vague distaste for "patriarchy"? The implication that I'd be idly accepting the traditions of male descent, and thereby going back on whatever pronouncement I'd made when I'd adopted Elman-Roche in the first place? The truth was the *Matthews* wouldn't take me far from the very spot I'd be in with *Roche,* and no one would think of it as my mom's long-discarded name, anyway. My grandmother was still alive, but this was, above all, my dead grandfather's name. When I wrote *Matthews, Matthews, Matthews,* I might as well have been making sketches of his large-jowled face.

For two months I tested another alternative—like a man preparing for a sex-change operation going out in a dress and a wig. I dropped my entire last name and used my middle name in its place. I put *Daniel Michael* on my mailbox, and received letters from friends who'd agreed to address them that way. I made reservations at restaurants, "Michael, party of two."

I liked the rat-tle rat-tle rhythm of *Daniel Michael.* The simplicity. I even liked the nostalgia of remembering my dad bellowing that name whenever I was in trouble. They weren't strong reasons, but they were enticing ones. But before I went any further, I finally thought to look in the phone book and see with whom I might be throwing in my lot. There were about a dozen Michaels. I couldn't imagine how I'd explain clearly why I wasn't related to any of them.

I WAS SLOWLY growing accustomed to the idea that I was going to be divorced. In the midst of a culture of divorce (the news-magazine tag for our age), I didn't have to worry about "what people would think." It was America, in 1991, and as someone divorced, I was almost in the majority. My parents and my close friends, like me, in some ways had been preparing for this split for years. "It's the right thing," they generally said. They didn't invite me to wallow in self-pity, angst, resentment—the smorgasbord of emotional options. I didn't get advice about crying, or support groups, or killing myself. And for the most part, my divorce washed over them like a story on the news. I understood completely, since I felt pretty much the same way myself. The one exception was my old roommate Phil. "You must be going through *something* anyway," he wrote, "and I hope you know that if you want to talk, I'll be glad to come down to Iowa City and we can get drunk or play tennis or whatever. You sounded fine on the phone, but I'm wondering how you'll feel over time." He added: "Going back and forth with Julie couldn't have been a fun thing— an emotional roller coaster." He suggested that a balance, "not without pain," could be a place to start something new. The idea was good, sincere. And there *was* pain, though so diffuse as to be inarticulable. It hardly seemed worth chasing down. Now that I was off the roller coaster, what I truly felt (which I was willing to admit, even wallow in) was relief. When I let myself do that, I was "fine."

BUT ALL MY emotional "health" was belied by the fact that I found myself unable to talk about things freely, keeping a strong undertow of pain and anger submerged. If I had convinced myself that I was fine, why, then, did I wait *weeks* before telling Maura about the divorce, even though I had begun courting her?

I use that word because that is really how I saw my actions—I'd stop by her apartment, call her up to go for walks, go out with her to the movies. But I'm sure she had no idea what I was doing, because I didn't tell her. I politely mentioned *nothing* about my wife. No openings, I kept telling myself, no right moments. I swore I didn't care what the world at large thought of me, but I cared deeply about what *she* would think. Weeks—maybe a full month or more—into my romancing, I still hadn't told her. She politely didn't ask. Then, finally, came an opening I couldn't ignore.

We were at a bar, in a booth next to the jukebox. Patsy Cline's "Crazy" had worked us into a conversation about our greatest tragedies. Maura was telling me of her father's death five years before. I listened and watched while she played with a small darning needle that she'd taken out of her sweater pocket. She traced the names scratched into the wooden table. There was a suitable pause. Then I said that I thought my greatest tragedy was going on right then. "What?" she said, surprised, concerned. "I'm getting divorced," I said. "It's . . . in the works." She immediately zeroed in on me. She shook her head; my silence had given her no clues about what I was going through. But I'd looked at her face when I broke the news and saw her taking it in like a fish she'd been feeling on the end of a line.

JULIE CALLED on her thirty-first birthday, January 24, 1991, to tell me that the divorce was final. She'd taken off work that afternoon and gone to the courthouse to witness the papers being signed—a weighty present. I hadn't sent her a birthday card (rituals had to end, and she hadn't sent me one in December), but I had thought of her almost all day, the most consistently she'd been on my mind since I'd left Knoxville. My thinking of her was part nostalgia and part sadness. But even as I listened to Julie speak, I felt my sadness as an impermanent thing, like a fog. I was sure that I'd dwell in it a while, then it would lift and I'd march onward, drier and wiser. I thought about her, though, because there was no one else in the world with whom I could share the moment in the same way. It seemed to me our last intimacy.

But how much did I *want* to share this moment with Julie? My brother Steve once told me that the worst thing about divorce was the way it left you alone with your memories. "You can have a whole duffel bag of pictures and no one to share them with." Julie and I had said our good-byes months before, in the hot parking lot in Knoxville. And we had been saying them gradually long before that, and in the time since. What more was there to say? There *were* duffel bags full of pictures, and we could've spent the evening recalling, evaluating, reliving every turn of our marriage. But I didn't want to, partly because I knew that all of the photographs and memories were there, and that I *could* get Julie to sift through it with me if I wanted. That was my defense against sentimentality. That and the ponderous reality of the word *divorced,* its sudden tangibility. It meant that I was now truly cut legally and socially from Julie "forever." I tried to wrap my mind around it.

"It was like . . . nothing," Julie said of her moments in the court-house. "Like a parking ticket. The judge called me up to the bench and asked if the information on the documents was right; then he signed them. It was . . . anticlimactic."

Her report was cordial, casual, with a hint of amazement over the lack of whatever she had expected. "Nothing." I took it to mean the ritual, the ceremony—though she could have been talking about her feelings. She didn't break down. I'd asked her that. "No, I didn't cry," she'd said.

Nor did I. I stood in the kitchen with the phone to my ear, half expecting to feel a *ker-pow,* an iron skillet over the head, a mask ripped off my face to reveal a new essence. I thought back to the time when I'd stood with a phone to my ear and listened to Colleen chew me out for ending our affair. I remembered the epiphany I'd had in that moment—the realization that I'd completely missed most of what was going on. This conclusion was nothing like that one. I'd thought too long and too thoroughly about moving on to be cold-cocked. This experience just weighed more, as if I'd moved closer to the center of the earth.

I FLOATED for months on my hyphenation. Karl told me I was merely hanging on to the last vestige of Julie, but I pointed out that my place was lousy with vestiges of her. More likely, I theorized, I was hanging on to the last vestige of the person I'd been for eight years.

"Well, same thing," he said.

Of course it wasn't. Hanging on to Julie herself would have been a question of love—or of a dependence that would have made me feel weak. Perhaps instead I was missing the idea of Julie, of a wife and all that being married implied.

The hyphen remained for me a symbol of one significant accomplishment within my marriage—a striving for fairness, equality. But slowly, through the spring and summer, I could feel the *Elman* melting off the front of my name. My world was becoming large again in other ways, and perhaps as a result, the stone cabin I was living in began to feel ridiculously small. I had begun to spend more time outside, or over at Maura's. "You're not skeptical about moving into another relationship?" one friend asked me. Not skeptical exactly; cautious, hesitant. But the better I got to know Maura, the less I felt those things.

In early spring I got terribly sick with a bronchial infection. Maura hovered above me, a cool cloth always ready, with a firm insistence that I not try to get up to go to class. She took her nursing duties seriously, and my convalescence was a turning point. At the end of that week, I discovered that she'd fallen in love with me, and to my surprise and pleasure, I with her. My desire for isolation had become a growing craving for connection. I was ready to get on with my life, and I had to do something about my name.

My reasoning probably wasn't as solid this time, reducing itself at last to "Ah, fuck it." I could say that aloud, not knowing whether there was anything behind it besides a gut feeling, a lack of any better alternatives, a wish for simplicity, and a hunch that while the *Elman* wasn't going to do me any good anymore, the *Roche* might come in handy. That, plus thirty dollars for the paperwork, was enough. I hoofed it to the courthouse again; no one in the system was any more interested in my reasons than they had been the first time.

I suppose I was relieved, even thrilled in some ways, with the homecoming aspect of it. I'd expected to have been away long enough for the name to feel different. But I only noticed two changes. I felt as if I had to sign my name *Daniel Michael Roche* because I was so used to extra letters, and my cousin had had a son whom he'd named Daniel. So now there were two Dan Roches in the family. Maura was relieved and could more confidently identify me as the guy she was dating. And my father, I must say, was happiest of all. "It's like the greatest thing in his life," my mom told me after I broke the news. An exaggeration, sure. But I was happy I could please.

SOMEWHERE ALONG the way, Julie disappeared. We simply quit trying to stay in touch, and let other channels carry information back and forth between us. I heard secondhand that she'd moved that spring back to Boston, and moved in with a boyfriend. My sister, who also was living in Boston, ran into Julie's father at a health club. He told her that Julie was out of the newspaper business temporarily, working instead at the family store (then, soon after, for a computer firm). Every six months or so the phone would ring and it would be her, or I'd get a sudden urge and write her a letter. Ours was the most casual of connections, and felt, in truth, like the most satisfying of reliefs. Wherever Julie went—Boston, the woods, the North Pole— I had no duty or desire to map the route.

But even at so great a physical and emotional distance, she was nowhere near completely gone. When I had hyphenated my name years before, my mom addressed letters to me incorrectly for almost two years. For at least that long after my divorce, it seemed no easier for my family to submerge my eight-year marriage than it was for me. They asked every few weeks on the phone whether I'd heard from Julie. They were questions filled with sincere curiosity for someone they liked, but not at all tinged (I think) with hopes of a reconciliation. Maura theorized that they couldn't figure out why we had gotten divorced. No bloody fights, no running off with other people, no door slammed in finality.

"It was more complicated than that," I said.

"But the complications are . . . invisible," she said. "I don't completely understand what they were."

She wasn't asking for an explanation—at least not right then—and I didn't want to try to give her one. I had even less interest in broaching the subject with my parents. But I think partially as a result of their not understanding (or maybe of it simply not occurring to them), their house remained pockmarked with reminders of Julie: portraits she took, the small round mirror in the hallway that she and I gave them one Christmas, the blue-and-white quilt we bought for them another year. But I supposed those things reminded me more than they did my parents, in whose minds they had as strong a connection to me as to Julie.

During the summer of 1992, before Maura's first visit to Dayton, my mom had finally taken down the wedding pictures of Julie and me that for years had been displayed in the living room. I'd had to call and ask her, but she'd willingly tucked them in a drawer. She didn't, however, sweep clean the rest of the house. A hundred more family pictures hung on the walls. When I took Maura on her first tour of them, she stopped at a color snapshot taken in the summer. The whole family was in shorts and t-shirts, packed onto the front porch underneath a blooming purple fuchsia. Julie was a face in the crowd—tanned, smiling broadly like the others—but as distinct as if she had been highlighted in a small oval of yellow. She was sitting on my lap.

"Who's this sitting on your lap?" Maura asked, leaning closer. She had never seen Julie. I saw the realization hit her before she got to the end of her question. "Oh," she said, leaning even closer to inspect.

She looked only for a few polite seconds, her face reflected in the glass, then smiled at me and said, "She's pretty."

The picture was enclosed with ten or twelve others in an intricately matted and framed collage. Disassembling it would be a job, the slowness of it undercutting any drama I could achieve by ripping the picture in half right in front of Maura. Stashing the whole thing in a closet would only stir up my parents to ask, "What happened to the pictures that were here?"

When I caught my mom by herself, I whispered, "There's still a picture of Julie on the wall. Sitting on my *lap*."

"Oops," she said sympathetically. But the picture was still there at Christmas.

WITH ENOUGH effort, everything can go. You can blot out as much of your life as you want, if you have enough persistence. With me, some things disappeared naturally, like my energy to keep up with Julie. Next was much if not all of the sadness I'd felt when the judge signed the divorce papers and Julie called to report the news. That took six months, maybe eight. By then I no longer felt sad about anything having to do with Julie. But there wasn't a void. As the sadness evaporated, what arose in its place was anger.

My marriage began to scratch at the inside of my chest, and like someone slowly realizing he's been duped, I continually thought of new things to resent. I'd been too self-sacrificing. I'd given up too much of my ambitions so Julie could have her career. I'd convinced myself I didn't want kids when I really did want them. I'd cooked more often than Julie had. I'd lived for two years in goddamned West Virginia. I'd gone quietly to sleep too many nights because she was worn out or immersed in her own thoughts. Those were sensations that I hadn't expected. I thought I was past the opportunity for anger—or the peril of it. But I won't say that to discover otherwise didn't feel good.

As the dimensions of my new post-Julie life grew, however, my thoughts of and attachments to the past faded ever more quickly. Near the end of that summer, Maura and I began planning to get married. And, to my surprise, we decided that if we were going to do it, there were compelling reasons to get married in the Catholic church. We both were Catholic, for one, though I hadn't been to church regularly since the first year or two of my marriage to Julie (she always stayed home on Sunday morning, and asked me how it was when I got back). Maura had been away from the routine for about as long. Our families thought a church wedding was a good idea, too, with varying degrees of certainty about how necessary it was for a priest to say the magic words. I hoped I wasn't getting old and conservative, but I felt that I'd already experimented with worlds outside my own. Now the idea of doing something familiar held powerful sway.

A priest has more interest in your motivations than the government does. To get a priest to make a change for you, you've got to come up with some convincing arguments. This I found out when we asked Father Fitzpatrick if he would hitch us. First step, he said, was to wipe the slate clean.

What he wanted to know was whether Julie and I had been properly married. In the eyes of the church, we'd been about as improper as you could get. A civil ceremony. No blessing from a priest. The wedding in an unsanctified building, "chapel" or not.

"This should be no trouble," Father Fitzpatrick said. "We'll send all the information off to the diocese in Davenport, and they ought to approve what we call a 'Lack of Form.' "

"Sloppiness?" I said.

He smiled thinly and nodded his head.

Six weeks later the decree arrived.

> *Since it appears evident from the certified and authentic*
> *documents that at the time of the attempted civil marriage of*
> ### *DANIEL M. ROCHE, a Catholic*
> *with JULIE M. ELMAN [born: Elman], a non Catholic*
> *the Catholic party was bound to observe the canonical form of*
> *marriage [Canons 1108, 1117, 1124], we declare that this*
> *marriage from the very beginning was*
> ### *NULL AND VOID*
> *due to the*
> ### *LACK OF LEGITIMATE CANONICAL FORM.*

I read it twice, put it back in its envelope, and went for a walk. I'd been expecting something as fat and ponderous as our divorce papers, something in which the words' meaning was buffered by their multitude. This notice was bare—the cover letter even chummy, explaining that the Matrimonial Tribunal was "pleased to inform" me of the news, appreciated my "timely remittance" of thirty dollars, and sent "best wishes" to me and Maura.

I walked down by the Iowa River and through City Park, following the asphalt bike path that wound its way past the ferris wheel and through the begging ducks. When I got to the Little League fields, I sat on a set of wooden bleachers. Two kids were tossing a ball around the infield.

When I thought back on my marriage to Julie, "null" was not the word that came to mind. I understood that the church meant "invalid" and "not binding." But there were other implied definitions that I heard loud and clear in my head: "nonexistent, amounting to nothing"; "having or associated with the value zero." In language the pope wouldn't use, a fuck-up.

What got to me was anybody's characterizing my marriage when they couldn't know what it was. I certainly wasn't bragging about having been married for (by my count) eight years, three months, and nine days, but I *could* get defensive about the fact that I had been. People liked to categorize, to pass judgment. How easily everybody called the marriage a failure! I recoiled from the word just as strongly.

I watched the kids alternate grounders with pop flies and some full-body heaves meant to show they could get the ball from the fence to home plate if they had to. And I decided that the only response to this decree was to categorize *it*—a ritual designed by someone else holding real meaning only for that someone else. A hoop to jump through. There was the legal mumbo-jumbo, there was the religious mumbo-jumbo, and then there was what I knew. *Null and void* didn't apply. *Failure* wasn't right. But what was?

Maybe my marriage—any marriage—wasn't reducible. Because even if you said a marriage "worked," what did that mean? That it lasted? That the people in it seemed happy? That it had never veered into tough times, or that it had elbowed its way through some real horribleness? Wasn't saying that a marriage worked about as informative as saying that your day was "fine"? Wasn't calling it a failure just about as imprecise and simplistic? Julie and I had had goals: to be in love; to avoid the worst traps of conventional marriage; to balance our individuality within our identity as a couple; to stay married until we kicked off at ninety-five. We achieved more of them than we didn't. Some of our early goals evolved into different ones, and I think one of the unstated reasons we actually got married was to find out what the hell marriage was about. And I didn't think we'd failed at that, or that what we'd found was something invalid. We had been in love, and I had loved her deeply. Now I didn't. Life goes on, but the life you had before isn't lessened for it.

I was mad at the church for making me feel compelled to defend a marriage against which I had enough anger rising already. But I left the ballfield and walked home to tell Maura that I was free and clear. And the next day I took the decree into Father Fitzpatrick and had him sign us up for the required marriage-preparation classes. I would need a more personal ritual, though, to get me completely ready for Marriage Number Two. A real flood.

WASHING AWAY

JUNE 1993. IOWA CITY. THE FOOTBRIDGE WAS A LONG SERIES OF three-foot-wide wooden planks hanging off the side of a railroad bridge, with a three-tier metal pipe railing to keep you from toppling into the river. According to the morning paper, the river was at 27.8 feet, six feet over flood stage. The day's rain—and there was rain almost every day that summer, sometimes two or three thunderstorms coming through at intervals like trains—hadn't started yet. But the wind had kicked up, and the clouds hovered low and leaden. Orange plastic snow fence—recently strung across each end of the bridge by the city—snapped and billowed like a bedsheet. I clambered past a small white sign that, underneath loopy swirls of black spray paint, announced, "DANGER: PEDESTRIANS KEEP OFF BRIDGE." Trains weren't coming through anyway, because the tracks were submerged in different places all across Iowa. I put my foot on top of the fence and pushed it down to the rail, then swung my other leg over.

Normally, crossing that bridge, I'd have to stretch my neck over the pipe railing to see clear to the water below me. I'd lob rocks I'd scooped from the railroad bed, then peer over to watch them hit. The drop was thirty or forty feet, enough for the rocks to gain speed and describe a gentle arc. The impact occurred so far down that I'd see the splash and then wait for the plunk to rise slowly after it. On this day, though, I could almost have dangled my feet in the river. It was running fast, foamy and muddy. I stopped in the middle of the bridge and felt barely suspended above the current. The bridge's piers seemed to have sunk up to their shoulders in the mud. It would have been a short jump—a stepping off, really, as into a pool—and I thought about it simply because it was right *there*, and because it felt almost as damp in the humid open air as it would have underwater.

I didn't have my usual handful of rocks. And I wasn't trespassing on the railroad company's property as a shortcut, my usual excuse. I was there that day with my old wedding ring, sitting as heavy as a stone in my jeans pocket.

I was throwing it in the river because Plan A had failed. Cold, unsentimental, Plan A was to sell the ring. I'd taken it to a jeweler downtown, a silent fat man who lifted the ring from my hand without looking at me, and scraped at the gold with a penknife. He tossed the ring into the metal tray of a scale, where it clanked around like a coin, then murmured an offer of twelve bucks. I had to ask him to repeat himself. The ring was only a quarter-inch gold band, but I'd expected at least to pay the phone bill with it.

Plan B hit me the moment I turned my back on the jeweler's fluorescent-lit cases. I walked the four sloping blocks west to the river as if I'd been going there all along. I was glad, I realized, that the jeweler had been cheap. With one good heave into the river, I'd cleanse myself of the ring without soiling myself with cash. Cast deep into the water, the ring would never end up on someone else's finger or find its way back to me through the mysteriously circuitous routes that objects travel through the universe.

It was the summer of floods. The Midwest's worst floods, meteorologists theorized, in five hundred years. It rained seven and a quarter inches in Iowa City in May, well above average but not enough for anyone to suspect what was to come. It rained a half-inch on June 2, three-quarters on the fifth, an inch and a half on the eighth, eighteenth, and nineteenth. A few rainy days in between made almost eleven inches total for the month of June, more than thirteen total in July, another dozen in August. By September 25, we'd had more rain than in any of the previous 121 full years.

The rain felt cleansing to me, and by mid-June I had come to dwell on everything's washing away. It was hard to avoid such thoughts, with water in the streets constantly ankle deep, and some neighborhoods in town open only to canoes and hip-waders. Maura's and my basement floor was bisected by currents that seeped in along one wall and swirled toward the drain along the other. And the TV news showed constant footage of big things—cars, cows, houses—that actually *had* washed away.

In the midst of it, I felt that the last vestiges of my old marriage had not yet completely washed away. Out on the bridge, I wanted to make my ex-marriage ancient. I wanted *distance*, in time and in space. Sometimes I felt it, sometimes not. With my marriage only three years in the past, what I still had was a relatively young divorce.

But those mazy lines of communications between us still existed.

Enough to track each other's lives, but with time between those blips on our radar screens for eight years of marriage to fade like a book I hadn't read since I was fifteen.

I was striving to relegate my old marriage to history because that summer of floods was the summer of my marriage to Maura. I envied Deucalion and Pyrrha, the newlyweds in Ovid's *Metamorphoses* whose marriage gift from the gods is a flood that washes away everything in the known world except the boat in which they drift.

Ever since the divorce, the overlap of relationships had scared me, the possibility that some of the energy I wanted to give to Maura could be drawn off. People I know who've gotten married for the second time often have about them an air of concentration. I can see a determination right below the sheen of happiness, which proclaims that now they know what they're doing.

So why did I still have my old wedding ring? Three years, a spit of time, is nonetheless long enough to clear out all mementoes of a marriage—rings, books, corny poems, and all the other objects that have an intimacy only because you owned them together (a toaster, a hammer). Would Karl have diagnosed me as a hanger-on, someone who was trying to have it both ways? Was I afraid to make the clean break to which a divorce like mine—no kids, the two of us living a thousand miles apart—lent itself? Had I been waiting for this flood, trusting that some force higher than myself would tell me when the time was right to let go completely?

Sociologists have taken to calling them "starter marriages"—marriages that end in divorce by the time husband and wife reach thirty, with no children and little more joint property than a stereo. My friend Elizabeth, whose first marriage lasted five years during her twenties, simply calls it "the one that didn't take." At the end, Julie and I had shared three cats, a car with three years of payments left on it, books, a few secondhand pieces of furniture, and some well-used pots and pans.

Pitted against my family's forty- and fifty-year marriages, eight years is, anyway, succinct. But even a short marriage possesses the property of inertia. Like eating, giving birth, picking at a cracked fingernail, marriage is harder to stop than to start. For the term to be exact, a "starter marriage" would cut itself off like an ignition. People would move out of them the way they move out of starter homes. No one takes the shutters and doorknobs from their first home with them to their second.

I'd found the ring in a box in the hall closet, a few days after Maura and I got back from our honeymoon. (We went to Seattle, which was strangely sunnier than Iowa.) I tried to force myself to feel surprise when I discovered it there, but in truth I'd never really forgotten its presence. I'd stopped thinking about it, the way you stop thinking about a coat you haven't worn in years but never give away. I was going through the box looking for something else—a snapshot, a notebook, something innocuous. It was a mishmash box that I'd hefted from the closet to the dining room table and was picking through immunization certificates, birthday cards, and expired passports. On the bottom, alongside some Kennedy half-dollars my grandfather had given me twenty years before, lay the ring.

It hadn't moved an inch, hadn't tarnished, hadn't lost any of its scratches. It was only thicker than I'd remembered. I'd expected to find a ring as thin as gold leaf, as if I were remembering only the impalpable dissolution it had come to stand for rather than its initial weighty reality. But there it was. Ample.

How did this particular ring hang on to the soft flesh below my knuckle? I rolled it between my right thumb and index finger, measured its eye against the tip of my left index finger, tracing its circumference. In Jewish weddings it is traditional for the bride to slip a ring onto the tip of the groom's index finger while she recites her vows, and for the groom to do likewise, an allusion to the belief that a vein runs from the index finger straight to the heart. Slipping this ring on, I thought, would have felt like adultery—not a sensation I wanted two weeks into my new marriage. I bounced it in the palm of my right hand, weighing it, wondering what the price of gold was that day.

Out on the footbridge, what I wondered was how far the river would take it. As furiously as the water was running, I could easily imagine the ring's being washed quickly over the ten-foot dam a half-mile downstream. If the current held and the ring didn't lodge in the muddy bottom, it could even be swept past the flooded cornfields of southeastern Iowa, sixty miles into the engorged Mississippi, picking up steam down through St. Louis, Memphis, Vicksburg, New Orleans—into the Gulf of Mexico.

Or it could get lodged in a crevice south of town. Or in the sandbags that volunteers were stacking by a riverside trailer court. But that would be okay. I only wanted the ring—the instrument of this ritual—to suffer its own blows.

The next thunderstorm was bearing in from my right—as oppressive as the dozens preceding it. People were scurrying down the sidewalks on the riverbanks. Some of them glanced over at me and then at the bright orange snow fence, seeming to wonder how I'd gotten out on the bridge. I was leaning forward casually on the railing, the fingers of my hand that didn't hold the ring wrapped around the top bar. I looked nothing like someone who might be planning to jump to his death. And I tried to look nothing like someone who might be planning to perform a ritual. I adopted the guileless expression of a man who happened to find himself out on a railroad trestle in an approaching storm and was thinking through his options. But I didn't want to *perform* casually, didn't want my ceremonial casting off of the ring to be as perfunctory as flicking away a cigarette butt. I was making up the ritual as I went along, feeling my way into the realms of what final thing I needed this ring to give me. The jeweler's indifference had reversed my desire to have it all done with easily and profitably. The ring had taken on a completely different kind of value, which I could extract only by ridding myself of it in the proper way.

The Vacuum Theory of Prosperity says that getting rid of one thing in your life creates room for something else to arrive. The new arrival does not have to be something material—would not have to be, in my case, another ring.

IN NONFLOOD YEARS the Iowa River is often nearly stagnant. In the last few years of our marriage, I'd been moving away from Julie with the same sort of slowness. Our lives had diverged in ways I couldn't see at the time, and had a hard time pinpointing even those few years later. Maybe it would have been clearer, easier, with screaming fights, shrill markers on our timeline. But I doubted that even such drama could guarantee you *control* over the drift of your marriage.

Instead of fighting outright, Julie and I had shared deeply submerged dissatisfactions. Or we'd each come to have our own. We'd floated apart, steered in different directions, not realizing for the longest time that we'd been cutting new banks, that the one river we'd both been navigating had become two. The body of land that had come between us kept getting wider and wider. A glance at any atlas shows that a river that splits rarely comes back together. The two streams empty into different parts of the ocean, or end mysteriously in the middle of nowhere, hundreds of miles apart.

But in a divorce, you're supposed to despise each other. People expect you to be as passionate in your repulsion from each other as you were, in the now inconceivable beginning, in your attraction. You are supposed to blow up, storm out, camp on the couches of friends or relatives; make angry lists of who gave you the coffeemaker, the three-pronged sterling silver candlestick holder, the blender that still works but has a handle that needs to be glued back together. It is your duty to rifle the shelves at night and write your name in your future ex's books so you can claim them for your own. It's all part of the lore, the story our culture has created around the cycles of romance. Like everything linear and predictable, there is nothing more confining.

From the moment I'd first imagined myself as divorced (was it way back during Julie's first year of grad school?), I planned to be a good ex—staying above the frays that snared other couples. I knew even then that I wouldn't want a "typical" divorce any more than I'd wanted a "typical" marriage. I'd wavered from that resolution in the last moments, in Knoxville, when the imagination of being divorced inched closer and closer to reality. Then Julie had called me to my better senses. "Let's make it nice." And so our divorce became as amicable as a graduation.

Maybe my new marriage—this much more satisfying and balanced relationship—was the catalyst for the anger that finally, like a drowned body broken free from the bottom of a weedy lake, rose to the surface. And that anger had hung on; it was much slower to disappear than my sadness had been. Even in the first summer of my new marriage, I recalled my old one and wanted—in ways I never had while Julie was my wife—nothing more than to throw plates against a kitchen wall. My desire was frustrated, because the marriage seemed so *removed*, the grief therefore so inappropriate. Occasionally, when I got a letter from Julie, I threw that, but watching it flutter to the carpet only dissatisfied me more.

Out on that footbridge, though, I could finally define my anger. It came from having to feel the disappointment and muddiness of being an ex-husband, rather than simply the joy of being a new one. I reared back and slung the ring as far downstream as I could. I saw it sail through the mist. The rapids overwhelmed its tiny splash and the water's roar drowned out its plunk. I couldn't tell exactly where it hit.

How I wanted the moment to be dramatic! The weather was playing its part—raindrops had started to fall, thunder rumbled from the other side of the buildings on the riverbank. And I so much believed that witnessing the ring's actual submersion would ease some enmity inside me. I rested both empty hands on the rail, stared hard at the water.

The real plunk was inaudible. But something metaphoric rose from the physical act of throwing the ring. The realization was in my gut, and it held not so much its own drama as its own surprise. The river hurtled southward and the wind wailed from the west, and I realized this: It wasn't drama I wanted, but nothing. I wanted the ring to become as meaningless as a rock. I wanted not only to complete my divorce from Julie but to feel as if our marriage had never happened. I wanted what the Catholic church had already presumed to bestow upon me. But I wanted it from the inside.

I had a professor at the time, Carl, who told me that when he got divorced, in 1964, he received one piece of advice from a man who was ten years into his own divorce: "He said, 'Carl, you'll know you're better when you never think about your first marriage at all, when it never enters your mind.'" Carl laughed, a resonant bark. "Ha!"

"Did you try it?" I asked him.

It wasn't his style, not his way to cut connections so bloodlessly, he said. "But," he bunched his forehead in thought over the struggle, "in 1964, the act of forgetting made a lot of sense."

In 1993 it enticed me, too. Before me was my new marriage to Maura, and I wanted to be open to the simplicity of one love, the cleanliness of my married life to come. I was hoping that unburdening myself of the ring would create a vacuum to be filled emotionally, with a love and intimacy. On the other hand, there was Ovid. After the flood came and the newlyweds were set adrift, Deucalion "Looked out on silent miles of ebbing waters. He wept, called to his wife. 'Dear sister, friend, O last of women, look at loneliness. . . .' "

"Ha!" I barked. I'd felt that plunk in my gut, but around it bubbled up a suspicion that it was crazy, useless, selfish to wish that my first marriage could suddenly mean less then than it ever had. How do you rid yourself of your history? What is it that Carl's friend was getting "better" from? Why shouldn't you live a divorce as deeply as you're supposed to live a marriage? And is simplicity even something to be desired? I never strove for it in my first marriage. Isn't it really the complexities and layers that satisfy us, make us feel human?

Past the red-brick power plant downriver on the left, the water curved into a line of swaying trees. I peered at the point where it disappeared, where it rushed around its turn and headed for the Mississippi. There was a churning in the air, just as much as under water. Feeling it, I let myself think that one way to live in the joy and contentment of my new marriage was to let the best memories of my old marriage wash not away from me but over me.

EPILOGUE

JULIE THOUGHT FOR SURE I WANTED TO SEE THE CATS.

"Ah, the cats." Actually, what I wanted was to eat, to get Maura some food. But we stopped.

Julie's house was small and yellow but furnished comfortably. Big windows. Lots of bookshelves. The cats sauntered out of the bedroom and looked exactly the same as they had three and a half years before.

"Look!" Julie said. "They remember you! Look how they're coming to you."

"They do this to everybody," I said. I picked up Cider, listened to her purr. When I glanced at Pepper, she rolled over onto her back.

"She *still* rolls over anytime anyone looks at her," Julie said, as if she were newly astounded each time by such a trick.

The cats, in their invariability, were slipping us into the realm of memories—it felt like thin ice to me.

"Lunch?" I reminded her.

"Okay, okay." She paused. She wanted to give us a quick tour of the house—kitchen, living room, hallway, bedroom. And when we were in the bedroom she asked, "Can I show you a *couple* recent photographs? Then we'll go eat. I promise." She hunched her shoulders, pleading. I nodded. She rustled through notebooks and boxes on a shelf.

"You okay?" I mouthed to Maura while Julie's back was to us.

"Mm-huh," she hummed, holding up her hand.

"We'll eat soon," I whispered.

For me, looking at Julie's photographs was not an unwelcome change in direction. I trusted that Maura would have the reaction I used to depend on whenever I showed anyone Julie's pictures. She would be pulled into the stark and striking images. If I wanted Maura to understand what I'd been attracted to in Julie, she had to see this part.

"I've been shooting beauty pageants. This is my favorite." She handed us the photo from the top of the stack. It was a black-and-white eight-by-ten shot taken from the end of a short runway in a low-ceilinged bar. A banner tacked above the stage said "The Comedy Connection," and Julie had written under the image "Mrs. Greater Boston Pageant." Across the stage, eight women faced away from the camera, some of them broad-shouldered, all of them clenching their calves above high-heeled shoes, their swimsuits clinging, unflattering, to lax butts.

"Ugh," Maura said. "That's very disturbing."

"I think it's incredibly sad," said Julie.

We eased through the rest of the photographs, more images of sad, hopeful women, of small girls in malls being paraded in front of shoppers. Maura shook her head silently at each one.

"Hey, I've got news," Julie suddenly said. "I got a tattoo."

At that moment, I didn't know her body anymore. She had once given me a black-and-white self-portrait of her standing nude in the kitchen of the trailer outside Athens. I had kept it for years, then finally ripped it into small, unidentifiable pieces and buried it at the bottom of a garbage bag. This is what I thought: that my image of it from that black-and-white was no more indicative of her body's present state than the image of her face in our wedding pictures was of how she looked eleven years later. Both were recognizable, of course, but she'd taken possession of her own looks. And the *idea* of this tattoo—before I saw it, before I knew what or where it was— transported the rest of her body into an odd independence from my memories.

"Want to see it?"

I wasn't sure I did.

"You remember what my nickname was on the trail?" she asked. Almost every thru-hiker picked one up sooner or later, but hers wasn't coming back to me.

"Purple Rose of Cairo," she said. "I don't know where the name came from. I was walking up this hill one day and it popped into my head. So I got a purple rose, right here above my left breast."

She pulled at the collar of her white shirt with two crooked fingers. The fabric stretched down to the top of her breast, to where I saw the beginnings of an outward curve. On the skin above that, the rose floated dramatically but elegantly, like a holograph. Its stem was long and detailed, its petals watercolor purple, light and airy but stark at the same time. A minute seemed to pass.

"I've wanted one for years. You know that, Dan. I heard about this guy up in Maine, and I drove up one weekend to see his work. I *really* liked it. He wasn't the skulls and crossbones type."

"It's a lovely rose," I said. I turned slightly to glance at Maura without looking away from Julie's chest, and saw her leaning forward curiously, nodding politely. I had simultaneous déjà vu's: Julie growing the hair on her legs; Maura studying the picture of Julie on my parents' wall.

I looked fully back at Julie, who smiled broadly, arching her neck and pulling in her chin to look at the tattoo herself.

"Isn't it beautiful? I love to get out of the shower and see it in the mirror. It feels *right,* like I was meant to have it."

I told her I'd heard that tattoos are a form of psychic armor, that they can make people feel more confident and better about themselves.

"It's not that I felt bad about myself before," Julie said. "But this is like . . . a completion."

If the day was meant to be a sharing of new lives, a show-and-tell of "where we are now," what of myself could I expose for Julie? Nothing, of course, except Maura, who was beautiful and a completion of me in ways as magical as a holograph, and who was imprinted deep within my own skin in ways unseeable and indelible. We stood in Julie's bedroom, the cats nestled on her futon, and I held Maura's hand.

SO THE THREE of us went to lunch, and it was fine, comfortable. Our waiter was a tall Indian man, square-headed, square-shouldered, with arms the length of garden rakes. He didn't even have to bend at the waist to fill our water glasses. "Lurch for lunch," I whispered to Julie and Maura when he left. We ordered three dishes and shared them. And on that neutral ground we talked about our lives: Maura's and my work in grad school, families, the postcard beauty of Vermont, the flatness of the Midwest.

Once, we veered into Julie's memories of Iowa City—those cold winter months when she'd done almost nothing but take care of me. She told Maura stories of the low points of my recovery, of what I was like as a patient. Many were stories I'd forgotten or had never gotten around to telling Maura. Others were Julie's take on the events. I wondered as I listened to her who owned those stories. When I was the only one around who knew them, then I did. But sitting there with Julie, I felt them slipping out of my control. It wasn't a comfortable feeling. But I let them come out, let Maura hear them without my interruptions or contradictions.

Months later, I'd find myself on the other side of the issue, telling Julie that I wanted to write about our marriage and asking her how she felt about it. She said emphatically, "They're *your* memories. You had your own experience, and if I was telling it I'd tell it differently. At least in some places." She felt that I would be presenting a piece of her life to her, one filtered through my eyes and memories but true nonetheless. She thought the whole thing would be "enlightening."

Around that same time, I asked Maura what *she* thought about my closing myself in a room for hours on end, reliving this old love, this ex-marriage. "It's really an incredible gift," she said. "How many people get to know so many details of their spouse's previous life?" At that moment she was in an exceptionally openhearted mood. Later she would grow more philosophical, a bit more apprehensive about what this gift entailed. "It's one thing to know that someone's had a life, relationships before," she said, "and it's another to hear it, see it all in detail. At some level I want us to live our lives together right here, in the present. And for anybody, what that means to some extent is to forget the past, not think about it—even though thinking about it is inescapable, and useful in making sense of one's own present and future. It's just difficult for your spouse to have all that on the surface when you're trying to live with him or her in the present. I guess it's the same reason you were jealous of my old boyfriends before we got married."

"I was?"

She rolled her eyes.

For two hours over lunch the three of us talked—and performed, I thought, like reasonable adults, wise veterans of relationships, free of jealousies and possessiveness. The two of them seemed to be forging their own familiarity. Of course an overlapping of the romantic segments of one's life is a temporary state—a channel from one way of being to another. A process. You do it by yourself, or you do it, if you're lucky, with the person at the fresh end of that channel. You do it with the idea of its end in mind, and with an effort to bring about that end—for the sake, if nothing else, of that new person.

I waited months after throwing my old ring in the river before telling Maura about it. The ritual had been private, and I suppose I hadn't wanted her to know that I'd kept the ring even for that long. By the time I told her, much of my own anger was gone, but it was inevitable that I'd pulled her into the overlapping of my marriages still in progress. "What struck me," she admitted, "what gave me pause— I wouldn't say exactly discomfort, but sort of an Oh!—was the idea that you had still been coming off some of those feelings from your marriage and divorce the summer we were married." And my wish for her to meet Julie was as much as anything else, I think, a wish to let Maura witness—and share, as wife, as intimate and confidante—my movement even more completely into *our* marriage.

By then, too, it seemed possible to save something of the intimacy that I'd spent years forming with Julie. I didn't yet know exactly what, though I could say with certainty that I'd never backtracked, never felt any resurgence of romance, nor of anything physical. After the surprise of the tattoo had worn off, my image of her body was gone almost instantly, leaving me to concentrate on her face across the table, its ovalness, the way it had filled out into maturity.

"It's good that you and Julie can still stay friends," people have told me, though they never explain why. They say it in the same way they used to tell us that we were each so lucky to be able to do what we wanted in our marriage. I always thought, too, that being friends was much better than not being friends. And yet "friendship" with an old lover is a concept as ambiguous and reliant on improvisation for its moment-to-moment meaning as "marriage" had ever been for me. I believed (and believe) that not all intimacies are passionate, and the ones that are can relax into relationships of mutual trust and caring. Julie seemed to believe the same thing. That's the positive spin on it. The negative is that we both were wrong. Our desire to see each other again—and to bring Maura into the picture—signaled something larger, some sense of deep loss that each of us was trying to assuage. Perhaps the loss of history, or of opportunity. Maybe we needed to reconnect, to move onward in some sort of relationship, because we were scared of thinking our years of marriage were wasted, in the way we thought for a long time about our months in the Peace Corps. I don't know.

The conversation got more relaxed, and Julie wanted to tell the story of the time I had the runs in Antigua, wanted to get up between the tables and act it out. The story always made her double over with laughter.

"No," I pleaded.

She looked at Maura and whispered, "I'll tell you some other time."

And we came around to more recent events.

"Tell me about your *wedding*," Julie said. "I want to hear everything."

I swiveled toward Maura with an upturned palm.

"Me?"

She'd honed the story over the previous six months. I wanted to let it be fully hers. Because she told it better? (She did.) Because it was her only wedding, while I, fattened with two to draw from, could sit in the middle and share in the history of both? Or was a wedding "supposed" to belong to the bride?

"Okay," Maura said, squaring her shoulders toward Julie, "but I have to begin with buying the dress."

"Tell the whole thing," I told her.

Now and then I chipped in a detail or a punch line, smiled and nodded at Julie to warn her that a good part was coming up. But Maura held the floor, tossed in dramatic pauses, her hands flitting over the table like birds. Julie laughed and smiled, wanting to know more details, thought it all was beautiful.

THEN THE food was gone, our third pot of tea empty. *Where are we now?* I wanted to ask. *What kind of trio have we forged?* My brother Steve, a father and married at nineteen, divorced at twenty-two, faced the more typical dilemma: What kind of relationship could he have with his since-remarried ex-wife, who had custody of their son? How could he get along with her new husband, who was raising his son? He was forced into some kind of unifying relationship. In the six years I'd been watching him struggle with those dynamics, I'd been glad they weren't mine.

Still, the question of what forces act upon an ex hung with me, and those forces seemed neither escapable nor unpleasant. There was a centripetal feel to them, as if Julie and I would always be pulled, however slightly, toward some common center. The center was distant but tangible, the centripetal force not nearly as strong as the centrifugal one that was spinning Maura and me out into our own new territory, but it was comforting to discover once again that histories of intimacy are never null and void.

There was a moment of silence, then Julie said to Maura, "People used to say that Dan and I looked alike. But you two look much more alike."

Then another silence, in which Lurch cleared our plates and, on his way out of the room, belched.

"Hear that?" Julie whispered.

The place was empty except for us. Lurch was standing behind the swinging kitchen doors, letting loose. I turned once and saw the back of his square shoulder in the small window of the door.

Julie had a better view, peeked through the window surreptitiously. "He's just standing there," she reported, *"belching."*

It was low and rumbling and long, like an ancient furnace in the building's dusty basement.

"My god," Julie whispered.

And again. This time not from behind the door, but from the far corner of the dining room, where he was resetting a table.

We all giggled.

"I think he wants us to go home," Maura whispered.

"Clearly," I said.

We sat a little longer, testing how far he would go, and maybe not really knowing where we'd go next if we did get up and leave.

But finally we each pitched in some money for the check, added some extra to the tip for the entertainment, and then hiked back to Julie's house. We all piled into her car (our old car, still running) and let her drive us back in to Harvard Square. Maura sat up front with Julie, and I leaned up between the seats, listening to the last of the idle chat. Julie pulled up to the curb on the busy street outside a bakery we wanted to shop at and put on the flashers. She shook Maura's hand and said she hoped to see her again soon.

"If you're ever in Iowa . . ." I said. It was a line Maura and I could offer freely, because no one ever came to Iowa. Still, I wanted to mean it, and thought I *did* mean it.

"We'll keep in touch," she said. "I think we'll always keep in touch."

"We probably will," I said.

She twisted around, and we gave each other a hug as I began to get out of the car. Maura was already out, and I could see her black coat flapping in the breeze.